SECOND EDITION

PRODUCTS LIABILITY

A MANAGERIAL PERSPECTIVE

RICHARD J. HUNTER, JR., J.D.

Professor, Legal Studies
W. Paul Stillman School of Business
Seton Hall University

JOHN H. SHANNON, M.B.A., J.D.

Professor, Legal Studies
W. Paul Stillman School of Business
Seton Hall University

HENRY J. AMOROSO, J.D.

Associate Professor, Legal Studies
W. Paul Stillman School of Business
Seton Hall University

Products Liability

A Managerial Perspective

Second Edition

Richard J. Hunter, Jr. | John H. Shannon | Henry J. Amoroso

ISBN: 9781731150684

FOREWARD

Products Liability - A Managerial Approach is a specially created text and case book meant for the advanced undergraduate student of business and for the MBA student involved in any way in the business of creating, selling, or financing products or in managing these activities.

The authors have developed a unique text that combines knowledge gained from many functional areas of business—most notably marketing, management, finance, and business law—and places this knowledge in the context of modern products liability law and theory.

The chapters are arranged so that the student will think about products liability from both a theoretical and practical basis. Coverage begins with a discussion of the nature of product defects in the manufacturing, design and marketing of products. The discussion then moves to negligence, breach of warranty, fraud, and the core theories of liability, all leading to the creation of a modern theory of products liability, strict liability in tort. It then concludes by discussing the scope of liability in product cases, defenses available in product cases, and theories of damages in product cases. As a tool for managers, the text contains appendices with practical information, clear examples, and major traditional cases explaining and expanding upon the text materials.

The authors have provided relevant case questions, as well as problems that will help the students process the materials in a straightforward manner.

While the text contains traditional legal analysis (cases), it is meant to be a practical guide for students of business who are charged with managerial decision-making in fields that include pharmaceuticals, marketing and sales, management, finance and hospital administration.

We are indebted to our students at Seton Hall University for providing the authors with unique insights, practical information, and many interesting examples that have strengthened this text. We also wish to thank Professor Victor Metallo, Adjunct Professor, Seton Hall University, for his suggestions for additions and edits to this Second Edition.

We hope that we have met our objective of proving a hands-on managerial approach to this most relevant topical area in this Second Edition of the text.

RJH

TABLE OF CONTENTS

Notes

Chapter One

Introduction and Overview

The Defective Product

The area of law termed products liability is a hybrid of both contract law (involving either express or implied promises, found in the law of warranties) and tort law (based upon specific conduct, oftentimes reflected in a negligence standard, or actions based on fraud or misrepresentation). In general terms, products liability refers to the obligations or duties of manufacturers, wholesalers (or other middlemen), or retailers / sellers (as well as other parties) to consumers, purchasers, users, and even bystanders when a product is found to be defective. No matter what the theory of liability, the predicate of a suit in products liability is a defective product.

Three Sources Of A Defective Product

A defect in a product can arise from three common sources:

- A manufacturing or production defect — that occurs from a random and atypical breakdown in the manufacturing process;
- A design defect — that is characteristic of a whole product line (such as the Ford Pinto); or
- A marketing defect — involving inadequate warnings relating to risks or dangers, or inadequate instructions relating to how to properly or safely use a product. Many cases in the area of a marketing defect involve food, drugs, or more recently, children's toys, cribs, or car seats.

Three Theories to Bring Suit

Under the common law, there were three theories under which a plaintiff could bring a suit for personal injury or property or economic damage caused by a defective product.

Negligence, a tort action, focuses on the defendant's conduct or omission and whether that conduct or omission was unreasonable in light of the defendant's duty of due care for others. Negligence in a products liability action requires proof that a product was designed or manufactured in an unreasonable manner, or that the warnings or directions were inadequate under the circumstances. One of the features of a suit based on negligence is the requirement, in many cases, of expert proof that can be quite expensive for an ordinary plaintiff.

Another negative was the existence of the doctrine of privity. The the doctrine of privity made it difficult, if not impossible, to reach a negligent manufacturer with whom an injured plaintiff had not entered into a contract. What happened then if a plaintiff sued the retailer? The retailer was absolved from liability because the retailer had normally only passed on the product and was not ordinarily negligent.

Since there was no liability on the part of either the manufacturer or retailer, the common law doctrine of caveat emptor, or "let the buyer beware" was routinely applied to negligently made products. The requirement of vertical privity between the plaintiff and the manufacturer was later severely limited in the 1916 case of *MacPherson v. Buick Motors*.

A further negative was the defense of contributory negligence, which at common law, was an absolute bar to recovery by a plaintiff. Finally, the sometimes-tortured reasonable man standard could be problematic in negligence cases, more specifically, reaching a consensus on what would be the standard required of a reasonable manufacturer or reasonable designer or of a reasonable plaintiff or reasonable defendant under the circumstances of the case.

Misrepresentation and fraud actions focus on proof of a false representation or statement of a material fact (which may be found in words, actions, concealment, or in some cases silence where the common law found a duty to speak), upon which a plaintiff reasonably relied in entering into a contract. At common law, evidence of falsehood was required to prove misrepresentation, and proof of scienter, the intent to deceive (arising from either knowledge of falsity or reckless disregard for the truth), was a part of the prima facie proof required in cases of fraud. An assertion of safety or of a safe product formed the basis of many fraud claims.

A drawback to a suit based on fraud was the common belief or even expectation that all sellers would in fact engage in a certain amount of sales puffing or exaggeration regarding their products, and the common notion that no matter how careful a manufacturer might be, no one could absolutely guarantee the safety of any product in all cases, thus negating the element of reasonable reliance.

Actions for breach of warranty were essentially based on contract promises, either express or implied. Warranties were subject to disclaimers on the part of sellers and could also be severely limited in their scope. Warranty actions also were subjected to severe notice requirements (that is, the injured party had to give the party causing the injury a notice that damage/injury had occurred within a rather limited period of time). Another drawback is the plaintiff had to show that he or she relied upon specific words or promises made by a seller in order to maintain a warranty action.

Warranties under the Uniform Commercial Code (UCC) arose in cases involving the sale of goods, and not in the myriad of other types of transactions that resulted in goods or personal property reaching the hands of a consumer—most notably through leases or bailments.

Under the common law, there was also an aspect of privity – horizontal privity—that limited a manufacturer's liability under a warranty to the actual purchaser of a product and not to any other parties. Privity of contract was greatly expanded with the decision in *Henningsen v. Bloomfield Motors* (See Chapter 6 for the case), which saw the expansion of liability under the warranty of merchantability to persons other than the consumer/buyer (horizontal privity). This expansion of horizontal privity may be seen in UCC § 2-318, which significantly expanded the range of potential plaintiffs in a warranty action.

The drawbacks inherent in the three common law forms of action led to the development of the modern and now preferred theory in products liability cases—strict (or absolute) liability in tort. The theory of strict liability focuses exclusively on the existence of a product defect, and not on the nature of the conduct of the defendant (negligence), or on specific words or promises (warranty/misrepresentation/fraud). Strict liability permits an injured party (broadly defined) to sue a manufacturer directly, even in the absence of privity of contract and will not permit manufacturers to disclaim their duty of due care. Notice requirements under strict liability are less stringent than under warranty actions, which were often as short as three months. Actions under strict liability permit plaintiffs to sue within more generous statute of limitation time periods. (Under the Uniform Commercial Code, the Statute of Limitations can never be less than one year and may extend to no more than four years.)

What is a Product?

As a preliminary matter... a product can be defined by making reference, for example, to the definition of a good, found in UCC Section 2-105-1: A good is defined as an item of personal property that is both movable and tangible. By definition, pure services would be excluded from the area of products liability. In cases under the UCC where both a good and a service are involved, courts will use the "which predominates" test to determine if the transaction involved is a good or a service. According to the UCC, food or drink served in a restaurant is considered a good by definition.

The definition of product is also sufficiently broad to include certain intangibles such as electricity, some natural products (crops, pets, plants), some writings (like a navigation chart—

although in the case of certain writings, courts are properly solicitous of the implications of the First Amendment). In certain cases, real property, notably, defectively made mass produced or manufactured homes, may be considered as products, although there is still a pronounced reluctance to extend products liability to transactions involving land (real estate), buildings, or appurtenances (unattached buildings).

Questions

1. Find modern day examples of the following:
   a. Manufacturing or production defect
   b. Design defect
   c. Marketing defect
2. Given the shift from the three common law theories to the notion of strict liability, how is it different from its predecessors?
3. What were some of the drawbacks to the following common law theories:
   a. Negligence
   b. Misrepresentation & fraud
   c. Warranty Actions
4. How do courts use the "which predominates" test to determine if the transaction involved is a good or service under the UCC? Find a case to support this.
5. In the Ford Pinto case, which type of defect did the product exhibit? Moreover, which of the three common law theories can best be applied for the action?

Notes

Chapter Two

TYPES OF DEFECTS

A production or manufacturing defect exists "if the product differs from a manufacturer's intended result or if the product differs from apparently identical products from the same manufacturer." (A California judge's instruction to a jury regarding the nature of a manufacturing defect…)

There are various formulations concerning a production or manufacturing defect:

- A product which comes off the assembly line in a substandard condition in comparison with other identical units; called the deviation from the norm test—sometimes termed as the Lee Test.
- Manufacturing defects are imperfections that occur in a typically small percentage of products of a given design as a result of the failure in the manufacturing process. If there are a large number of individual defects, this will be seen as a design defect and not an isolated manufacturing or production defect.
- Products that do not conform to their intended design;
- Products that do not conform to the great majority of manufactured products within the design;
- Products that are misconstructed or misassembled;
- Defects which result from a mishap in the manufacturing process or from improper workmanship, or because defective materials were used. This standard is even applied to component parts assembled by the primary manufacturer;
- Products which do not conform to the manufacturers' own specifications.

In a large majority of manufacturing defect cases, courts use a simple test to determine if a product is defective: the reasonable expectations of the buyer / consumer. Let's look at one small wrinkle to this test!

Hunt v. Ferguson-Paulus Enterprises

Supreme Court of Oregon Department Two, 243 Ore. 546; 415 P.2d 13 (1966)

OPINION BY: LUSK, JUDGE

The plaintiff bought a cherry pie from the defendant through a vending machine owned and maintained by the defendant. On biting into the pie one of plaintiff's teeth was broken when it encountered a cherry pit. He brought this action to recover damages for the injury, alleging breach of warranty of fitness of the pie for human consumption. In a trial to the court without a jury the court found for the defendant and plaintiff has appealed.

Plaintiff assigns error to the court's failure to sustain his objection to a general finding entered in favor of the defendant and to the court's refusal to enter special findings requested by the plaintiff, among which the following presents the plaintiff's theory of the applicable law:

> *"Cherries in cherry pies are normally pit-less, and are offered to the public in that condition, and plaintiff did not reasonably expect to find a pit in the cherry pie and the defendants [sic] had no knowledge that any pits were baked into pies offered by it for sale."*

Plaintiff also requested the following conclusion of law which the court refused to make:

> *"That a consumer of a piece of cherry pie purchased from a vending machine to be consumed at the time of sale, does not reasonably expect to find a cherry pit in such pie."*

Under ORS 72.3150 if the cherry pie purchased by the plaintiff from the defendant was not reasonably fit for human consumption because of the presence of the cherry pit there was a breach of warranty and plaintiff was entitled to recover his damages thereby caused.

In the consideration of similar cases some of the courts have drawn a distinction between injury caused by spoiled, impure, or contaminated food or food containing a foreign substance, and injury caused by a substance natural to the product sold. In the latter class of cases, these courts hold there is no liability on the part of the dispenser of the food. Thus in the leading case of Mix v. Ingersoll Candy Co., 6 Cal 2d 674, 59 P.2d 144, the court held that a patron of a restaurant who ordered and paid for chicken pie, which contained a sharp sliver or fragment of chicken bone, and was injured as a result of swallowing the bone, had no cause of action against the restaurateur either for breach of warranty or negligence. Referring to cases in which recovery had been allowed the court said:

> *"All of the cases are instances in which the food was found not to be reasonably fit for human consumption, either by reason of the presence of a foreign substance, or an impure and noxious condition of the food itself, such as for example, glass, stones, wires or nails in the food served, or tainted, decayed, diseased, or infected meats or vegetables."*

The court went on to say that:

"* * * despite the fact that a chicken bone may occasionally be encountered in a chicken pie, such chicken pie, in the absence of some further defect, is reasonably fit for human consumption. Bones which are natural to the type of meat served cannot legitimately be called a foreign substance, and a consumer who eats meat dishes ought to anticipate and be on his guard against the presence of such bones."

Further the court said:

> *"Certainly no liability would attach to a restaurant keeper for the serving of a T-bone steak, or a beef stew, which contained a bone natural to the type of meat served, or if a fish dish should contain a fish bone, or if a cherry pie should contain a cherry stone—although it be admitted that an ideal cherry pie would be stoneless."*

The so-called "foreign-natural" test of the Mix case has been applied in the following cases: Silva v. F.W. Woolworth Co., 28 Cal App 2d 649, 83 P.2d 76 (turkey bone in "special plate" of roast turkey); Musso v. Picadilly Cafeterias, Inc. (La App), 178 S2d 421 (cherry pit in a cherry pie); Courter v. Dilbert Bros., Inc., 186 NYS2d (App Div) 334 (prune pit in prune butter); Adams v. Tea Co., 251 NC 565, 112 SE2d 92 (crystallized grain of corn in cornflakes); Webster v. Blue Ship Tea Room, Inc., 347 Mass 421, 198 NE2d 309 (fish bone in a fish chowder).

Other courts have rejected the so-called foreign-natural test in favor of what is known as the "reasonable expectation" test, among them the Supreme Court of Wisconsin, which, in Betehia v. Cape Cod Corp., 10 Wis. 2d 323, 103 NW2d 64, held that a person who was injured by a chicken bone in a chicken sandwich served to him in a restaurant, could recover for his injury either for breach of an implied warranty or for negligence. "There is a distinction," the court said, "between what a consumer expects to find in a fish stick and in a baked or fried fish, or in a chicken sandwich made from sliced white meat and in roast chicken. The test should be what is reasonably expected by the consumer in the food as served, not what might be natural to the ingredients of that food prior to preparation. What is to be reasonably expected by the consumer is a jury question in most cases; at least, we cannot say as a matter of law that a patron of a restaurant must expect a bone in a chicken sandwich either because chicken bones are occasionally found there or are natural to chicken." 10 Wis. 2d at 331-332.

Among other decisions adopting the reasonable expectation test are: Bonenberger v. Pittsburgh Mercantile Co., 345 Pa 559, 28 A2d 913, 143 ALR 1417, Annotation at page 1421 (oyster shell in canned oysters used in making oyster stew); Bryer v. Rath Packing Co., 221 Md. 105, 156 A2d 442, 77 ALR 2d 1 (chicken bone in chow mein); Varone v. Calarco, 199 NYS2d 755 (struvite in canned tuna).

Other decisions upon the question may be found reviewed in Hursh, American Law of Products Liability, §§ 12.33-12.35. See, also, the Annotation, 77 ALR 2d 7, at 79. The foreign-natural test is criticized in Dickerson, Products Liability and the Food Consumer 184-189, and in an article by Mitchel J. Ezer, "The Impact of the Uniform Commercial Code on the California Law of Sales Warranties," 8 UCLA California Law Review 281.

In view of the judgment for the defendant, we are not required in this case to make a choice between the two rules. Under the foreign-natural test the plaintiff would be barred from recovery as a matter of law. The reasonable expectation test calls for determination of a question of fact: Betehia v. Cape Cod Corp.; Bonenberger v. Pittsburgh Mercantile Co.; Bryer v. Rath Packing Co.; Dickerson, Products Liability and the Food Consumer, all supra. The court has found the fact in favor of the defendant and this court has no power to disturb the finding.

Plaintiff argues that the court based its decision on the foreign-natural rule. The court did so indicate in a letter to counsel announcing its decision, but in the same letter the court also spoke of what can be "reasonably anticipated and guarded against by the consumer" and said that the question was a "mixed question of law and facts." Further, the court, as above stated, refused to make a finding of fact requested by the plaintiff that the plaintiff "did not reasonably expect to find a pit in the cherry pie." The general finding entered by the court covered all the issues of fact in the case.

Plaintiff also assigns error to the admission in evidence of defendant's Exhibit A, a pamphlet issued by the United States Department of Agriculture entitled "United States Standards for grades of Frozen Red Tart Pitted Cherries." It is sufficient to say that on the trial plaintiff's counsel stipulated to the admission of the exhibit.

There are no other assignments of error and the judgment is affirmed.

In summary, *Hunt* discussed both the foreign-natural test, i.e., the *Mix* test, and the reasonable expectation test that is applied to impure food cases. The court also distinguished between an injury caused by "spoiled, impure, or contaminated food or food containing a foreign substance, and injury caused by a substance natural to the product sold."

After reading *Hunt*, which test is more favorable to plaintiffs? To manufacturers? What test seems most reasonable to you?

Design defects arise where the design of the product makes the product defective and unreasonably dangerous. Courts will use industry standards, trade customs or trade usage, applicable manufacturing codes, or consensus industry standards in order to determine the nature of any design defect. Design defect cases will always require expert proof, which must be authenticated, and the expert him/herself must be qualified to give objective/fact testimony or render a professional opinion. This requirement implicates what is called the *Daubert Rule* and requires a judge to act as a judicial gatekeeper in order to assure that any alleged expert testimony meets a basic level of fact based on real and not junk science.

A Few Words About The Use Of Expert Witnesses

Proof of a defect in a product may be shown at trial through the testimony of an expert witness, a witness who has knowledge of a technical subject. Technical experts can give opinions on scientific information that is beyond the general knowledge of the jurors. Because of his or her education, training or experience, an expert witness's testimony may help the jury understand complex technical issues. Scientific methodology is based on creating a supposition or premise and testing it to see if experiments support the supposition. If they do, the supposition is regarded as a valid scientific theory and may be presented to the jury as the trier of facts.

Junk Science

Product liability cases in the 1980s and early 1990s were often characterized by the "battle of the experts." Experts for both sides presented opinions that in many cases contradicted one another, leaving the jury to pick between the experts. It appeared that expert testimony was increasingly based on what some came to call junk science. Junk science refers to novel scientific theories that are based on biased data or inferences that are not scientifically proven.

Daubert Test or Standard for Expert Testimony

In 1993, the United States Supreme Court established principles for the admission of expert testimony in the landmark case *Daubert v. Merrell Dow Pharmaceuticals*. The court stated that trial judges should act as gatekeepers and exclude testimony based on junk science. Daubert determined that scientific evidence had to be both relevant and reliable.

The court listed four standards for admitting scientific evidence:

- Has the theory been tested?
- Has the theory been subjected to peer review and publication?
- What is the known or potential rate of error and are there controlling standards?
- Does the scientific community generally accept the theory?

The trial court must apply these standards in deciding whether to admit expert testimony.

State of the art testimony will be utilized to determine the technology available at the time the product left the manufacturer's hand in order to determine if a design defect exists.

Design defect cases recognize the fact that there is a risk involved in the production of many products. Then the question is asked: Did the manufacturer take reasonable steps to correct or at least minimize the risk?

In determining the existence of a design defect, courts must necessarily balance the economic interests of the manufacturer against the safety interests of the consumer. Courts hold that the proper standard to be applied is as follows:

"A product is defective because of its design and unreasonably dangerous if the reasonable seller, having been made aware of the danger involved, would not sell the product."

In many cases, courts will inquire whether or not the hazard, danger, or risk could have been obviated at a slight cost. (For example, selling or manufacturing a lawnmower without a dead man's (cut-off) switch which could have been added or supplied for less than $5.00 – *Burch v. Sears Roebuck.*)

New Jersey follows the majority view. New Jersey courts require a plaintiff to prove that there is a "practical and technically feasible" alternative design that will not impair the core function of the product or unreasonably increase its cost.

The *Boatland* case (below) discusses the issues of feasibility ("the more scientifically and economically feasible the alternative was, the more likely that a jury may find that the product was defectively designed.") This may be shown by proving that a safer alternative was available at the time of manufacture; or that there was evidence of the scientific and economic capacity to develop safer alternatives. *Boatland* also discusses "state of the art" evidence. After reading the case, which opinion (majority or dissent) seems more persuasive to you?

Today, many courts have imposed a duty on the part of a manufacturer to recall and/or possibly repair products which were not necessarily defective when they were designed but which may have become defective at a later date, perhaps through obsolescence or the passing of time—especially if there "is a substantial risk of harm to a large number of persons and if the change required to make the product safer or substantially more safe would be a minimal one." (See *Daubert v. Merrell Dow Pharmaceuticals*).

Boatland of Houston v. Bailey

Supreme Court of Texas, 609 S.W.2d 743 (1980) 26 U.S. 310 (1945)

OPINION BY: McGEE, JUDGE

This is a product defect case involving an alleged defect in the design of a 16-foot bass boat. The plaintiffs were the widow and adult children of Samuel Bailey, who was killed in a boating accident in May of 1973. They sued under the wrongful death statute, alleging that Samuel Bailey's death occurred because the boat he was operating was defectively designed. The boat had struck a partially submerged tree stump, and Bailey was thrown into the water. With its motor still running, the boat turned sharply and circled back toward the stump. Bailey was killed by the propeller, but it is unclear whether he was struck when first thrown out or after the boat circled back toward him.

Bailey's wife and children sought damages under a strict liability theory from the boat's seller, Boatland of Houston, Inc. At trial, they urged several reasons why the boat was defectively designed, including inadequate seating and control area arrangement, unsafe stick steering and throttle design, and the failure of the motor to automatically turn off when Bailey was thrown from the boat.

The trial court rendered a take-nothing judgment based on the jury's failure to find that the boat was defective and findings favorable to Boatland on several defensive issues. The court of civil appeals, with one justice dissenting, reversed and remanded the cause for a new trial because of errors in the admission of evidence and the submission of the defensive issues. We reverse the judgment of the court of civil appeals and affirm that of the trial court.

EVIDENCE OF DESIGN DEFECT

* * * In Turner v. General Motors Corp., this court discussed the strict liability standard of "defectiveness" as applied in design defect cases. Whether a product was defectively designed requires a balancing by the jury of its utility against the likelihood of and gravity of injury from its use. The jury may consider many factors before deciding whether a product's usefulness or desirability is outweighed by its risks. Their finding on defectiveness may be influenced by evidence of a safer design that would have prevented the injury. Because defectiveness of the product in question is determined in relation to safer alternatives, the fact that its risks could be diminished easily or cheaply may greatly influence the outcome of the case.

Whether a product was defectively designed must be judged against the technological context existing at the time of its manufacture. Thus, when the plaintiff alleges that a product was defectively designed because it lacked a specific feature, attention may become focused on the feasibility of that feature the capacity to provide the feature without greatly increasing the product's cost or impairing usefulness. This feasibility is a relative, not an absolute, concept; the more scientifically and economically feasible the alternative was, the more likely that a jury may find that the product was defectively designed. A plaintiff may advance the argument that a safer alternative was feasible with evidence that it was in actual use or was available at the time of manufacture. Feasibility may also be shown with evidence of the scientific and economic capacity to develop the safer alternative. Thus, evidence of the actual use of, or capacity to use, safer alternatives is relevant insofar as it depicts the available scientific knowledge and the practicalities of applying that knowledge to a product's design.

As part of their case-in-chief, the Baileys produced evidence of the scientific and economic feasibility of a design that would have caused the boat's motor to automatically shut off when Bailey fell out. According to the Baileys, the boat's design should have incorporated an automatic cut-off system or the boat should have been equipped with a safety device known as a "kill switch."

The deposition of J. C. Nessmith, president of Boatland, was read, in which he stated that there were presently several types of "kill switches" available, and that they were now installed by Boatland when it assembled and sold bass boats.

The deposition of Bill Smith, who was a passenger in the boat with Bailey at the time of the accident, was also read. Smith had not heard of automatic kill switches before the accident, but afterwards he got one for his own boat.

The deposition testimony of George Horton, the inventor of a kill switch designed for open-top carriers, was also introduced. Horton began developing his "Quick Kill" in November of 1972 and applied for a patent in January of 1973. According to Horton, his invention required no breakthroughs in the state of the art of manufacturing or production. He stated that his invention was simple: a lanyard connects the operator's body to a device that fits over the ignition key. If the operator moves, the lanyard is pulled, the device rotates, and the ignition switch turns off. When he began to market his "Quick Kill," the response by boat dealers was very positive, which Horton perceived to be due to the filling of a recognized need. He considered the kill switch to be a necessary safety device for a bass boat with stick steering. If the kill switch were hooked up and the operator thrown out, the killing of the motor would prevent the boat from circling back where it came from. Horton also testified that for 30 years racing boats had been using various types of kill switches. Thus, the concept of kill switches was not new.

Robert Swint, a NASA employee who worked with human factors engineering, testified that he had tested a bass boat similar to Bailey's. He concluded that the boat was deficient for several reasons and that these deficiencies played a part in Bailey's death. According to Swint, when the boat struck a submerged object and its operator became incapacitated, the seating and control arrangement caused the boat to go into a hard turn. If the operator were thrown out, the boat was capable of coming back and hitting him. Swint also stated that a kill switch would have cut off the engine and the motor would not have been operative when it hit Bailey.

Jim Buller, who was fishing in the area when Bailey was killed, testified that his own boat did not have a kill switch at that time, but he ordered one within "a matter of days."

Boatland elicited evidence to rebut the Baileys' evidence of the feasibility of equipping boats with kill switches or similar devices in March of 1973, when the boat was assembled and sold.

In response to the Baileys' evidence that the "Quick Kill" was readily available at the time of trial, Horton stated on cross-examination that until he obtained the patent for his "Quick Kill" in 1974 he kept the idea to himself. Before he began to manufacture them, he investigated the market for competitive devices and found none. The only applications of the automatic engine shut-off concept in use at the time were homemade, such as on racing boats. He first became aware of competitive devices in August of 1974.

Boatland introduced other evidence to show that kill switches were not available when Bailey's boat was sold. The deposition of Jimmy Wood, a game warden, was read in which he stated that he first became aware of kill switches in 1975. He testified that he had a "Quick Kill" on his boat since 1976, and he thought it was the only kill switch made. Willis Hudson, who manufactured the boat operated by Bailey, testified that he first became aware of kill switches in 1974 or 1975 and to his knowledge no such thing was available before then. Ralph Cornelius, the vice-president of a marine appliance dealership, testified that kill switches were not available in 1973. The first kill switch he saw to be sold was in 1974, although homemade "crash throttles" or foot buttons had long been in use.

* * * After considering the feasibility and effectiveness of an alternative design and other factors such as the utility and risk, the jury found that the boat was not defective. The trial court rendered judgment for Boatland. The Baileys complained on appeal that the trial court erred in admitting Boatland's evidence that kill switches were unavailable when Bailey's boat was assembled and sold. The court of civil appeals agreed, holding that the evidence was material only to the care exercised by Boatland and thus irrelevant in a strict liability case.

In its appeal to this court, Boatland contends that the court of civil appeals misconstrued the nature and purpose of its evidence. According to Boatland, when the Baileys introduced evidence that kill switches were a feasible safety alternative, Boatland was entitled to introduce evidence that kill switches were not yet available when Bailey's boat was sold and thus were not a feasible design alternative at that time.

The primary dispute concerning the feasibility of an alternative design for Bailey's boat was the "state of the art" when the boat was sold. The admissibility and effect of "state of the art" evidence has been a subject of controversy in both negligence and strict product liability cases. In negligence cases, the reasonableness of the defendant's conduct in placing the product on the market is in issue. Evidence of industry customs at the time of manufacture may be offered by either party for the purpose of comparing the defendant's conduct with industry customs. An offer of evidence of the defendant's compliance with custom to rebut evidence of its negligence has been described as the "state of the art defense." In this connection, it is argued that the state of the art is equivalent to industry custom and is relevant only to the issue of the defendant's negligence and irrelevant to a strict liability theory of recovery.

In our view, custom "...is distinguishable from "state of the art." The state of the art with respect to a particular product refers to the technological environment at the time of its manufacture. This technological environment includes the scientific knowledge, economic feasibility, and the practicalities of implementation when the product was manufactured. Evidence of this nature is important in determining whether a safer design was feasible. The limitations imposed by the state of the art at the time of manufacture may affect the feasibility of a safer design. Evidence of the state of the art in design defect cases has been discussed and held admissible in other jurisdictions. In this case, the evidence advanced by both parties was relevant to the feasibility of designing bass boats to shut off automatically if the operator fell out, or more specifically, the feasibility of equipping bass boats with safety switches.

The Baileys offered state of the art evidence to establish the feasibility of a more safely designed boat: They established that when Bailey's boat was sold in 1973, the general concept of a boat designed so that its motor would automatically cut off had been applied for years on racing boats. One kill switch, the "Quick Kill," was invented at that time and required no mechanical breakthrough. The Baileys were also allowed to show that other kill switches were presently in use and that the defendant itself presently installed them.

Logically, the plaintiff's strongest evidence of feasibility of an alternative design is its actual use by the defendant or others at the time of manufacture. Even if a safer alternative was not being used, evidence that it was available, known about, or capable of being developed is relevant in determining its feasibility. In contrast, the defendant's strongest rebuttal evidence is that a particular design alternative was impossible due to the state of the art. Yet the defendant's ability to rebut the plaintiff's evidence is not limited to showing that a particular alternative was impossible; it is entitled to rebut the plaintiff's evidence of feasibility with evidence of limitations on feasibility. A suggested alternative may be invented or discovered but not be feasible for use because of the time necessary for its application and implementation. Also, a suggested alternative may be available, but impractical for reasons such as greatly increased cost or impairment of the product's usefulness. When the plaintiff has introduced evidence that a safer alternative was feasible because it was used, the defendant may then introduce contradictory evidence that it was not used.

Thus in response to the Baileys' evidence of kill switch use in 1978, the time of trial, Boatland was properly allowed to show that they were not used when the boat was sold in 1973. To rebut proof that safety switches were possible and feasible when Bailey's boat was sold because the underlying concept was known and the "Quick Kill," a simple, inexpensive device had been invented, Boatland was properly allowed to show that neither the "Quick Kill" nor any other kill switch was available at that time.

It could reasonably be inferred from this evidence that although the underlying concept of automatic motor cut-off devices was not new, kill switches were not as feasible an alternative as the Baileys' evidence implied. Boatland did not offer evidence of technological impossibility or absolute nonfeasibility; its evidence was offered to show limited availability when the boat was sold. Once the jury was informed of the state of the art, it was able to consider the extent to which it was feasible to incorporate an automatic cut-off device or similar design characteristic into Bailey's boat. The feasibility and effectiveness of a safer design and other factors such as utility and risk, were properly considered by the jury before it ultimately concluded that the boat sold to Bailey was not defectively designed.

In cases involving strict liability for defective design, liability is determined by the product's defective condition; there is no need to prove that the defendant's conduct was negligent. Considerations such as the utility and risk of the product in question and the feasibility of safer alternatives are presented according to the facts as they are proved to be, not according to the defendant's perceptions. Thus, even though the defendant has exercised due care his product may be found defective. When the Baileys introduced evidence of the use of kill switches, Boatland was entitled to introduce rebuttal evidence of nonuse at the time of manufacture due to limitations imposed by the state of the art. Evidence offered under these circumstances is offered to rebut plaintiff's evidence that a safer alternative was feasible and is relevant to defectiveness. It was not offered to show that a custom existed or to infer the defendant's compliance therewith. We would be presented with a different question if the state of the art in 1973 with respect to kill switches had not been disputed and Boatland had attempted to avoid liability by offering proof that Bailey's boat complied with industry custom.

CONCLUSION

For the reasons stated above the judgment of the court of civil appeals is reversed. The judgment rendered by the trial court, that the Baileys take nothing against Boatland, is affirmed.

POPE, J., concurring, in which BARROW, J., joins.

CAMPBELL, Justice, dissenting.

I dissent.

"State of the art" does not mean "the state of industry practice." "State of the art" means "state of industry knowledge." At the time of the manufacture of the boat in question, the device and concept of a circuit breaker, as is at issue in this case, was simple, mechanical, cheap, practical, possible, economically feasible and a concept seventy years old, which required no engineering or technical breakthrough. The concept was known by the industry. This fact removes it from "state of the art."

Boatland is a retail seller. It is not the manufacturer. From the adoption of strict liability in this case, and consideration of public policy, each entity involved in the chain of commercial distribution of a defective product has been subject to strict liability for injuries thereby caused, even though it is in no way responsible for the creation of a defective product or could not cure the defect. The remedy for a faultless retail seller is an action for indemnity against the manufacturer.

In products liability, the measure is the dangerously defective quality of the specific product in litigation. The focus is on the product, not the reasoning behind the manufacturer's option of design or the care exercised in making such decisions. Commercial availability or defectiveness as to Boatland is not the test. Defectiveness as to the product is the test. If commercial unavailability is not a defense or limitation on feasibility to the manufacturer, it cannot be a defense to the seller.

The manufacturer of the boat, Mr. Hudson, testified as follows as concerns the concept of a "kill switch." It is practically without dispute that this is one of the simplest mechanical devices and concepts known to man. Its function is, can be, and was performed by many and varied simple constructions. It is more a concept than an invention. The concept has been around most of this century. It is admittedly an easily incorporated concept. Was an invention required in order to incorporate a circuit breaker on a bass boat? Absolutely not! Did the manufacturer have to wait until George Horton invented his specific "Quick Kill" switch before it could incorporate a kill switch of some sort on its bass boats? Absolutely not! Mr. Hudson uses an even simpler electrical circuit breaker on his boats.

Mr. Hudson testified he could have made a kill switch himself, of his own, and of many possible designs, but simply did not do it. Why didn't he do it? He didn't think about it. He never had any safety engineer examine his boats. He hadn't heard of such, he puts them on now, but still thinks people won't use them.

What is this Court faced with in this case? Nothing more than a defendant seller attempting to avoid liability by offering proof that Bailey's boat complied with industry practice (which it did at that time) but not because of any limitations on manufacturing feasibility at that time. This is an industry practice case. The evidence does not involve "technological feasibility."

There is no dispute that commercially marketed "kill switches" for bass boats were unavailable to Boatland at the time it sold the boat. Horton's "Quick Kill" was unavailable. The important point is that there is no dispute that at the time of the manufacture of Mr. Bailey's boat, a circuit breaker, whether electrical or mechanical could have easily and cheaply been incorporated into the boat.

I would hold that the trial court erred in permitting such evidence by Boatland to go to the jury, and would affirm the judgment of the Court of Civil Appeals.

I further disagree with the majority opinion and agree with the Court of Civil Appeals on the submission of the issues pertaining to Bailey's conduct in handling the boat. There is no evidence that Bailey was struck when first thrown from the boat. The evidence is that he was hit when the boat circled.

The theory of Valerie Bailey's lawsuit is that if the manufacturer had incorporated a circuit breaker in the manufacture of the boat, the boat motor would have cut off when Mr. Bailey was first thrown from the boat. The boat would not have circled back to where he was thrown and struck him with a rapidly spinning propeller. Under this theory, Mr. Bailey's conduct is not determinative of anything. The result would have been the same if he had been in a stump-free lake, hit a submerged log which had just drifted in, and had been thrown from the boat.

The evidence stated in the opinion of the Court of Civil Appeals clearly shows the alleged conduct of Mr. Bailey in operating the boat was reasonably foreseeable by Boatland. The foreseeability of that deviation in the manufacturer's intended use of the product is relevant to the basic question of whether the product was unreasonably dangerous when and as it was marketed. General Motors Corp. v. Hopkins, 548 S.W.2d 344 (Tex.1977).

The harmful effect of the submission of these issues cannot be more vividly displayed than by considering the emphasis placed on them by counsel for Boatland in his argument to the jury. I would affirm the judgment of the Court of Civil Appeals.

RAY, J., joins in this dissent.

Failure To Warn

In general, in order for a warning to be adequate, it must make the product safe for both its intended and foreseeable uses, including any potential foreseeable misuse, especially by children. A warning must also take into account the "environment of use" of a product.

There are three criteria that are used by the courts to determine the adequacy of warnings:

- A warning must be displayed in such a way as to reasonably catch the attention of the person expected to use the product. This element deals with such factual questions as size, position, and even the color of the warnings.
- A warning must fairly apprise a reasonable user of the nature and extent of the danger and not minimize any danger associated with the use of a product.
- A warning must instruct the user how to use the product in such a way so as to avoid the danger—essentially how to safely use the product.

Courts emphasize that manufacturers must anticipate reasonable risks and warn of these risks. Manufacturers must also appreciate the "environment of use" of a product—as will be seen in *Spruill v. Boyle-Midway, Inc.* in the next chapter.

Think about ads for drugs or medical devices that you have either recently heard on the radio or seen on TV. Do these ads really warn the consumer about real risks? Is there such a thing as information overload? Do consumers sometimes turn a "blind eye or a deaf ear" to product warnings?

We will discuss products warnings in great detail in the next chapter.

Questions

1. Find a recent manufacturing defect case. How does the product exhibit a manufacturing defect, given its definition?
2. What flaw to the reasonable expectations test was revealed in *Hunt v. Ferguson-Paulus Enterprises*?
3. *Boatland of Houston* creates and designs boats. Samuel Bailey was operating one of these boats when it hit a partially submerged tree stump, causing Bailey to be thrown into the water. With its motor still running, the boat came back and killed Bailey after being struck by the propeller. It is unclear whether he was struck when he was first thrown out or after the boat came back. At the trial, the family of the deceased presented several reasons why the boat was defectively designed such as inadequate seating and control arrangement, unsafe steering and throttle design, and a failure of the motor to automatically shut off when Bailey was thrown from the boat.
   a. Does the doctrine of strict liability apply to this case? If so, how?
   b. Was the boat defective?
   c. Is Boatland of Houston liable?
4. Ferguson-Paulus Enterprises, the defendant, owns and maintains a vending machine. Hunt, the plaintiff, bought a cherry pie from the vending machine. Upon biting the pie, the plaintiff's tooth broke when it hit a cherry pit. He brought action to recover damage for his injury. Additionally, the plaintiff asserted that "a consumer of a piece of cherry pie purchased from a vending machine does not reasonably expect to find a cherry pit in such pie."
   a. Does the foreign-natural test apply to this case? If so, how?
   b. Is Ferguson-Paulus Enterprises liable for Hunt's injuries?

Chapter Three

PRODUCT WARNINGS

PRODUCT WARNINGS

"... an insufficient warning is in legal effect no warning..." (Spruill v. Boyle-Midway, Inc.)

SPRUILL V. BOYLE-MIDWAY, INC.

United States Court of Appeals for the Fourth Circuit, 308 F.2d 79 (1962)

OPINION BY: BELL, JUDGE

This is an appeal by the defendants, Boyle-Midway, Incorporated, from a judgment of the District Court for the Eastern District of Virginia entered upon a jury verdict for the plaintiffs in a wrongful death action. The defendants having preserved their right by proper motions throughout the trial now ask us to set aside the judgment and rule that the case ought properly not to have gone to the jury; or that if it was properly submitted to the jury that the evidence in the case does not support the verdict.

The defendants are manufacturers and distributors of a product identified as 'Old English Red Oil Furniture Polish'. The plaintiffs in the court below were the parents and siblings of a fourteen months old infant who died as a result of chemical pneumonia caused by the ingestion of a small quantity of the defendant's product.

The mother of the deceased stated that she had purchased the polish on the morning of November 13, 1959, and later in the day was using it in her home to polish furniture. While using it in the deceased's bedroom she noticed a catalog which her mother had asked to see. While still in the course of polishing the furniture, she left the room and took the catalog next door to her mother's home. She testified that she was out of the room for four or five minutes.

At the time she left the room the deceased was in his crib in one corner of the room which was near one end of a bureau. The child could reach the end of the bureau nearest the crib but could not reach articles beyond the very edge of the bureau. The mother placed the polish, prior to leaving the room, upon the end of the bureau that was out of the child's reach. When she returned she found that the child had pulled a cover-cloth which was on the bureau into the crib, and the bottles and other articles sitting on the cloth came into the crib with it. The child had removed the cap of the bottle and had consumed a small portion of the polish.

The child was admitted to a hospital that same day, and according to the testimony of Dr. Barclay ultimately died on November 15th from hydrocarbon pneumonia. This particular type of pneumonia is a form of chemical pneumonia which usually results from the ingestion or inhalation of the petroleum distillate.

Old English Red Oil Furniture Polish is a liquid of a bright cherry red color contained in a clear glass bottle which is about 6 3/4' tall and 2 1/4' in diameter. The bottle has a red metal cap. The evidence shows that there are one and one-half to two threads upon the neck of the bottle and the cap.

The ingredients of Old English Red Oil Furniture Polish are 98.2% mineral seal oil, 1.8% cedar oil, a trace of turpentine, and oil soluble red dye. Chemical analysis of the product states: 'This preparation consists almost entirely of (a) petroleum distillate which is somewhat heavier than kerosene and commonly designated as Mineral Seal Oil, or 300 degree oil, as it distills near 300 degrees C.'

The label consists of a piece of paper of deep red hue which passes completely around the bottle at its center. On the front part of the label appear the words 'Old English Brand Red Oil Furniture Polish' in large letters; beneath this in small letters 'An all purpose polish for furniture, woodwork, pianos, floors'. The reverse side of the label, the background of which is white, contains the following printed matter: at the top in red letters about 1/8th of an inch in height, all in capitals, 'CAUTION COMBUSTIBLE MIXTURE'. Immediately beneath this in red letters 1/16th of an inch high 'Do not use near fire or flame'; several lines down, again in letters 1/16th of an inch in height, in brown ink, all in capitals, the word 'DIRECTIONS'; then follow seven lines of directions printed in brown ink in letters about 1/32nd of an inch in height. On the eighth line in letters 1/16th of an inch high in brown ink appear the words 'Safety Note'; following this in letters approximately 1/32nd of an inch in height:

> *'Contains refined petroleum distillates. May be harmful if swallowed, especially by children.'*

Following this is the name of the manufacturer and various other information with which we are not here concerned.

There was testimony that mineral seal oil is a toxic substance, and that it is a petroleum distillate. The defendants' expert chemists testified that one teaspoonful of this product would kill a small child. There was uncontroverted evidence of several doctors that the child died of hydrocarbon pneumonia resulting from the ingestion of the defendants' polish. Dr. Julius Caplan, one of the doctors treating the deceased, attributed death to the nature of the polish, and stated that because of its toxic quality it was capable of penetrating the intestinal tract, thus getting into the blood stream and thereby setting up fatal lung damage. Dr. James Morgan, another treating physician, testified that this polish contained a hydrocarbon that was toxic and that such resulted in the death of the child.

The mother testified that she had no knowledge that the defendants' product would have caused injury or death to her child. She stated that she had read the statement at the top of the label in large colored letters 'Caution Combustible', but did not read the directions because she knew how to use furniture polish.

At the trial the plaintiffs were allowed to put into evidence certain interrogatories they had served upon the defendants together with the defendant's answers and admissions which showed that the defendants had knowledge or notice of at least thirty-two cases of chemical pneumonia since 1953 resulting from the ingestion of this product. Ten of these thirty-two cases resulted in death. At least seven of these thirty-two cases were infants; four of these infants died as a result of chemical pneumonia. The defendants vigorously objected to the admission of this testimony, and on this appeal assigned its admission as error.

The jury in returning its verdict excluded the mother from sharing in any part of the judgment. The defendants made no request for a special verdict; therefore, the jury returned a general verdict. It was in favor of the plaintiffs other than the child's mother.

* * * The defendants here have at no time raised the issue of lack of privity between themselves and the deceased and it appears that the point is conceded. In any event it is apparent that this case comes within the exception to the doctrine of Winterbottom v. Wright, 10 Mees & W. 109, 152 Eng. Reprint 402 (1842) which is made for inherently dangerous products. There can be no doubt but that this exception to that doctrine is well established in Virginia. General Bronze Corp. v. Kostopulos, 203 Va. 66, 122 S.E.2d 548 (1961); Norfolk Coca-Cola Bottling Works v. Krausse, 162 Va. 107, 173 S.E. 497 (1934); Robey v. Richmond Coca-Cola Bottling Works, 192 Va. 192, 64 S.E.2d 723 (1951). Indeed it is significant to note that the product involved in the leading case of Thomas v. Winchester, 6 N.Y. 397, 57 Am. Dec. 455 (1852), which firmly established the exception made for inherently dangerous products, was a poison.

Within the last year the courts of Virginia held that the test of whether a product is inherently dangerous is whether, 'the danger of injury stems from the product itself, and not from any defect in it.' General Bronze Corp. v. Kostopulos, supra. We hold that the danger of injury from the product stems from the product itself and nor from any defect arising out of, or resulting from, negligence in the course of manufacture. It is therefore, an inherently dangerous product.

The defendants have contended throughout that they are liable only for injuries caused in the course of the intended use of their product. Since their product was not intended to be consumed, they say, there is no liability for death or injury resulting from consumption of it. We agree with the general principle but the application the defendants would have us make of it here is much too narrow. Intended use' is but a convenient adaptation of the basic test of 'reasonable foreseeability' framed to more specifically fit the factual situations out of which arise questions of a manufacturer's liability for negligence. 'Intended use' is not an inflexible formula to be apolitically applied to every case. Normally a seller or manufacturer is entitled to anticipate that the product he deals in will be used only for the purposes for which it is manufactured and sold; thus he is expected to reasonably foresee only injuries arising in the course of such use.

However, he must also be expected to anticipate the environment which is normal for the use of his product and where, as here, that environment is the home, he must anticipate the reasonably foreseeable risks of the use of his product in such an environment. These are risks which are inherent in the proper use for which his product is manufactured. Thus where such a product is an inherently dangerous one, and its danger is not obvious to the average housewife from the appearance of the product itself, the manufacturer has an obligation to anticipate reasonably foreseeable risks and to warn of them, though such risks may be incidental to the actual use for which the product was intended. As the courts of Virginia have stated it,

'The common law requires a higher degree of care and vigilance in dealing with a dangerous agency than in required in the ordinary affairs of life and business which involve small risk of injury.' American Oil Co. v. Nicholas, 156 Va. 1, 157 S.E. 754, 757 (1931). See also Standard Oil Co. v. Wakefield, 102 Va. 824, 47 S.E. 830, 66 L.R.A. 792 (1904).

We have no doubt but that under the circumstances of its use the courts of Virginia would regard Old English Red Oil Furniture Polish as a dangerous agency. A very small quantity of it is lethal to children and extremely dangerous to adults, yet the product gives no indication by its appearance of its life endangering capacity. It appears as harmless as a bottle of soft drink, yet this product is sent daily into thousands of homes in which dwell persons incompetent to safely judge its capacity for harm. It goes there without any reasonable indication from its natural character of its death dealing power if improperly used. It would be quite reasonable to anticipate that in the process of using it for its intended purpose it would be placed in close proximity to children. They certainly cannot be expected to recognize it as a lethal poison. Under these circumstances we think that a reasonable jury could properly find that it was foreseeable that sooner or later some child would draw the fatal draught.

* * * However, even though a reasonable manufacturer should have foreseen that the product would have been consumed by humans, that manufacturer may not be liable if it has adequately warned of the danger to be reasonably foreseen. But a mere indication of danger, in and of itself, does not accomplish an inevitable tergiversation of liability. If warning of the danger is given and this warning is of a character reasonably calculated to bring home to the reasonably prudent person the nature and extent of the danger, it is sufficient to shift the risk of harm from the manufacturer to the user. To be of such character the warning must embody two characteristics: first, it must be in such form that it could reasonably be expected to catch the attention of the reasonably prudent man in the circumstances of its use; secondly, the content of the warning must be of such a nature as to be comprehensible to the average user and to convey a fair indication of the nature and extent of the danger to the mind of a reasonably prudent person.

The only protection available to children living in homes where this product is used is the caution of their parents, who are incapable of recognizing this harmless looking product for the dangerous agency it is. Without additional warning these adults have not the knowledge to invoke their caution on behalf of their young.

Under such circumstances as these the Virginia Courts have imposed upon the manufacturer or seller of the product a duty to warn of the danger.

'A person who knowingly sells or furnishes an article which, by reason of defective construction or otherwise, is eminently dangerous to life or property, without notice or warning of the defect or danger, is liable to third persons who suffer therefrom.' (Emphasis added.) McClanahan v. California Spray-Chemical Corp., supra; quoting with approval, 3 Cooley, Torts, § 498 at 467 (4th ed., 1932).

Where one is under a duty to warn another of danger and he fails to perform this duty by giving adequate warning, he is liable to the person to whom the duty is owed for injuries he suffers due to ignorance of the danger. Low Moore Iron Co. v. La Bianca, 106 Va. 83, 55 S.E. 532 (1906). The sufficiency of the warning is to be judged on the basis of the nature of the danger, and the degree of care required is 'commensurate with the risk therefrom reasonably to be foreseen'. Sadler v. Lynch, 192 Va. 344, 64 S.E.2d 664 (1951).

The duty to call attention to the danger is properly on defendant under the Virginia law. Moreover the question of the sufficiency of the warning is normally for the jury. McClanahan v. California Spray-Chemical Corp., supra; American Oil Co. v. Nicholas, supra; C. F. Maize v. Atlantic Refining Co., 352 Pa. 51, 41 A.2d 850, 160 A.L.R. 449 (1945) quoted with approval in McClanahan, supra. See generally Dillard and Hart, 'Product Liability: Directions For Use And The Duty To Warn', 41 Va. L. Rev. 145, 177-78 (1955).

* * * Keeping in mind the nature of the danger as described above we think reasonable men

could properly differ as to the sufficiency of the notice here given, and that the finding of insufficiency of notice made by the jury in this case is amply supported by the evidence. The notice here given was not printed on the label in such a manner as to assure that a user's attention would be attracted thereto. Indeed, we think one might reasonably conclude that it was placed so as to conceal it from all but the most cautious users. It is located in the midst of a body of print of the same size and color, with nothing to attract special attention to it except the words 'Safety Note'.

Further, even if the user should happen to discover the warning it states only 'contains refined petroleum distillates. May be harmful if swallowed especially by children'. The first sentence could hardly be taken to convey any conception of the dangerous character of this product to the average user. The second sentence could be taken to indicate to the average person that harm is not certain but merely possible. The expert medical evidence in this case shows that 'harm' will not be contingent but rather inevitable, to young and old alike. Moreover, over, the last phrase of the sentence hardly conveys the thought that a very small quantity of the polish is lethal to children.

There were two elements of danger inherent in this product, first, its character as a lethal poison, and second, its combustibility. We think that a reasonable jury could conclude that the greater danger in the environment of the modern home, and therefore the danger which due caution would require to be given the greater prominence on the label, was its poisonous character. Certainly a reasonable jury could conclude that this danger was required to be given a prominence at least equal to that arising from its combustible nature. A jury convinced that the poisonous character of this polish poses the greater danger could reasonably conclude that a manufacturer which hides its warning of the greater danger within its warning of the lesser is indulging its mercantile interests at the expense of the duty of due care it owes to the purchasing public.

The defendants contend, however, that,

> *'The question of the sufficiency of the warning is alleviated by the mother's admission that she never read the label. Not having availed herself of the information contained on the bottle she cannot be permitted to ask for a more explanatory label.'*

The short answer to this is that where the manufacturer is obligated to give an adequate warning of danger the giving of an inadequate warning is as complete a violation of its duty as would be the failure to give any warning. In this case had the warning been in a form calculated to attract the user's attention, due to its position, size, and the coloring of its lettering, and had words used therein been reasonably calculated to convey a conception of the true nature of the danger, this mother might not have left the product in the presence of her child. Indeed, she might not have purchased the product at all, a fact of which the manufacturer appears to be aware. Having deprived the mother of an adequate warning which might have prevented the injury, it cannot be permitted to rely upon a warning which was insufficient to prevent the injury. This is the reasoning behind

> the rule laid down by the courts of Virginia that, '* * * An insufficient warning is in legal effect no warning'. Sadler v. Lynch, 192 Va. 344, 347, 64 S.E.2d 664, 666 (1951); McClanahan v. California Spray-Chemical Corp., supra. The jury in this case could reasonably find that the warning given was insufficient both in form and in content, and did, in fact, so find. The warning being insufficient, defendants cannot be permitted to take aid and comfort from it to any extent.
>
> Perceiving no error by the court below, we Affirm.

There is a close relationship between a defect arising because of a failure to warn and a defect arising because of a defect in the design of a product. In some jurisdictions, the failure to warn may be seen as evidence of a design defect in the product itself because proper instructions and warnings are seen as an integral part of the design of a product.

The *Spruill* case was decided within the context of "inherently dangerous products" (the issue discussed in *Thomas v. Winchester*), where the "danger of injury stems from the product itself, and not from any defect in it" or not resulting from negligence in the course of manufacture.

The requirement of *Spruill* that the product must be inherently dangerous in order for there to be a duty to warn is no longer the law. A warning is required for any product, which may be considered dangerous if used in its intended fashion - encompassing a wide variety of consumer products, food products, and pharmaceuticals.

Spruill establishes that the basic test in a product warning case should be reasonable foreseeability and that a manufacturer must anticipate the environment which is normal for the use of its product.

By focusing on the warnings, the jury may be persuaded that a manufacturer should have changed or modified its warnings rather than change the design of the product. However, in either case, the product may be judged to be defective and liability would follow.

Here are some important points about "warnings."

A warning is not adequate if it minimizes the danger associated with a product, especially if there is a known and documented problem. An example can be seen in the following warning: Inhalation of asbestos in excessive quantities over long periods of time may be harmful. In *In re: Asbestos, Plaintiffs v. Bordelon, Inc.*, the court held that this warning was not adequate to inform insulation workers of the substantial risk of contracting asbestosis and cancer because of the presence of the word may in the warning.

A majority of courts have ruled that there is no duty to warn about obvious or known dangers or where it can be shown that the plaintiff has actual knowledge of a danger. This is substantially the assumption of risk defense that we will discuss in greater detail in the materials on negligence.

Restatement 402A, Comment j tracks this point and states: "A seller is not required to warn with regard to products, or ingredients in them, when the danger or potentiality of danger, is generally known and recognized."

In such a case, it is argued that the warning would serve no practical purpose because it would tell the user nothing that he does not already know. Look at some examples of warnings that would probably not be required under Comment j:

- "Drinking of excessive amounts of alcohol can result in death";
- "Diving into a 4 foot pool can cause spinal cord injury";
- "Falling off a horse can result in injury";
- "Cigarettes cause cancer."

What about the following warnings?

- "Pregnant women should not drink alcohol"; or
- "Keeps arms and feet inside the car on the roller coaster ride."

Some states, like New Jersey, require that warnings must still be given (and posted conspicuously) - even about obvious dangers - because of overriding public policy considerations.

There are several other important issues relating to product warnings:

- Warnings must be given to the user or consumer, but not to the general public, because it might be difficult or impossible to effect or monitor such warnings.
- Where products are sold to sophisticated industrial users for their use in the manufacturing process, the manufacturer or supplier is not required to warn the purchaser's employees. The supplier can escape liability by adequately warning and training the purchaser. This rule would only apply to producer goods, as opposed to consumer goods, which are defined as goods purchased for personal, family or household use.
- Prescription Drugs: A manufacturer's duty to warn is limited to an obligation to advise the prescribing physician or pharmacist of any potential dangers that may result from the drug's use. This is called the learned intermediary exception. Manufacturers, thus, have no duty to warn the patient directly. As to nonprescription (over-the-counter) drugs, the manufacturer must warn consumers directly by and through adequate labels, warnings, and directions.

This learned intermediary exception does not generally apply where a prescription drug such as a vaccine is distributed in a mass immunization program in which the drug manufacturer participated, where required by the FDA, or where a drug is distributed through public health clinics. In these cases, the role of the physician is minimal or perhaps practically nonexistent. Therefore, there is a duty on the part of a manufacturer to directly warn the consumer.

There are also significant minority views, especially regarding common drugs—most notably some antibiotics and birth control pills—because of their routine use and prescription, and again, because of the limited role of the physician. The FDA now requires direct consumer warnings.

Should there be a requirement of a duty to warn after the purchase of a product? A manufacturer or retailer may incur liability for failing to warn relating to dangers in the use of a product which come to its attention after manufacture or sale which occur as a result of advancements in the state of the art, or through the manufacturer being made aware of accidents or problems involving dangers in the use of the product.

Whether such a warning must be given depends on:

- The degree of danger involved;
- The number of instances reported; and
- The cost of any change to the product that might be required in relation to the danger perceived.

What about the nature of such post-manufacture/sale warnings? Courts would have to balance the following:

- The nature and extent of any harm that may result from the continued use of a product without any such notice;
- The burden on the manufacturer involved in locating persons to whom the notice is required to be given;
- The attention expected from the recipient;
- The kind of product involved and the number of products manufactured or sold.

Manufacturers will frequently attempt to warn consumers through issuing a product recall. Look at the number of mass recalls in the past few years! Be attentive to consumer recalls initiated by the Consumer Product Safety Commission. Note how many of these warnings apply to children's toys, baby cribs, and car seats!

Anderson v. Weslo, Inc.

Court of Appeals of Washington, Division 2, 906 P.2d 336 (1995)

OPINION BY: FLEISHER, JUDGE.

After he was injured while jumping on a trampoline, Anderson sued the owner and the manufacturer, alleging failure to warn, unreasonably dangerous design, and inadequate product warnings. He appeals the trial court's granting of summary judgment for the defendants. We affirm, holding that: (1) premises liability has not been established; (2) the trampoline's design is not unreasonably dangerous; and (3) with regard to the manufacturer's warnings, Anderson has not shown proximate cause.

FACTS

Sixteen-year-old David Anderson was injured on May 8, 1990, while attempting to do a double flip on a trampoline manufactured by Weslo and owned by the Iszlers. Anderson landed on his head on the trampoline mat, fracturing a cervical vertebra.

After Anderson was injured, he brought a negligence/products liability action against the Iszlers and Weslo. He alleged that the Iszlers and Weslo's user's manual failed to warn him of the kinds of injuries that could result from doing somersaults on the trampoline. Anderson also alleged that the trampoline's design is unreasonably dangerous. The trial court granted the defendants' motion for summary judgment, and Anderson appeals.

Manufacturers' liability for their defective products or warnings is covered by RCW 7.72.030, which states in pertinent part:

(1) A product manufacturer is subject to liability to a claimant if the claimant's harm was proximately caused by the negligence of the manufacturer in that the product was not reasonably safe as designed or not reasonably safe because adequate warnings or instructions were not provided.

. . . .

(3) In determining whether a product was not reasonably safe under this section, the trier of fact shall consider whether the product was unsafe to an extent beyond that which would be contemplated by the ordinary consumer.

The standard for allegations of defective design and of inadequate warnings is one of strict liability…

FAILURE TO PROVIDE ADEQUATE WARNINGS

Anderson argues that a question of material fact exists with regard to whether the warnings Weslo, Inc. provided were adequate. RCW 7.72.030(1)(b) states:

(b) A product is not reasonably safe because adequate warnings or instructions were not provided with the product, if, at the time of manufacture, the likelihood that the product would cause the claimant's harm or similar harms, and the seriousness of those harms, rendered the warnings or instructions of the manufacturer inadequate and the manufacturer could have provided the warnings or instructions which the claimant alleges would have been adequate.

As with a claim of defective design, a plaintiff may thus establish liability through either this "risk-utility" test or the "consumer expectations" test of RCW 7.72.030(3). But a plaintiff must first show that the lack of adequate warnings or instructions proximately caused his or her injury.

Therefore, we first address the issue of proximate cause, which can be resolved as a matter of law when no reasonable persons would differ. A plaintiff must show both components of proximate cause: cause in fact and legal causation. Cause in fact refers to the "but for" connection between an act and an injury, while legal causation requires a determination of whether liability should attach, based on logic, common sense, policy, and similar considerations.

Here, Weslo provided numerous warnings. Detailed warnings and rules for use are in the user's manual, a placard with safety rules listed is provided for posting near the trampoline, and warning stickers are attached to the metal frame and sewn into the mat. Among the warnings listed in the safety section of the user's manual is the following:

CAUTION SHOULD BE USED TO AVOID THE FOLLOWING TYPES OF ACCIDENTS

4. Landing incorrectly on the trampoline mat.

The list of rules in the user's manual and on the safety card posted near the trampoline also contains this statement:

9. Do not attempt somersaults without proper instruction and competent coaching and supervision, or without the aid of safety apparatus such as overhead suspension, training rig, or spotting machine. Most serious trampoline injuries occur during somersaults.

With regard to cause in fact, when a person is aware of a risk and chooses to disregard it, the manufacturer's warning "serves no purpose in preventing the harm." Thus, the Washington Supreme Court held that inadequate warnings were not the cause in fact of an injury that occurred when two young boys rode their mini-bikes on a public street in disregard of the manufacturer's warnings. Similarly, because Anderson was aware of the risks of injury, yet paid so little attention to the warnings that were given, it is unlikely that he would have changed his behavior in response to even more detailed warnings. Thus, Anderson has not established cause in fact.

But even if cause in fact presents a jury issue in this case, without the existence of legal causation, proximate cause has not been established. In Baughn, the court also found that there was no legal causation. The court pointed out that "[m]any products used by children may be capable of causing injury, but that alone does not mean they should be removed from the market...." On the other hand, the Ayers court held that the legal causation requirement was met when Johnson & Johnson failed to warn of the dangers of aspirating baby oil.

> These cases demonstrate that determining the existence of legal causation is driven by policy considerations and common sense, which in turn stem from the particular facts of the case. Here, unlike in Ayers, detailed warnings were provided. Again, no matter how many warnings are given, or how detailed they are, it is simply impossible completely to prevent trampoline injuries. As one court has pointed out, providing more detailed warnings may very well reduce the chances they will be read, thereby increasing the risk of injury.
>
> Anderson alleges the warnings were inadequate because they did not inform him of every possible injury that could occur or of the mechanism that would cause injury. But he was warned of the general risk of injury and of the serious risk of injury when doing somersaults. Moreover, a manufacturer does not have a duty to warn of obvious or known dangers. The risk of falling or landing incorrectly while jumping on a trampoline is obvious. Logic dictates that if that risk is obvious, it is also obvious that one could land on any part of one's body, including the head, neck, or back, causing very serious injury. For these reasons, we hold that Weslo's warnings adequately informed users of the risk, and therefore, that proximate cause has not been established as a matter of law.
>
> JUDGMENT AFFIRMED

This duty to warn is especially relevant in prescription drug and automobile (and perhaps automobile tire) cases. In other cases, however, there is no general duty to warn regarding changes in technology that might improve safety. In these cases, courts will look to the nature of any industry; the life of any machinery; the shelf life of any drugs; the number of units sold, etc. And one other factor: In general, there might not be high consumer expectations regarding outdated products.

The continuing duty to warn problem is accentuated by difficulties in locating present owners and effectively communicating with them which ranges from difficult in some cases to impossible to others.

Questions

1. Find a product that features some form of risk associated with its use. What makes its warning sufficient/adequate?
2. In Thomas v. Winchester, was the product inherently dangerous? Is the defendant liable?
3. Should states require warnings about obvious dangers due to overriding public policy considerations?
4. Antonio dies from the use of a prescription drug. The manufacturer of the drug advised the prescribing physician of any potential dangers associated with the drug's use.
5. Is the physician liable? Is the manufacturer?
6. How did the duty to warn factor into the defects associated with Firestone tires?
7. Boyle-Midway Inc., the defendant, manufactures and distributes Old English Red Oil Furniture Polish. The Spruill family, the plaintiffs, brought suit for the death of their 14 month old infant, who died as a result of ingesting a small quantity of the defendant's product. Additionally, it should be noted that on the eighth line of the label on the product are the words 'Safety Note' in letter 1/16th of an inch high. Following this, in letters approximately 1/32nd of an inch in height are the words contains refined petroleum distillates. May be harmful if swallowed, especially by children.
   a. Was the warning sufficient?
   b. Does the doctrine of reasonably foreseeability apply? If so, how?
   c. Is Boyle-Midway Inc. liable?
   d. Why were certain parties excluded from receiving any of the damages?

Appendix 3.1

Warnings Relating To Over-The-Counter Drugs

The U.S. Food and Drug Administration (FDA) requires all over-the-counter (OTC) medications to have a Drug Facts label. This label provides basic information about a drug's ingredients, instructions for use, and important safety cautions and interactions. This information will help you to select the correct medication and to use it properly.

The Drug Facts label is only required for OTC drugs, and it is not used for dietary supplements, such as vitamins, minerals, and herbal remedies.

THE DRUG FACTS LABEL:

Whenever you use an over-the-counter (OTC) medicine, reading the drug product's labeling is important for taking care of yourself and your family. The label tells you what the medicine is supposed to do, who should or shouldn't take it, and how to use it. The labeling of OTC medicines has always contained usage and safety information for consumers. With the introduction of the "Drug Facts" label, the information is more uniform and easier to read and understand.

In the Federal Register of March 1999, the Food and Drug Administration published the OTC Drug Facts Label regulation. This regulation required most OTC drug products to comply with the new format and content requirements by May 2002. Manufacturers may continue to use old-format labels until their inventories are exhausted.

The OTC labeling rule applies to more than 100,000 OTC drug products.

Before simplifying the OTC label, the FDA conducted extensive research on how consumers use OTC drug product labels. One major problem has been the readability of the labels, especially for older Americans, who purchase almost 30 percent of the OTC drugs sold in the United States. The FDA also found that consumers thought words like "indications," "precautions," and "contraindications" were confusing and not easily understood.

Previously, information about product directions, warnings, and approved uses appeared in different places on the label depending on the OTC product and brand. Finding information about inactive ingredients has also been a challenge for those who may be allergic to an ingredient in a drug product.

Patterned after the Nutrition Facts food label, the Drug Facts label uses simple language and an easy-to-read format to help people compare and select OTC medicines and follow dosage instructions. The following information must appear in this order:

> The product's active ingredients, including the amount in each dosage unit.
>
> The purpose of the product.
>
> The uses (indications) for the product.
>
> Specific warnings, including when the product should not be used under any circumstances, and when it is appropriate to consult with a doctor or pharmacist. This section also describes side effects that could occur and substances or activities to avoid.
>
> Dosage instructions--when, how, and how often to take the product.
>
> The product's inactive ingredients, important information to help consumers avoid ingredients that may cause an allergic reaction.

Along with the standardized format, the label uses plain-speaking terms to describe the facts about each OTC drug. For example, "uses" replaces "indications," while other technical words like "precautions" and "contraindications" have been replaced with more easily understood words and phrases. The label also requires a type size large enough to be easily read and specific layout details--bullets, spacing between lines, and clearly marked sections--to improve readability.

If you read an OTC medicine label and still have questions about the product, talk to your doctor, pharmacist, or other health care professional.

See the example of an OTC medicine label on the next page.

Drug Facts

Active ingredient (in each tablet)	***Purpose***
Chlorpheniramine maleate 2 mg	Antihistamine

Uses temporarily relieves these symptoms due to hay fever or other upper respiratory allergies:
■ sneezing ■ runny nose ■ itchy, watery eyes ■ itchy throat

Warnings

Ask a doctor before use if you have
■ glaucoma ■ a breathing problem such as emphysema or chronic bronchitis
■ trouble urinating due to an enlarged prostate gland

Ask a doctor or pharmacist before use if you are taking tranquilizers or sedatives

When using this product
■ You may get drowsy ■ avoid alcoholic drinks
■ alcohol, sedatives, and tranquilizers may increase drowsiness
■ be careful when driving a motor vehicle or operating machinery
■ excitability may occur, especially in children

If pregnant or breast-feeding, ask a health professional before use.
Keep out of reach of children. In case of overdose, get medical help or contact a Poison Control Center right away.

Directions

adults and children 12 years and over	take 2 tablets every 4 to 6 hours; not more than 12 tablets in 24 hours
children 6 years to under 12 years	take 1 tablet every 4 to 6 hours; not more than 6 tablets in 24 hours
children under 6 years	ask a doctor

Other information store at 20-25° C (68-77° F) ■ protect from excessive moisture

Inactive ingredients D&C yellow no. 10, lactose, magnesium stearate, microcrystalline cellulose, pregelatinized starch

Appendix 3.2

Recall Letter

Here is an example of a manufacturer (Honda of America) attempting to notify its buyers of a post-purchase problem through a recall letter:

December 2011

NHTSA Recall 11V-260 | Safety Recall: Driver's Airbag Inflator

Dear Honda Owner:

This notice is sent to you in accordance with the requirements of the National Traffic and Motor Vehicle Safety Act.

What is the reason for this notice?

Honda has decided that a defect related to motor vehicle safety exists in certain 2001-2002 model year Accord vehicles, 2001-2003 model year Civic and Odyssey vehicles, 2002 model year CR-V vehicles and 2003 model year Civic Hybrid and Pilot vehicles. In some vehicles, the driver's airbag inflator could produce excessive internal pressure. If an affected airbag deploys, the increased internal pressure may cause the inflator to rupture. Metal fragments could pass through the airbag cushion material possibly causing injury or fatality to vehicle occupants.

What should you do?

You must have your vehicle's driver's airbag inflator replaced; this work will be done free of charge. You must have the inflator replaced even if, earlier this year, you 1) had your vehicle inspected and were told that the driver's airbag inflator did not need to be replaced, as we have now determined that the inflator must be replaced, or 2) received a separate driver's airbag recall notification letter and did not take any action in response to it. In all case, call any authorized Honda dealer and make an appointment to have the driver's airbag inflator replaced. The replacement process may be completed in approximately 30 minutes; however, your vehicle will need to be at the dealer for a longer period of time. We recommend that you plan to leave your vehicle for half a day to allow the dealer flexibility in scheduling.

Who to contact if you experience problems?

If you are not satisfied with the service you receive from your Honda dealer, you may write to:

American Honda Motor Co., Inc.
Honda Automobile Customer Service
Mail Stop 500-2N-7A
1919 Torrance Blvd.
Torrance, CA 90501-2746

If you believe that American Honda or the dealer has failed or is unable to remedy the defect in your vehicle, without charge, within a reasonable period of time (60 days from the date you first contact the dealer for a repair appointment), you may submit a complaint to:

Administrator
National Highway Traffic Safety Administration
1200 New Jersey Ave., SE
Washington, DC 20590

You can also call the toll-free Safety Hotline at (888) 327-4236 [TTY (800) 424-9153], or go to http://www.safercar.gov.

Lessor Information.

Federal law requires that any vehicle lessor receiving this recall notice must forward a copy of this notice to the lessee within 10 days.

If you have questions.

If you have any questions about this notice, or need assistance with locating a Honda dealer, please call Honda Automobile Customer Service at (800) 999-1009, and select option 4. You can also locate a dealer online at wwwHondacars.com.

We apologize for any inconvenience this campaign may cause you.

Sincerely,

American Honda Motor Co., Inc. | Honda Automobile Division

Campaign #Q96 / Service Bulletin #08-093 the airbag cushion material possibly causing injury or fatality to vehicle occupants.

Appendix 3.3

The Black Box Warning

A black box warning is the sternest warning by the U.S. Food and Drug Administration (FDA) that a medication can carry and still remain on the market in the United States.

A black box warning appears on the label of a prescription medication to alert you and your healthcare provider about any important safety concerns, such as serious side effects or life-threatening risks.

A black box warning, also known as a black label warning or boxed warning, is named for the black border surrounding the text of the warning that appears on the package insert, label, and other literature describing the medication, e.g., magazine advertising. It is the most serious medication warning required by the FDA.

When Does the FDA Require a Boxed Warning?

The FDA requires a black box warning for one of the following situations:

The medication can cause serious undesirable effects (such as a fatal, life-threatening or permanently disabling adverse reaction) compared to the potential benefit from the drug. Depending on your health condition, you and your doctor would need to decide if the potential benefit of taking the drug is worth the risk.

A serious adverse reaction can be prevented, reduced in frequency, or reduced in severity by proper use of the drug. For example, a medication may be safe to use in adults, but not in children.

Or, the drug may be safe to use in adult women who are not pregnant.

What Information Does the FDA Require in the Black Box?

The FDA requires the boxed warning to provide a concise summary of the adverse side effects and risks associated with taking the medication. You and your doctor need to be aware of this information when deciding to start the drug or if you should switch to another medication altogether. Understanding side effects will help you make a better informed decision.

Examples of Black Box Warnings

The following are examples of black box warnings that have been required for some commonly used medications:

Fluoroquinolone Antibiotics

According to the FDA, people taking a fluoroquinolone antibiotic have an increased risk of tendinitis and tendon rupture, a serious injury that could cause permanent disability. The FDA warning includes Cipro (ciprofloxacin), Levaquin (levofloxacin), Avelox (moxifloxacin) and other medications containing fluoroquinolone. (Warning issued July 2008.)

Diabetes Medications

According to the FDA, people with diabetes taking Avandia (rosiglitazone) have an increased risk of heart failure or heart attack if they already have heart disease or are at high risk of suffering a heart attack. (Warning issued November 2007.)

Antidepressant Medications

According to the FDA, all antidepressant medications have an increased risk of suicidal thinking and behavior, known as suicidality, in young adults ages 18 to 24 during initial treatment (generally the first one to two months). The FDA warning includes Zoloft (sertraline), Paxil (paroxetine), Lexapro (escitalopram), and other antidepressant medication. (Warning issued May 2007.)

What Does a Black Box Warning Look Like?

The following excerpt from the prescription label of Zoloft is an example of a black box warning.

Suicidality in Children and Adolescents

Antidepressants increased the risk of suicidal thinking and behavior (suicidality) in short-term studies in children and adolescents with Major Depressive Disorder (MDD) and other psychiatric disorders. Anyone considering the use of Zoloft or any other antidepressant in a child or adolescent must balance this risk with the clinical need. Patients who are started on therapy should be observed closely for clinical worsening, suicidality, or unusual changes in behavior. Families and caregivers should be advised of the need for close observation and communication with the prescriber. Zoloft is not approved for use in pediatric patients except for patients with obsessive compulsive disorder (OCD).

Medication Guides

Along with a black box warning, the FDA also requires a drug company to create a medication guide that contains information for consumers on how to safely use a specific medication. The guides contain FDA-approved information that can help you avoid a serious adverse event.

These guides are meant to be given out by your pharmacist at the time you have your prescription filled. The guides are also available online from the drug company and from the FDA. For example, the medication guide for Avandia (rosiglitazone) is available from GlaxoSmithKline, the manufacturer of Avandia, and from the FDA Center for Drug Evaluation and Research.

If you are concerned that your medication has a black box warning, ask your pharmacist and, if available, obtain a printed copy of the medication guide.

Appendix 3.4

Reporting An Unsafe Product

Taken From The Office Of Compliance Of The Consumer Product Safety Commission:

This chapter contains information to familiarize companies with their reporting obligations under the Consumer Product Safety Act (CPSA). Companies that distribute consumer products subject to the provisions of the Federal Hazardous Substances Act (FHSA), Flammable Fabrics Act (FFA), Poison Prevention Packaging Act (PPPA), and Refrigerator Safety Act (RSA) also must comply with these reporting requirements. The information which follows will help you to recognize potentially hazardous consumer products at an early stage, and will assist you in understanding when you are legally obligated to report information about the product to the Commission.

The information contained in this Handbook does not replace the Commission Statutes or Commission Interpretative Regulations set forth in 16 C.F.R. parts 1115 and 1116. For more information about reporting, see also the Commission's Statement of Enforcement Policy, 51 FR 23410 (1986) which may be obtained from the Regional Office.

Statutory Requirements | Reporting Under Section 15 of the CPSA

Section 15(b) of the CPSA defines responsibilities of manufacturers, importers, distributors and retailers of consumer products. Each is required to notify the Commission if it obtains information which reasonably supports the conclusion that a product.

- fails to comply with a consumer product safety standard or banning regulation established by the Commission or a voluntary consumer product safety standard upon which the Commission has relied under section 9 of the CPSA;
- contains a defect which could create a substantial product hazard described in section 15(a)(2) of the CPSA; or
- creates an unreasonable risk of serious injury or death.

The Commission's interpretative regulation (16 C.F.R. part 1115, as amended following the enactment of the Consumer Product Safety Improvement Act of 1990) explains the company's obligations and those of the Commission. A copy of the regulations is included with the LOA or will be provided by the Regional Office upon request.

Reporting Products Involved in Lawsuits

In addition to the amendments to section 15 of the CPSA, a new section 37 reporting requirement has been added to the CPSA. This new section requires manufacturers (including importers) of a consumer product to report to the Commission if (1) a particular model of a consumer product is the subject of at least three civil actions that have been filed in Federal or State court, (2) each suit alleges the involvement of that model in death or grievous bodily injury (as defined in section 37(e)(1)), and (3) at least three of the actions result in a final settlement involving the manufacturer or in a judgment for the plaintiff within any one of the two year periods specified in section 37(b). The first two year period began to run on January 1, 1991 and ends on December 31, 1992. The second two year period starts on January 1, 1993; the third, on January 1, 1995; and so forth. Manufacturers must file a report within 30 days after the settlement or judgment in the third civil action to which the section 37 reporting requirement applies.

Why Reporting Is Required

The intent of Congress in enacting section 15(b) and section 37 of the CPSA was to encourage widespread reporting of potential product hazards. Congress sought not only to have the Commission uncover substantial product hazards, but also to identify risks of injury which the Commission could attempt to prevent through its own efforts, such as information and education programs, safety labeling, and adoption of product safety standards.

Although CPSC relies on sources other than company reports to identify substantial product hazards, reporting by companies under section 15 and section 37 provisions is invaluable because firms often learn of product safety problems long before the Commission does. For this reason, any company involved in the manufacture, importation, distribution or sale of consumer products should develop a system of reviewing and maintaining consumer complaints, inquiries, product liability suits and comments on the products they handle.

If a firm reports to the Commission under section 15 of the CPSA, it does not necessarily mean there is a substantial product hazard. Section 15 simply requires firms to report whenever a product (1) fails to comply with a consumer product safety rule; (2) fails to comply with a voluntary standard upon which the Commission has relied; (3) contains a defect that could create a substantial product hazard; or (4) creates an unreasonable risk of serious injury or death. Thus, a product need not actually create a substantial product hazard to trigger the reporting requirement.

When To Report

It is the Commission's view that a firm should take that all important first step of notifying the Commission when the information available to the company reasonably indicates that a report is required. It is in the company's interest to assign the responsibility of reporting to someone in executive authority. The individual's knowledge of the product and the reporting requirements of section 15 and section 37 are valid reasons for assigning the responsibility.

Reporting Procedures

A company is considered to have knowledge of product safety information when such information is received by an employee or official of the firm who may reasonably be expected to be capable of appreciating the significance of that information. Under ordinary circumstances, five (5) days is the maximum reasonable time for that information to reach the chief executive officer or other official assigned responsibility for complying with the reporting requirements. Weekends and holidays are not counted in that timetable.

The Commission will evaluate whether or when a firm should have reported. This evaluation will be based, in part, on what a reasonable person, acting under the circumstances, knows about the hazard posed by the product. Thus, a firm shall be deemed to know what it would have known if it had exercised due care ascertaining the accuracy of complaints or other representation.

If the company is uncertain whether the information is reportable, the firm may elect to spend a reasonable time investigating the matter, but no evaluation should exceed ten (10) days unless the firm can demonstrate that a longer timetable for the investigation is reasonable. If a firm elects to conduct an investigation to decide whether it has reportable information, the Commission will deem that, at the end of ten (10) days, the firm has received and considered all information which would have been available to it had a reasonable, expeditious, and diligent investigation been undertaken.

Penalties For Failure To Report

Failure to report in accordance with the above referenced requirement is a prohibited act under section 19(a) of the CPSA which states: It shall be unlawful for any person to - (4) fail to furnish information required by section 15(b); (11) fail to furnish information required by section 37.

Any person who commits a prohibited act is subject to civil penalties under section 20 of the CPSA, including fines up to $1.25 million for a related series of violations, and criminal penalties under section 21 of the CPSA, which includes fines up to $500,000 or imprisonment not more than one year, or both. Chapter 1 of this Handbook provides additional details regarding the penalties.

… excerpted from the REGULATED PRODUCTS HANDBOOK, U.S. Consumer Product Safety Commission, Office of Compliance, February 1994 - 2nd Edition*

Brought to you by - The 'Lectric Law Library: The Net's Finest Legal Resource for Legal Pros & Laypeople Alike, http://www.lectlaw.com

Appendix 3.5

Some Examples Of Recent Product Recalls

May 05, 2016

BRP Recalls Side-by-Side Off-Road Vehicles Due to Loss of Steering Control and Crash Hazard (Recall Alert)

The steering coupling can strip on the rack and pinion assembly and result in a loss of steering control.

May 05, 2016

Munchkin Recalls Latch Lightweight Pacifiers & Clips Due to Choking Hazard

The clip cover can detach from the pacifier's clip.

May 03, 2016

Cascade Designs Recalls Avalanche Rescue Probes Due to Risk of Suffocation

The lock button on the probe can fail to engage and lock, causing the probe not to function as intended. This can interfere with finding someone buried beneath snow.

May 03, 2016

Walmart Recalls Rival Electric Water Kettles Due to Burn and Shock Hazards

The heating element can fail and rupture, posing shock and burn hazards to the user.

April 29, 2016

Cub Cadet Recalls Challenger Off-Road Utility Vehicles Due To Crash Hazard (Recall Alert)

The parking brake cable can fail, posing a crash hazard.

April 26, 2016

Stile Products Expands Recall of Tern Folding Bicycles Due to Fall Hazard

The bike's frame can crack at the hinge on the top tube.

April 26, 2016

One World Technologies Recalls Snow Blowers Due to Fire and Burn Hazards; Sold Exclusively at Home Depot

The snow blowers can overheat.

April 26, 2016

Alltrade Tools Recalls Ratcheting Tie Downs Due to Injury Hazard; Sold Exclusively at Sam's Club

The ratchet handle can fail during use, releasing the secured load, posing an injury hazard to consumers.

US Consumer Product Safety Commission – Excerpts from "Recent Recalls and Product Safety News"

Lacrosse Helmets Recalled by Easton Sports Due to Facial Injury Hazard (Thu, 22 Mar 2012 16:00:00 GMT) The chin bar can break, causing the wearer to suffer a jaw or facial injury.

Adjustable Mattress Bases Recalled by Leggett & Platt Due to Fire Hazard (Thu, 22 Mar 2012 15:00:00 GMT) Electrical components in the motor control board can fail and short causing overheating, which poses a fire hazard.

Safety 1st Cabinet Locks Recalled Due to Lock Failure; Children Can Gain Unintended Access to Dangerous Items (Thu, 22 Mar 2012 11:00:00 GMT) Young children can disengage the cabinet locks, allowing access to cabinet contents and posing the risk of injury, due to dangerous or unsafe items.

Ceiling Fans Recalled by Westinghouse Lighting Due to Shock and Fire Hazards (Wed, 21 Mar 2012 19:45:00 GMT) The two 60-watt light bulbs included with the ceiling fans exceed the fan's maximum wattage, which can cause the ceiling fans to overheat or fail. This poses fire and shock hazards to consumers.

Bon Hiver Recalls Freebase Snowboard Bindings Due To Fall Hazard (Tue, 20 Mar 2012 14:30:00 GMT) The binding's base plate can fracture from impact during use, posing a fall hazard to snowboarders.

North American Product Safety Agencies Team Up in the Name of Poison Prevention (Mon, 19 Mar 2012 17:00:00 GMT) As the United States marks the 50th anniversary of National Poison Prevention Week from March 18-24, the U.S. Consumer Product Safety Commission (CPSC) is teaming up with product safety counterparts in Canada and Mexico to call attention to the dangers of unintentional poisoning.

Kawasaki USA Recalls Utility Vehicles due to Fire Hazard (Thu, 15 Mar 2012 14:00:00 GMT) The fuel tube can scrape against the air cleaner housing and develop holes, posing a fire hazard.

Hydrostatic Lawn Tractors Recalled by Hydro-Gear Due to Crash Hazard (Tue, 13 Mar 2012 16:00:00 GMT) A drive gear in the lawn tractor's hydrostatic transaxle can fail causing brake failure, posing a crash hazard to consumers.

Guidecraft Recalls Children's Play Theaters Due to Tip-over Hazard (Tue, 13 Mar 2012 15:00:00 GMT) The recalled children's toys can unexpectedly tip over during play, posing an entrapment hazard to young children.

Umbro Boys' Jackets with Drawstrings Recalled; Waist Drawstrings Pose Entrapment Hazard; Sold Exclusively at Ross Stores (Thu, 08 Mar 2012 16:30:00 GMT) The boys' jacket has a retractable elastic drawstring at the waist with a toggle that could become snagged or caught in small spaces or doorways, which poses an entrapment hazard to children.

Lenovo Recalls ThinkCentre Desktop Computers Due to Fire Hazard (Thu, 08 Mar 2012 15:30:00 GMT) A defect in an internal component in the power supply can overheat and pose a fire hazard.

Locker Brand Recalls Rx Lockers Due to Failure Leading to Allowing Unauthorized Access to Medicine Containers (Wed, 07 Mar 2012 18:00:00 GMT) The medicine container can open by applying pressure to the latch when it is locked. This could result in unauthorized access to medicine bottles in the container.

Change Batteries in Smoke and CO Alarms This Weekend (Wed, 07 Mar 2012 17:00:00 GMT) The U.S. Consumer Product Safety Commission (CPSC) is urging consumers to replace the batteries in their smoke and carbon monoxide (CO) alarms this weekend for Daylight Saving Time. This year, Daylight Saving Time begins on Sunday, March 11. Fresh batteries allow smoke and CO alarms to do their jobs saving lives by alerting families of a fire or a buildup of deadly carbon monoxide in their homes.

Notes

Chapter Four

Tests Of A Product Defect

How do we know if a product is defective in either design or manufacture? This area of law is very complex and no single rule or test will apply uniformly throughout the United States. Thus, courts will use one of the following: consumer expectations, assumption of risk analysis, or the risk-utility (risk-benefit) test.

Consumer Expectations Test

This test addresses the reasonable expectations of the consumer or purchaser. The test requires that the product must be dangerous to an extent beyond that which would be contemplated by the ordinary consumer who purchases it, with the ordinary knowledge common to the community as to its characteristics.

This is the test discussed in *Gray v. Manitowoc Co., Inc.*, which has its basis in Comment I of Section 402A of the Restatement of the Law of Torts.

Dean Prosser, the main author of the Restatement of the Law of Torts, restated the test as follows: *"Would the ordinary consumer expect to encounter such a risk in using a product?"*

Case Study: Gray v. Manitowoc Co, Inc.

Procedural Posture

Defendant manufacturer appealed from the judgment of United States District Court for the Southern District of Mississippi, which denied defendant's motions for Judgment n.o.v. and for a new trial following a jury verdict in favor of plaintiffs husband and wife. Defendant claimed there was insufficient evidence to support recovery on plaintiffs' theories of strict liability, implied warranty, and negligence.

Overview

Plaintiff husband was injured at his construction job when he was struck by the boom of a crane manufactured by defendant manufacturer. Plaintiffs husband and wife brought an action against defendant for strict liability in tort, implied warranty, and negligence, alleging that plaintiff's injuries were caused by a design defect in the crane which prevented the crane operator from seeing to his left when the crane was operated in the "boom down" position. After a jury verdict for plaintiffs, the trial court denied defendant's motions for judgment n.o.v. and for new trial. On appeal, the court determined that the defect of which plaintiffs complained was well known in the construction industry and thus was a patent or obvious hazard. Applying state law, the court held that a manufacturer's liability for product defects under any of plaintiffs' theories of liability could not, as a matter of law, be premised on the existence of an obvious hazard in a product which functioned properly for its intended purpose. As a result, the court reversed the judgment of the trial court and rendered judgment for defendant.

Outcome

The court reversed the judgment of the trial court and rendered judgment in favor of defendant manufacturer because it held that plaintiffs husband and wife had failed to establish liability for a design defect under theories of strict liability, implied warranty or negligence. The court held that the defect which plaintiffs complained of was obvious and within the expectation of the ordinary consumer who purchased it.

Note the similarity to the reasonable man test formulated in negligence cases, discussed earlier. Note also the intentional use of the word "ordinary" as a synonym for the word reasonable.

As will be seen in Chapter 9, this standard of consumer expectations is very close to that of merchantability found in the UCC, where in order to be merchantable, goods sold must be fair, average quality and fit for their ordinary purpose as determined by the ordinary or reasonable consumer.

Defects in products are of two general types: patent (or obvious) and latent (or hidden). Generally, courts apply the consumer expectations test more rigidly where a defect is latent because the consumer is completely unaware of any danger posed by a product and would therefore reasonably expect the product to be safe.

Brawner v. Liberty Industries, Inc.

Court of Appeals of Missouri, St. Louis District, Division One, 573 S.W.2d 376 (1978)

OPINION BY: SMITH, JUDGE

Plaintiff appeals the order of the trial court dismissing with prejudice his suit against defendants brought under a theory of strict liability in tort. We affirm.

Plaintiff is seven years old and was burned when he and Ray Middleton, Jr., also seven years old, removed the lid from a gasoline storage container and the gasoline ignited. The gasoline container was manufactured by defendant Liberty Industries, Inc., and purchased by Ray Middleton (presumably the younger Middleton boy's father) from defendant National Food Stores, Inc. and its store manager defendant Ipellito. The allegation upon which plaintiff sought to invoke the strict liability doctrine was:

> *"That the failure of said gasoline storage container to be equipped with an opening device which would render same to unable to be opened by a child of seven years constitutes a defect in design and an unreasonably dangerous condition of said gasoline storage container."*

In Keener v. Dayton Electric Mfg. Co., 445 SW2d 362 (Mo. 1969), Missouri adopted the theory of strict liability in tort set forth in Restatement of Torts 2d, Sec. 402 A as follows:

> *"One who sells any product in a defective condition unreasonably dangerous to the user or consumer or to his property is subject to liability for physical harm thereby caused to the ultimate user or consumer or to his property, . . ."*

In Missouri a defect in design can meet the requirement of "defective condition". See Keener, supra; Higgins v. Paul Hardeman, Inc., 457 SW2d 943 (Mo. App. 1970).

Under Comments to Sec. 402 A para. (g), we find that a defective condition is a "condition not contemplated by the ultimate consumer which will be unreasonably dangerous to him." Paragraph (i) of the Comments states that "Unreasonably dangerous" means "The article sold must be dangerous to an extent beyond that which would be contemplated by the ordinary consumer who purchases it, with the ordinary knowledge common to the community as to its characteristics." A gasoline container which does not have a child-proof spout does not meet the definition of either defective or unreasonably dangerous. A manufacturer is not an insurer nor must he create a product which is accident proof. See Royal v. Black and Decker Manufacturing Co., 205 So.2d 307 (Fla. App. 1968); Vincer v. Esther Williams All-Aluminum Swimming Pool, 69 Wis. 2d 326, 230 NW2d 794 (1975); Belotte v. Zayre Corp. 352 A.2d 723, 116 N.H. 52 (1976). We have found no case, nor have we been cited to one, where a product made for adult use is deemed defective and unreasonably dangerous solely because it has not been made child-proof. The trial court correctly dismissed plaintiff's petition.

Plaintiff objects to the trial court's failure to allow plaintiff an opportunity to amend. Initially, the record does not indicate plaintiff ever requested such an opportunity. Secondly, plaintiff has not indicated what amendment he would or could make to state a cause of action.

Judgment affirmed. All concur.

Brawner makes an important point, noting that a manufacturer is not an insurer; that is, a manufacturer does not promise or guaranty that he has manufactured a product that is accident-proof or safe under all circumstances. In *Brawner*, the court held that a product that is made safe for adult use is not necessarily defective and unreasonably dangerous solely because it has not been made childproof. There is no reasonable expectation that the product would, in fact, be childproof. Remember, however, the concept of the environment of use found in *Spruill*. If it could be foreseen that the product might or would be used by a child, the application of the consumer expectations test might lead to the conclusion that the product was defective. In *Keller v. Welles Department Store of Racine* (a design defect case), the court noted:

> *"If the average consumer would not reasonably anticipate the dangerous condition of the product and not fully anticipate the attendant risk of injury, it would be unreasonably dangerous and defective."*

A problem with the consumer expectations test arises in design cases because the product may be too complex to generate any concrete consumer expectations. Consumer expectations about safety are often vague or will oscillate between "it will never happen to me" or "all products are poorly made." There is thus an anomaly that since most consumers are highly skeptical about products, it might never be seen as a reasonable expectation that a product is safe!

Keller v. Welles Department Store Of Racine

Court of Appeals of Wisconsin, 88 Wis. 2d 24; 276 N.W.2d 319 (1979)

OPINION BY: BODE

This is a products liability case. On October 21, 1971, two and one-half year old Stephen Keller was playing with two year old William Sperry in the basement of the Sperry home. The boys were playing with a gasoline can which had been filled with gasoline by Wayne Sperry, William's father. The can was manufactured by Huffman Manufacturing Company, Inc. (Huffman) and was purchased by Wayne Sperry at Welles Department Store (Welles). The children were near a gas furnace and a hot water heater when gasoline, which they had poured from the can, was ignited. Stephen Keller was severely burned. Although Mrs.

Sperry was home at the time of the accident, the two boys were unsupervised.

The sole issue before this court is whether the complaint states a cause of action against the manufacturer and retailer of a gasoline can, in either strict liability or negligence, for injuries sustained by Stephen Keller resulting from the ignition of gasoline poured from a gasoline can without a child-proof cap.

In this case, plaintiff attempts to state causes of action both in strict liability and in negligence. Each theory will be considered separately.

STRICT LIABILITY

In Dippel v. Sciano, 37 Wis.2d 443, 155 N.W.2d 55 (1967), the Wisconsin Supreme Court adopted sec. 402A of Restatement, 2 Torts 2d, thereby accepting the concept of strict liability. The court immediately hastened to add, and has since reiterated, that strict liability makes a manufacturer neither an insurer nor absolutely liable for any harm resulting from the use of his product. On the contrary, to recover under the theory of strict liability the plaintiff must still prove:

(1) that the product was in defective condition when it left the possession or control of the seller, (2) that it was unreasonably dangerous to the user or consumer, (3) that the defect was a cause (a substantial factor) of the plaintiff's injuries or damages, (4) that the seller engaged in the business of selling such product . . ., and (5) that the product was one which the seller expected to and did reach the user or consumer without substantial change in the condition it was when he sold it. Dippel, 37 Wis.2d at 460, 155 N.W.2d at 63.

To state a cause of action under strict liability then, the plaintiff must essentially allege that the product was defective and unreasonably dangerous. In the present case, the complaint clearly alleges that the defendants respectively manufactured or sold a gasoline can which was defective and unreasonably dangerous to children such as the plaintiff. The defect complained of was the failure to design the can with a cap sufficient to prevent children from removing it.

* * * The defendants contend that the motion to dismiss should have been granted because, as a matter of law, no jury could have reasonably concluded that the gasoline can was either defective or unreasonably dangerous. In support of their argument, the defendants rely on Vincer v. Esther Williams All-Aluminum Swimming Pool Co., 69 Wis.2d 326, 230 N.W.2d 794 (1975).

In Vincer, a young boy was visiting his grandparents' home. While unsupervised, he fell into a swimming pool, remained there for a prolonged period of time, and sustained severe brain damage. The allegation was that a retractable ladder to the aboveground pool had been left in the down position, thereby providing easy access to the pool. The parents brought suit against the manufacturer of the swimming pool claiming that the pool was defectively designed in that it failed to provide a self-latching and closing gate to prevent entry to the pool. The Esther Williams Company demurred to the complaint for failure to state a cause of action. The trial court sustained the demurrer and the supreme court affirmed.

In its opinion, the court determined as a matter of law that the pool did not contain an unreasonably dangerous defect. The defendants believe the principles enunciated in Vincer mandate a similar outcome in the instant case. We disagree.

Comment g to sec. 402A of Restatement, 2 Torts 2d, states that a product is in a defective condition when "at the time it leaves the seller's hands, [it is] in a condition not contemplated by the ultimate consumer, which will be unreasonably dangerous to him." While this comment serves as a guideline, there is no general definition for "defect," and a decision on whether a defect exists must be made on a case-by-case basis. Jagmin v. Simonds Abrasive Co., 61 Wis.2d 60, 66, 211 N.W.2d 810, 813 (1973).

The Vincer court concluded that the swimming pool could not have been defective for failure to have the suggested gate because it had a retractable ladder which rendered the pool "as safe as it reasonably could be." Vincer, 69 Wis.2d at 331, 230 N.W.2d at 798. The product at issue here, a gasoline can, was not as safe as was reasonably possible since the cap was not designed in such a way as to prevent young children from removing it. Equipping the gasoline can with a child-proof cap would have rendered the can substantially safer and entailed only a nominal additional cost. The practical value of such a cap may readily be seen since gasoline cans, while not intended to be used by children unable to appreciate the attendant dangers of gasoline, are customarily stored in places accessible to children.

The second element to be considered is whether the defective product, the gasoline can, was unreasonably dangerous. Comment i to sec. 402A of the Restatement, in part, describes an article as unreasonably dangerous when it is "dangerous to an extent beyond that which would be contemplated by the ordinary consumer who purchases it, with the ordinary knowledge common to the community as to its characteristics." In Arbet v. Gussarson, 66 Wis.2d 551, 225 N.W.2d 431 (1975), the distinction between dangers which are latent or hidden and those which are obvious was explored in the context of this Restatement comment. The court observed that since an ordinary consumer would expect a Volkswagen to be less safe in an accident than a larger car, the small size would not make the Volkswagen unreasonably dangerous. Arbet itself dealt with a design defect in a Rambler Station Wagon which resulted in gasoline being retained in the passenger compartment. Since the danger arising from this defect was hidden rather than obvious, the supreme court reversed the trial court and upheld the complaint as against the demurrer of the car manufacturer.

Vincer noted that the patent-danger rule discussed in Arbet and stated that the Wisconsin test of whether a product contains an unreasonably dangerous defect was as follows: "If the average consumer would reasonably anticipate the dangerous condition of the product and fully appreciate the attendant risk of injury, it would not be unreasonably dangerous and defective." Vincer, 69 Wis.2d at 332, 230 N.W.2d at 798. The court then concluded that the swimming pool did not contain an unreasonably dangerous defect for two reasons: first, because the absence of a self-latching gate was an obvious condition and second, because the average consumer would recognize the inherent danger of a retractable ladder in the down position when unsupervised children are about.

We think a different result is warranted in the present case. While the defect in the gasoline can was not concealed, this court is unable to conclude, as a matter of law, that the absence of a child-proof cap was an obvious as opposed to a latent condition. Nor do we believe the dangers to unsupervised children from a gasoline can without a child-proof cap are so apparent that the average consumer would be completely aware of them.

In this regard the factual circumstances in this case are clearly distinguishable from those in Vincer. It is common knowledge that children are attracted to swimming pools and that precautions must therefore be taken. See McWilliams v. Guzinski, 71 Wis.2d 57, 62, 237 N.W.2d 437, 439 (1976) (holding that an insufficiently guarded swimming pool in a residential area is an attractive nuisance to a four year old child). The danger to a young child from a swimming pool is obvious. The hazards to a child arising from a gasoline can without a child-proof cap are not so readily apparent. A child is not so clearly attracted to this product that an adult would immediately be put on guard to take precautions for the child's safety.

Based on the foregoing discussion, we conclude the complaint stated a cause of action in strict liability.

Assumption of Risk Analysis

If a reasonable consumer knows about a risk and nevertheless proceeds to use a product, it may be said that the consumer has assumed the risk of such use.

These are the two elements of the defense of assumption of risk: knowledge of a risk, and voluntary acceptance of that risk. If there were a known risk (a patent or obvious risk), then a reasonable consumer would not have the expectation that the product is completely safe and would be expected to act accordingly. In that sense, the assumption of risk defense may be another formulation of the consumer expectations test.

The Risk-Utility Test or Risk-Benefit Test

This test looks to what a reasonable seller/manufacturer would do in the face of a product that carries with it a risk or a danger. It is essentially a negligence standard, based on the expected conduct of a reasonable manufacturer. This test has enormous ethical and social responsibility aspects! The risk-utility test places the burden of proof on a manufacturer in a design case to justify why a certain product was manufactured.

The risk-utility test often revolves around a simple concept: Whether the cost of making a safer product is greater than the risk from using the product in its present form. If the cost of making the change is greater than the risk created by not making the change then the utility of keeping the product as is outweighs the risk and the product is not defective. If the cost of making the change is minimal or is less than the risk created by not making the change, then the benefit or utility of keeping the product as is outweighed by the risk and the product is defective. This is obviously a balancing act - a judgment call - on the part of the trier of fact. In many cases, the cost of effecting any change will be the most significant or overriding factor in applying the risk-benefit/risk-utility test. The lower the cost, the more likely that a court or jury will find that the product without the change is in fact defective!

Case Study: Phillips v. Kimwood Machine Company

Overview

Plaintiff appealed a judgment of the lower court directing a verdict for defendant in product liability case. The court reversed and found that defendant did not warn plaintiff's employer about possible problems that could arise because of the lack of safety devices on the sanding machine. The court found, in determining whether a design is unreasonably dangerous, the fact finder must look at the surrounding circumstances and knowledge at the time the product was sold, and whether a reasonably prudent manufacturer would have designed and sold the product if he had known of the risks. Here, the court found the jury could find the product was unreasonably dangerous and defective because the manufacturer had knowledge of the product and inspected plaintiff's machine before the accident. Further, the lack of warning to plaintiff of possible dangers associated with the use of the machine may have rendered the machine dangerously defective.

Outcome

The court reversed the judgment and remanded for a new trial because the jury could find the machine was dangerously defective, and the jury should decide whether the injury resulted from a design defect or misuse.

The common standards or factors used for determining risk-utility or risk-benefit are found in footnote number 13 in *Phillips*. They include:

- The usefulness and desirability of the product: There are some products that have little or no utility and would not even pass this ''threshold" test. Such products today might include assault weapons for skeet shooting, some large "home use" fireworks displays, or lawnmowers or boats without a 'dead mans' switch;
- The likelihood and probable seriousness of injury from the product as it is manufactured;
- The availability of a substitute product that would meet the same needs of the consumer and not be unsafe. If there are no substitute products, it might be difficult to find this particular product defective. Think of this in terms of an experimental drug used to treat cancer or AIDS. This drug may be very dangerous, but still may have a very high utility;
- The manufacturer's ability to eliminate the danger without impairing the usefulness of the product or making the product too expensive. This is the essence of the standard from the standpoint of the manufacturer! If a product becomes "too expensive," no one would be able to purchase it at all!;
- Given the nature of a danger, the user's ability to avoid the danger—especially with proper warnings or instructions);
- The user's anticipated awareness of the danger;
- The feasibility, on the part of the manufacturer, of spreading the risk by pricing decisions or through the purchase of insurance.

Under a risk-utility analysis, we are asked to determine that the product should never have been manufactured in the first place! Examples of such products might include the four foot high swimming pool with a diving/platform board attached; an assault weapon that the manufacturer advertised would be suitable for "backyard" shooting practice; or home-use bottle rockets (in effect, mini-mortars) for "safe use," during the July Fourth holiday. Think about the risk-utility test in conjunction with the manufacturing of the Pinto automobile.

Phillips makes an important point in the following statement:

> *"A dangerously defective article would be one which a reasonable person would not put into the "stream of commerce" if he had knowledge of its harmful characteristics."*

This is a "presumed knowledge" standard that assumes that the manufacturer in fact knew of the danger or harmful characteristics of a product.

As noted, *Phillips* also suggests that if a change in a product could have been effected at a relatively small price, there is a good chance liability will be imposed for not making the change. This may be the most important consideration for a jury!

In sum, in employing the risk-utility test, manufacturers, first, and then courts must balance several factors:

- Product cost: the relative cost both to the manufacturer and the consumer of producing, distributing, and selling the original product as compared to the product with the alternative design;
- Technological feasibility of an alternative design (e.g., a child's crib with larger slats, thus with smaller gaps);
- Time lag required to effect necessary changes or within which to implement the alternative design; (the shorter the time period needed to correct a problem, the more likely that a court would require the change to be made);
- The effect the new design has on product performance. Cars that travel at five miles per hour would be much safer but would they be practical or have any utility? Apple pie or coffee served by McDonald's at room temperature would be much safer but would anyone want to purchase such a product?

Case Study: Liebeck v. McDonald's

Overview

There is a lot of hype about the McDonalds' scalding coffee case. No one is in favor of frivolous cases of outlandish results; however, it is important to understand some points that were not reported in most of the stories about the case. McDonalds coffee was not only hot, it was scalding -- capable of almost instantaneous destruction of skin, flesh and muscle. Here's the whole story.

Stella Liebeck of Albuquerque, New Mexico, was in the passenger seat of her grandson's car when she was severely burned by McDonalds' coffee in February 1992. Liebeck, 79 at the time, ordered coffee that was served in a styrofoam cup at the drive through window of a local McDonalds.

After receiving the order, the grandson pulled his car forward and stopped momentarily so that Liebeck could add cream and sugar to her coffee. (Critics of civil justice, who have pounced on this case, often charge that Liebeck was driving the car or that the vehicle was in motion when she spilled the coffee; neither is true.) Liebeck placed the cup between her knees and attempted to remove the plastic lid from the cup. As she removed the lid, the entire contents of the cup spilled into her lap.

The sweatpants Liebeck was wearing absorbed the coffee and held it next to her skin. A vascular surgeon determined that Liebeck suffered full thickness burns (or third-degree burns) over 6 percent of her body, including her inner thighs, perineum, buttocks, and genital and groin areas. She was hospitalized for eight days, during which time she underwent skin grafting. Liebeck, who also underwent debridement treatments, sought to settle her claim for $20,000, but McDonalds refused.

During discovery, McDonalds produced documents showing more than 700 claims by people burned by its coffee between 1982 and 1992. Some claims involved third-degree burns substantially similar to Liebecks. This history documented McDonalds' knowledge about the extent and nature of this hazard.

McDonalds also said during discovery that, based on a consultants advice, it held its coffee at between 180 and 190 degrees Fahrenheit to maintain optimum taste. He admitted that he had not evaluated the safety ramifications at this temperature. Other establishments sell coffee at substantially lower temperatures, and coffee served at home is generally 135 to 140 degrees.

Further, McDonalds' quality assurance manager testified that the company actively enforces a requirement that coffee be held in the pot at 185 degrees, plus or minus five degrees. He also testified that a burn hazard exists with any food substance served at 140 degrees or above, and that McDonalds coffee, at the temperature at which it was poured into styrofoam cups, was not fit for consumption because it would burn the mouth and throat. The quality assurance manager admitted that burns would occur, but testified that McDonalds had no intention of reducing the "holding temperature" of its coffee.

Plaintiffs' expert, a scholar in thermodynamics applied to human skin burns, testified that liquids, at 180 degrees, will cause a full thickness burn to human skin in two to seven seconds. Other testimony showed that as the temperature decreases toward 155 degrees, the extent of the burn relative to that temperature decreases exponentially. Thus, if Liebeck's spill had involved coffee at 155 degrees, the liquid would have cooled and given her time to avoid a serious burn.

McDonalds asserted that customers buy coffee on their way to work or home, intending to consume it there. However, the company's own research showed that customers intend to consume the coffee immediately while driving.

McDonalds also argued that consumers know coffee is hot and that its customers want it that way. The company admitted its customers were unaware that they could suffer third-degree burns from the coffee and that a statement on the side of the cup was not a "warning" but a "reminder" since the location of the writing would not warn customers of the hazard.

Outcome

The jury awarded Liebeck $200,000 in compensatory damages. This amount was reduced to $160,000 because the jury found Liebeck 20 percent at fault in the spill. The jury also awarded Liebeck $2.7 million in punitive damages, which equals about two days of McDonalds' coffee sales.

Post-verdict investigation found that the temperature of coffee at the local Albuquerque McDonalds had dropped to 158 degrees Fahrenheit.

The trial court subsequently reduced the punitive award to $480,000 -- or three times compensatory damages -- even though the judge called McDonalds' conduct reckless, callous and willful.

No one will ever know the final ending to this case.

The parties eventually entered into a secret settlement which has never been revealed to the public, despite the fact that this was a public case, litigated in public and subjected to extensive media reporting. Such secret settlements, after public trials, should not be condoned.

... excerpted from ATLA fact sheet. © 1995, 1996 by Consumer Attorneys of California Brought to you by - The 'Lectric Law Library, The Net's Finest Legal Resource For Legal Pros & Laypeople Alike. (http://www.lectlaw.com)

Manufacturers also may wish a court to take into account the benefits to the economy from continuing to provide a product in terms of employees hired, taxes paid or generated, charitable activities engaged in by a business, or other intangible benefits to society, e.g., the utility of an experimental vaccine during an epidemic. Note that in New Jersey and in many other states, courts will not permit the introduction of any evidence regarding any supposed benefits to society - with the possible exception of the benefits derived from an experimental drug.

Cigarette manufacturers have frequently attempted to introduce this type of "beneficial evidence" in cases involving potential liability (the most recent example were in Washington and Oregon) and cite to the "amazing work" of the various cigarette manufacturers or their substantial charitable foundations as evidence of their product's utility or value to society.

Take careful note of the alternative theories under which a plaintiff can recover. The plaintiff can select either the consumer expectations test or the risk-utility test as a theory of recovery. If the plaintiff can prove either that the product fails the consumer expectations test or that its risk outweighed its utility, then the product would be defective.

Barker v. Lull Engineering Co.

Supreme Court of California, 20 Cal.3d 413, 143 Cal.Rptr. 225, 573 P.2d 443 (1978)

TOBRINER, JUDGE

Plaintiff was injured at a construction site while operating a high-lift loader manufactured by defendant. The loader tipped partially over, and plaintiff jumped off the loader and attempted to scramble away. He was injured when some lumber on the lift fell and hit him. Plaintiff claimed that the loader was defectively designed in several respects, including that it should have been equipped with "outriggers," a roll bar, and seat belts. [Plaintiff] instituted the present tort action seeking to recover damages for his injuries. The jury returned a verdict in favor of defendants, and plaintiff appeals from the judgment entered upon that verdict, contending primarily that in view of this court's decision in Cronin v. J.B.E. Olson Corp. (1972) 8 Cal.3d 121, 104 Cal.Rptr. 433, 501 P.2d 1153, the trial court erred in instructing the jury "that strict liability for a defect in design of a product is based on a finding that the product was unreasonably dangerous for its intended use * * *."

* * *

As we noted in Cronin, the Restatement draftsmen adopted the "unreasonably dangerous" language primarily as a means of confining the application of strict tort liability to an article which is "dangerous to an extent beyond that which would be contemplated by the ordinary consumer who purchases it, with the ordinary knowledge common to the community as to its characteristics." (Rest.2d Torts, ?402A, com. i.) In Cronin, however, we flatly rejected the suggestion that recovery in a products liability action should be permitted only if a product is more dangerous than contemplated by the average consumer, refusing to permit the low esteem in which the public might hold a dangerous product to diminish the manufacturer's responsibility for injuries caused by that product. As we pointedly noted in Cronin, even if the "ordinary consumer" may have contemplated that Shopsmith lathes posed a risk of loosening their grip and letting a piece of wood strike the operator, "another Greenman" should not be denied recovery. (8 Cal.3d at p. 133, 104 Cal.Rptr. 433, 501 P.2d 1153.) Indeed, our decision in Luque v. McLean (1972) 8 Cal.3d 136, 104 Cal.Rptr. 443, 501 P.2d 1163 - decided the same day as Cronin - aptly reflects our disagreement with the restrictive implications of the Restatement formulation, for in Luque we held that a power rotary lawn mower with an unguarded hole could properly be found defective, in spite of the fact that the defect in the product was patent and hence in all probability within the reasonable contemplation of the ordinary consumer.

Thus, our rejection of the use of the "unreasonably dangerous" terminology in Cronin rested in part on a concern that a jury might interpret such an instruction, as the Restatement draftsman had indeed intended, as shielding a defendant from liability so long as the product did not fall below the ordinary consumer's expectations as to the product's safety (footnote excluded). As Luque demonstrates, the dangers posed by such a misconception by the jury extend to cases involving design defects as well as to actions involving manufacturing defects: indeed, the danger of confusion is perhaps more pronounced in design cases in which the manufacturer could frequently argue that its product satisfied ordinary consumer expectations since it was identical to other items of the same product line with which the consumer may well have been familiar.

Accordingly, contrary to defendants' contention, the reasoning of Cronin does not dictate that the decision be confined to the manufacturing defect context. Indeed, in Cronin itself we expressly stated that our holding applied to design defects as well as to manufacturing defects (8 Cal.3d at pp. 134-135, 104 Cal.Rptr. 433, 501 P.2d 1153), and in Henderson v. Harnischfeger Corp. (1974) 12 Cal.3d 663, 670, 117 Cal.Rptr. 1, 527 P.2d 353, we subsequently confirmed the impropriety of instructing a jury in the language of the "unreasonably dangerous" standard in a design defect case. (See also Foglio v. Western Auto Supply (1976) 56 Cal.App.3d 470, 475, 128 Cal.Rptr. 545.) Consequently, we conclude that the design defect instruction given in the instant case was erroneous.

* * *

Defendants contend, however, that if Cronin is interpreted as precluding the use of the "unreasonably dangerous" language in defining a design defect, the jury in all such cases will inevitably be left without any guidance whatsoever in determining whether a product is defective in design or not. * * * Amicus California Trial Lawyer Association (CTLA) on behalf of the plaintiff responds by suggesting that the precise intent of our Cronin decision was to preclude a trial court from formulating any definition of "defect" in a product liability case, thus always leaving the definition of defect, as well as the application of such definition, to the jury. As we explain, neither of these contentions represents an accurate portrayal of the intent or effect of our Cronin decision.

* * *

Our decision in Cronin did not mandate such confusion. Instead, by observing that the problem in defining defect might be alleviated by reference to the "cluster of useful precedents," we intended to suggest that in drafting and evaluating instructions on this issue in a particular case, trial and appellate courts would be well advised to consider prior authorities involving similar defective product claims.

* * *

In general, a manufacturing or production defect is readily identifiable because a defective product is one that differs from the manufacturer's intended result or from other ostensibly identical units of the same product line. For example, when a product comes off the assembly line in a substandard condition it has incurred a manufacturing defect.

* * * A design defect, by contrast, cannot be identified simply by comparing the injury-producing product with the manufacturer's plans or with other units of the same product line, since by definition the plans and all such units will reflect the same design. Rather than applying any sort of deviation-from-the-norm test in determining whether a product is defective in design for strict liability purposes, our cases have employed two alternative criteria in ascertaining, in Justice Traynor's words, whether there is something "wrong, if not in the manufacturer's manner of production, at least in his product." (Traynor, The Ways and Meanings of Defective Products and Strict Liability, supra, 32 Tenn. L. Rev. 363, 366.)

First, our cases establish that a product may be found defective in design if the plaintiff demonstrates that the product failed to perform as safely as an ordinary consumer would expect when used in an intended or reasonably foreseeable manner. This initial standard, somewhat analogous to the Uniform Commercial Code's warranty of fitness and merchantability (Cal.U.Com.Code, §2314), reflects the warranty heritage upon which California product liability doctrine in part rests. As we noted in Greenman, "implicit in [a product's] presence on the market * * * [is] a representation that it [will] safely "do the jobs for which it was built." (59 Cal.2d at p. 64, 27 Cal.Rptr. at p. 701, 377 P.2d at p. 901.) When a product fails to satisfy such ordinary consumer expectations as to safety in its intended or reasonably foreseeable operation, a manufacturer is strictly liable for resulting injuries. * * * Under this standard, an injured plaintiff will frequently be able to demonstrate the defectiveness of a product by resort to circumstantial evidence, even when the accident itself precludes identification of the specific defect at fault. * * *

As Professor Wade has pointed out, however, the expectations of the ordinary consumer cannot be viewed as the exclusive yardstick for evaluating design defectiveness because "[i]n many situations * * * the consumer would not know what to expect, because he would have no idea how safe the product could be made." (Wade, On the Nature of Strict Tort Liability for Products, supra, 44 Miss.L.J. 825, 829.) Numerous California decisions have implicitly recognized this fact and have made clear, through varying linguistic formulations, that a product may be found defective in design, even if it satisfies ordinary consumer expectations, if through hindsight the jury determines that the product's design embodies "excessive preventable danger," or, in other words, if the jury finds that the risk of danger inherent in the challenged design outweighs the benefits of such design. * * *

A review of past cases indicates that in evaluating the adequacy of a product's design pursuant to this latter standard, a jury may consider, among other relevant factors, the gravity of the danger posed by the challenged design, the likelihood that such danger would occur, the mechanical feasibility of a safer alternative design, the financial cost of an improved design, and the adverse consequences to the product and to the consumer that would result from an alternative design. * * *

Although our cases have thus recognized a variety of considerations that may be relevant to the determination of the adequacy of a product's design, past authorities have generally not devoted much attention to the appropriate allocation of the burden of proof with respect to these matters. * * * The allocation of such burden is particularly significant in this context inasmuch as this court's product liability decisions, from Greenman to Cronin, have repeatedly emphasized that one of the principal purposes behind the strict product liability doctrine is to relieve an injured plaintiff of many of the onerous evidentiary burdens inherent in a negligence cause of action. Because most of the evidentiary matters which may be relevant to the determination of the adequacy of a product's design under the "risk- benefit" standard -- e.g., the feasibility and cost of alternative designs are similar to issues typically presented in a negligent design case and involve technical matters peculiarly within the knowledge of the manufacturer, we conclude that once the plaintiff makes a prima facie showing that the injury was proximately caused by the product's design, the burden should appropriately shift to the defendant to prove, in light of the relevant factors, that the product is not defective. Moreover, inasmuch as this conclusion flows from our determination that the fundamental public policies embraced in Greenman dictate that a manufacturer who seeks to escape liability for an injury proximately caused by its product's design on a risk-benefit theory should bear the burden of persuading the trier of fact that its product should not be judged defective, the defendant's burden is one affecting the burden of proof, rather than simply the burden of producing evidence. * * *

Thus, to reiterate, a product may be found defective in design, so as to subject a manufacturer to strict liability for resulting injuries, under either of two alternative tests. First, a product may be found defective in design if the plaintiff establishes that the product failed to perform as safely as an ordinary consumer would expect when used in an intended or reasonably foreseeable manner. Second, a product may alternatively be found defective in design if the plaintiff demonstrates that the product's design proximately caused his injury and the defendant fails to establish, in light of the relevant factors, that, on balance, the benefits of the challenged design outweigh the risk of danger inherent in such design.

* * *

Finally, contrary to the suggestion of amicus CTLA, an instruction which advises the jury that it may evaluate the adequacy of a product's design by weighing the benefits of the challenged design against the risk of danger inherent in such design is not simply the equivalent of an instruction which requires the jury to determine whether the manufacturer was negligent in designing the product. (See, e.g., Wade, On the Nature of Strict Tort Liability for Products, supra, 44 Miss.L.J. 825, 835.) It is true, of course, that in many cases proof that a product is defective in design may also demonstrate that the manufacturer was negligent in choosing such a design. As we have indicated, however, in a strict liability case, as contrasted with a negligent design action, the jury's focus is properly directed to the condition of the product itself, and not to the reasonableness of the manufacturer's conduct.

* * *

> Thus, the fact that the manufacturer took reasonable precautions in an attempt to design a safe product or otherwise acted as a reasonably prudent manufacturer would have under the circumstances, while perhaps absolving the manufacturer of liability under a negligence theory, will not preclude the imposition of liability under strict liability principles if, upon hindsight, the trier of fact concludes that the product's design is unsafe to consumers, users, or bystanders. * * *
>
> The judgment in favor of defendants is reversed.

Thus, a product may be found defective in design even if it satisfies normal consumer expectations, if through hindsight, the jury determines that the design embodies excessive preventable danger, or if the risk of danger, inherent in the challenged design, outweighs the benefits of the design.

Barker states that the burden of proof is shifted to the manufacturer, once the plaintiff proves that a design defect caused the injury. Under the risk-utility test, the defendant must then prove that on balance, the benefits of the challenged design outweigh the risk of danger in such a design.

Note that *Barker* is contrary to the view that the plaintiff must present evidence of a feasible, alternative, and safer design and places the burden of proof on the defendant-manufacturer. The shifting in the burden of proof to the defendant seems to be in line with the general philosophy of strict products liability cases which places the burden on the party best able to pay or absorb this cost. Thus, *Barker* may represent the future trend in products liability cases that places the clear burden on the manufacturer-defendant rather than on the person who suffered injury.

QUESTIONS

1. Manitowoc Co, Inc., the defendant, is a manufacturer of cranes. Gray, the plaintiff, was injured at his construction job when he was struck by the boom of the crane manufactured by the defendant. Plaintiff asserted that the design of the crane prevented the crane operator from seeing to his left when the crane was operated in the boom down position.

   a. Does the consumer expectations test apply to this case? If so, how?

   b. Was the product defective?

   c. Is Manitowoc Co, Inc. liable?

2. Brawner, the seven year old child of the plaintiff, was burned when he removed the lid from a gasoline storage container that ignited shortly after. The container was manufactured by Liberty Industries Inc., the defendant. Plaintiff brought suit under the claim that the product was defective because it lacked a mechanism to prevent it being opened by a seven year old.

   a. How does the consumer expectations test come into play?

   b. Was the container defective?

   c. Does the concept of environment of use apply to this case? Is so, how?

   d. Is Liberty Industries Inc. liable?

3. Two and a half year old Stephen Keller was playing with his 2 year old friend in the basement of his friend's home. They were playing with a gasoline can, which had been filled with gasoline by the friend's father. The can was manufactured by Huffman Manufacturing Company Inc. and sold by Welles Department Store to the friend's father. The children were near a gas furnace and a hot water heater when the gasoline was ignited.

   a. Would the average consumer reasonably anticipate the dangerous condition of the product?

   b. Does the doctrine of strict liability or negligence apply? If so, how?

   c. Is Welles Department Store liable? Is Huffman Manufacturing Company Inc. liable?

4. What is the flaw with the consumer expectation test? What is the alternative?

5. Kimwood Machine Company, the defendant, manufactures sanding machines. The

defendants did not warn the plaintiff's employer about possible problems that could arise because of the lack of safety devices on the machine.

a. Did the lack of a warning make the product defective?

b. Does the risk-benefit/risk utility test apply? If so, how?

c. Is Kimwood Machine Company liable?

6. Stella Liebeck, the plaintiff, was in the passenger seat of her grandson's car when she was severely burned by McDonald's coffee in February 1992. The coffee was not only hot; it was scalding, capable of almost instantaneous destruction of skin, flesh, and muscle. A surgeon determined that Liebeck suffered full thickness burns on over 6% of her body, in particular, her inner thighs, perineum, buttocks, and genital and groin area.

    a. How does the consumer expectations test apply?

    b. Does the risk-utility test apply? If so, how?

    c. Was the coffee defective?

    d. Is McDonald's liable?

7. The plaintiff, Barker, was injured at a construction site while operating a high-lift loader manufactured by defendant, Lull Engineering Co. The loader ripped open and the plaintiff jumped off the loader. Consequently, he was injured when some lumber fell on him. Plaintiff asserted that the product was defectively designed due to its lack of the following: outrigger, roll bar, and seat belts.

    a. Did the design defect cause the injury?

    b. Where did the shift of burden move to?

    c. How did the risk-benefit test apply?

    d. Is Lull Engineering liable?

Notes

Chapter Five

UNAVOIDABLY DANGEROUS PRODUCTS, NEGLIGENCE PER SE, AND PREEMPTION

UNAVOIDABLY DANGEROUS PRODUCTS

> *"There are simply some products which, in the present state of human knowledge, are quite incapable of being made safe for their intended and ordinary use... Such a product, properly prepared, and accompanied by proper directions and warnings, is not defective, nor is it unreasonably dangerous." (Feldman v. Lederle Laboratories, quoting Comment k to the Second Restatement.)*

Examples of unavoidably dangerous products are especially common in the fields of drugs, vaccines, blood products, medical devices, and especially new or experimental medications. Recent examples are the host of drugs used in the treatment of AIDS - and perhaps handguns in the future.

MCCARTHY V. OLIN CORP.

United States Court of Appeals, Second Circuit, 119 F.3d 148 (1997)

MESKILL, Circuit Judge:

Plaintiffs include two surviving victims and the estate of one deceased victim of the December 7, 1993 assault on the 5:33 p.m. Long Island Railroad commuter train. The bullets used in the shootings were Winchester "Black Talon" hollowpoint bullets, designed to enhance the injuries of their victims. This action was brought in New York State Supreme Court against, inter alios, Olin Corporation, the manufacturer of the bullets. The complaint asserted causes of action in the negligent manufacture, advertising and marketing of a product that was unreasonably designed and ultrahazardous, the making of an unreasonably dangerous product and strict liability in tort…The district court, Baer, J., granted the motion, finding that the complaint failed to state any claim under New York law upon which relief could be granted…Plaintiffs appeal from the order dismissing their suit, or in the alternative ask us to certify the question of ammunition manufacturer liability to the New York Court of Appeals. Finding sufficient precedents in New York law to evaluate the merits of plaintiffs' claims, we decline to grant certification and affirm the judgment of the district court.

BACKGROUND

On December 7, 1993, Colin Ferguson boarded the Long Island Railroad's 5:33 p.m. commuter train departing from New York City and opened fire on the passengers. Six people, including Dennis McCarthy, were killed and nineteen others, including Kevin McCarthy and Maryanne Phillips, were wounded in the vicious attack. Ferguson was armed with a 9mm semiautomatic handgun, which was loaded with Winchester "Black Talon" bullets (Black Talons). The injuries to Dennis and Kevin McCarthy and Maryanne Phillips were enhanced by the ripping and tearing action of the Black Talons because, unfortunately, the bullets performed as designed.

The Black Talon is a hollowpoint bullet designed to bend upon impact into six ninety degree angle razor-sharp petals or "talons" that increase the wounding power of the bullet by stretching, cutting and tearing tissue and bone as it travels through the victim. The Black Talon bullet was designed and manufactured by Olin Corporation (Olin) through its Winchester division and went on the market in 1992. Although the bullet was originally developed for law enforcement agencies, it was marketed and available to the general public. In November 1993, following public outcry, Olin pulled the Black Talon from the public market and restricted its sales to law enforcement personnel. Colin Ferguson allegedly purchased the ammunition in 1993, before it was withdrawn from the market.

Plaintiffs brought this action against Olin, Sturm, Ruger & Company Inc., the manufacturer of the handgun used by Ferguson, and Ram-Line Inc., the manufacturer of the fifteen round capacity magazine used with the handgun, in New York State Supreme Court to recover for the injuries of Kevin McCarthy and Maryanne Phillips and the death of Dennis McCarthy. The complaint was based on various theories of negligence and strict liability…

Olin moved to dismiss the complaint pursuant to Fed.R.Civ.P. 12(b)(6) for failure to state a claim upon which relief can be granted. The district court granted the motion. First addressing the issue of negligence, the court held that plaintiffs' negligence theories must fail because Olin owed no duty to plaintiffs to protect them from criminal misuse of the Black Talon ammunition. With respect to the strict liability claims, the court held that plaintiffs failed to allege the existence of a design defect in the Black Talon because the ammunition must by its very nature be dangerous to be functional. Id. at 370-71. The risk of the Black Talon arises from the function of the product, not from a defect in the product.

Id. at 371. The court noted that to state a claim in either negligence or strict liability, plaintiff must demonstrate that defendant's breach was the proximate cause of their injuries. Here, Ferguson's conduct was an extraordinary act which broke the chain of causation…

Plaintiffs appeal the dismissal of their complaint, claiming that the issue of whether they will ultimately prevail is a matter to be determined on a factual basis and not merely on the pleadings...

DISCUSSION …

Appellants argue that in New York, there is no definite rule of law as to liability for ammunition manufacturers, especially ammunition designed to cause enhanced injuries beyond ordinary bullets, and therefore the district court erred in dismissing their complaint…

Strict Liability

Appellants' first argument is that Olin should be held strictly liable for their injuries because the Black Talon ammunition was defectively designed and the design and manufacture of the bullets were inherently dangerous.

Design Defect

A manufacturer who places into the stream of commerce a defective product which causes injury may be held strictly liable. In New York, there are three distinct claims for strict products liability: (1) a manufacturing defect, which results when a mistake in manufacturing renders a product that is ordinarily safe dangerous so that it causes harm; (2) a warning defect, which occurs when the inadequacy or failure to warn of a reasonably foreseeable risk accompanying a product causes harm, and (3) a design defect, which results when the product as designed is unreasonably dangerous for its intended use. Appellants argue that the Black Talons were defectively designed because the expansion mechanism of the bullets, which causes ripping and tearing in its victims, results in enhanced injuries beyond ordinary bullets. The district court rejected this argument because the expanding of the bullet was an intentional and functional element of the design of the product. We agree.

To state a cause of action for a design defect, plaintiffs must allege that the bullet was unreasonably dangerous for its intended use. "[A] defectively designed product is one which, at the time it leaves the seller's hands, is in a condition not reasonably contemplated by the ultimate consumer." (applying the Robinson standard). "This rule, however, is tempered by the realization that some products, for example knives, must by their very nature be dangerous in order to be functional." The very purpose of the Black Talon bullet is to kill or cause severe wounding. Here, plaintiffs concede that the Black Talons performed precisely as intended by the manufacturer and Colin Ferguson.

Sadly it must be acknowledged that: [m]any products, however well-built or well-designed may cause injury or death. Guns may kill; knives may maim; liquor may cause alcoholism; but the mere fact of injury does not entitle the [person injured] to recover ... there must be something wrong with the product, and if nothing is wrong there will be no liability...

Appellants have not alleged that the bullets were defective. "As a matter of law, a product's defect is related to its condition, not its intrinsic function." The bullets were not in defective condition nor were they unreasonably dangerous for their intended use because the Black Talons were purposely designed to expand on impact and cause severe wounding.

Appellants next argue that under the risk/utility test analysis applied by New York courts, appellee should be held strictly liable because the risk of harm posed by the Black Talons outweighs the ammunition's utility. The district court properly held that the risk/utility test is inapplicable "because the risks arise from the function of the product, not any defect in the product." McCarthy, 916 F.Supp. at 371. "There must be `something wrong' with a product before the risk/utility analysis may be applied in determining whether the product is unreasonably dangerous or defective." Addison v. Williams) (holding that Olin Corp. could not be held strictly liable for the manufacture of steel jacketed ammunition capable of causing enhanced injuries) (citing Note, Handguns and Products Liability, 97 Harv. L.Rev.1912, 1915 (1984)).

The purpose of risk/utility analysis is to determine whether the risk of injury might have been reduced or avoided if the manufacturer had used a feasible alternative design. (burden of proving product is unreasonably dangerous requires showing that product could have been designed more safely). However, the risk of injury to be balanced with the utility is a risk not intended as the primary function of the product. Here, the primary function of the Black Talon bullets was to kill or cause serious injury. There is no reason to search for an alternative safer design where the product's sole utility is to kill and maim. Accordingly, we hold that appellants have failed to state a cause of action under New York strict products liability law.

Inherently Dangerous Product

Appellants also argue that Olin should be held strictly liable because the Black Talon ammunition is "unreasonably dangerous per se." According to the appellants' theory, a product is unreasonably dangerous per se if a reasonable person would conclude that the danger of the product, whether foreseeable or not, outweighs its utility. As the district court held, this is essentially a risk/utility analysis, which we have refused to apply. Under New York's strict products liability jurisprudence, there is no cause of action for an unreasonably dangerous per se product. Thus, this claim was properly dismissed.

Negligence

In their complaint, appellants asserted causes of action for the negligent marketing and manufacture of Black Talon bullets. On appeal, appellants do not appear to pursue their negligent manufacturing claim but rather focus their argument on Olin's negligent marketing of the ammunition. For the reasons discussed below, appellants cannot assert a cause of action under either theory of negligence.

The crux of appellants' negligence theory is that Olin negligently marketed and placed the Black Talon ammunition for sale to the general public. Appellants argue that because of the severe wounding power of the bullets, Olin should have restricted sales to law enforcement agencies, for whom the bullet was originally designed. They also argue that Olin should have known that their advertising, which highlighted the ripping and tearing characteristics of the bullet, would attract "many types of sadistic, unstable and criminal personalities," such as Ferguson.

To state a cause of action for negligence, the plaintiffs must show: (1) that Olin owed them a "duty, or obligation, recognized by law", (2) a breach of the duty, (3) a "reasonably close causal connection between [defendant's] conduct and the resulting injury" and (4) loss or damage resulting from the breach. W. Page Keeton et al., Prosser and Keeton on the Law of Torts § 30, at 164-65 (5th ed.1984) (hereinafter Prosser & Keeton). Becker v. Schwartz. "In the absence of a duty, as a matter of law, no liability can ensue." Gonzalez v. Pius. "Thus it may be said that the defendant was negligent, but is not liable because he was under no duty to the plaintiff not to be." Prosser & Keeton, § 30 at 164.

In tort cases, foreseeability is often confused with duty. Foreseeability "is applicable to determine the scope of duty — only after it has been determined that there is a duty." Pulka v. Edelman. "The mere fact that a consequence might foreseeably result from an action or condition does not serve to establish a duty owing from a defendant to a plaintiff." The existence of a duty is a question of law to be decided by the court. New York courts are reluctant to impose a duty of care where there is little expectation that the defendant could prevent the actions of a third party. See Pulka, 40 N.Y.2d at 786, 390 N.Y.S.2d at 397, 358 N.E.2d at 1022 ("While a court might impose a legal duty where none existed before, such an imposition must be exercised with extreme care, for legal duty imposes legal liability." (citation omitted)). "[C]ommon law in the State of New York does not impose a duty to control the conduct of third persons to prevent them from causing injury to others. This is so ... even where as a practical matter defendant could have exercised such control." While there are of course many exceptions to this rule, we find that none of them is applicable here.

New York courts do not impose a legal duty on manufacturers to control the distribution of potentially dangerous products such as ammunition. Accordingly, although it may have been foreseeable by Olin that criminal misuse of the Black Talon bullets could occur, Olin is not legally liable for such misuse. As the district court pointed out, appellants have not alleged that any special relationship existed between Olin and Ferguson. Here, Olin could not control the actions of Ferguson. "[I]t is unreasonable to impose [a] duty where the realities of every day experience show us that, regardless of the measures taken, there is little expectation that the one made responsible could prevent the ... conduct [of another]." Pulka, 40 N.Y.2d at 785, 390 N.Y.S.2d at 396, 358 N.E.2d at 1022; see also Forni, 648 N.Y.S.2d at 74 ("Plaintiffs did not, nor could they, show that defendants-manufacturers owed plaintiffs a duty of care.... New York does not impose a duty upon a manufacturer to refrain from the lawful distribution of a non-defective product.").

It is "the responsibility of courts in fixing the orbit of duty, to limit the legal consequences of wrongs to a controllable degree and to protect against crushing exposure to liability." To impose a duty on ammunition manufacturers to protect against criminal misuse of its product would likely force ammunition products — which legislatures have not proscribed, and which concededly are not defectively designed or manufactured and have some socially valuable uses — off the market due to the threat of limitless liability. Because Olin did not owe a legal duty to plaintiffs to protect against Colin Ferguson's horrible action, appellants' complaint does not state a cause of action for negligence and the claim was properly dismissed.

CONCLUSION

Because we hold that the Black Talon bullets were not defectively designed, we must affirm the dismissal of appellants' strict liability claims. We also hold that Olin was under no legal duty to prevent criminal misuse of its product and therefore affirm the dismissal of the negligence claims. Although appellants are the victims of a horrible tragedy, under New York law, they have failed to state a cause of action upon which relief can be granted — in sum, New York law does not afford them a remedy. Accordingly, we affirm the judgment of the district court.

JUDGMENT AFFIRMED

In *Wilkinson v. Bay Shore Lumber* (1986), the court held that "the few reported decisions which refer to comment k overwhelmingly involve products such as drugs, vaccines, blood, and medical devices such as intrauterine devices and breast implants." In these cases, courts are reluctant to apply strict liability, but not blanket immunity in all cases. The plaintiff can still win a case but must prove negligence, i.e., in manufacturing, preparation, or warnings or directions.

As we have discussed, in such a case the manufacturer would be required to adequately warn the physician (prescription drugs) or the consumer (nonprescription drugs) concerning issues of safety, fitness, suitability, or compatibility with other medications. Note Comment k which addresses the basis of liability:

> *"The seller of such products... is not to be held to strict liability for unfortunate consequences attending their use, merely because he has undertaken to supply the public with an apparently useful and desirable product, attended with a known but apparently reasonable risk."*

Effects of Statutes and Regulations

Courts may adopt as the standard of conduct of a reasonable man either a law (statute) or an administrative regulation. This raises the stakes considerably in products cases!

In these cases, an unexcused violation of a statute or of an administrative regulation is termed *negligence per se,* and creates a presumption of negligence on the part of the actor that may only be overcome by strong, powerful, and conclusive evidence. The following are examples of possible excused violations of a statute or regulation: the inability to comply; an emergency situation; or where compliance would involve a greater risk of harm than non-compliance. Courts construe these examples very narrowly.

However, on the other side of the equation, compliance with a statute or regulation is not necessarily proof that a party acted reasonably and would not be a bar to recovery or a finding of negligence if a reasonable man [manufacturer] would have taken additional reasonable precautions. The statute or regulation is seen as the legally minimum standard, although in most states, compliance with the law or statute would be given a strong presumption—termed as a rebuttable presumption—that a party had acted reasonably under the circumstances.

A rebuttable presumption either of negligence or that a party has not been negligent is a marker, laid down by a court as a matter of law, but may be countered by clear and convincing proof or evidence to the contrary.

Examples of some actions that have resulted in imposition of negligence per se include failing to follow the proper steps in gaining approval of a drug (following the FDA Protocol); failing to file required health and safety reports; or filing such reports in a non-timely manner.

See *The Drug Development and Approval Process* found at the end of this Chapter for a depiction of the Drug Approval process.

Preemption

The doctrine of preemption can be found in the Supremacy Clause of the United States Constitution, which defines federal law as "Supreme," provided that the federal law falls within the powers granted within Article I of the Constitution.

Congress is restricted to exercising the powers contained in Article I; therefore anything not mentioned in Article I is "reserved to the states" under the Tenth Amendment.

The Supremacy Clause, Article IV, Clause 2, states:

> *"This Constitution, and the Laws of the United States which shall be made in pursuance thereof; and all treaties made, or which shall be made, under the authority of the United States, shall be the supreme law of the land; and the judges in every state shall be bound*

thereby, anything in the constitution or laws of any state to the contrary notwithstanding."

Congress' intent in enacting a wide variety of statutes in the context of preemption is often unclear as to how much state authority has been displaced or preempted.

The United States Supreme Court case may be found at 505 U.S. 504 (1992).

Did federal law preempt any or all of the state common law claims brought by the Cipollone's? The plaintiffs sued on the basis of the theory that the defendant had failed to provide adequate warnings relating to the cigarettes they manufactured and sold. Section 1333 of the *Federal Cigarette Labeling and Advertising Act* provided for the required warnings.

In order to determine the validity of a claim of preemption, courts will initially look to the actual words of a statute, and to the legislative history of this act. There are four considerations in the preemption discussion; that is, in deciding whether a specific state regulation would or would not be preempted in the absence of an express preemption clause:

- Congress may intend to occupy the field in a given area because federal regulations may be so pervasive or the federal interest so dominant (*Silkwood v. Kerr-McGee Corp.*), as in federal labor legislation or in nuclear waste disposal;
- Where a state law or statute conflicts with a federal rule;
- Where a state law or statute stands as an obstacle to the accomplishment and execution of the purposes of a federal law as determined by Congress;
- Where it would be a physical impossibility to comply with both federal and state law.

In these cases, state regulations or causes of action based upon a state regulation or a state statute would be preempted. In *Cipollone* (which is important as well from an historical point of view- outlining the history of the required warnings on cigarette packages and the evolving form of the warning itself so as not to minimize the danger of smoking), the United States Supreme Court held that federal law preempts only those actions that related to the required warnings, advertising, or promotion of cigarettes. Other actions or theories of recovery offered by the plaintiffs, with the exception of those based on the required warnings, were not preempted and could proceed.

Cipollone v. Liggett Group, Inc.

United States Court Of Appeals For The Third Circuit, 789 F.2d 181 (1986)

HUNTER, Circuit Judge:

This case, before the court on the district court's certification pursuant to 28 U.S.C. § 1292(b) (1982), presents the question whether the Federal Cigarette Labeling and Advertising Act, 15 U.S.C. §§ 1331-1340 (1982) (the "Act"), preempts any or all of the state common law claims brought by appellee Antonio Cipollone and his wife Rose in the district court. Several of the claims in the Cipollones' complaint concern the alleged failure of the defendants, Liggett Group, Inc. ("Lorillard"), to provide an adequate warning of the dangers of the cigarettes that they manufactured and sold. Because these claims implicate the legislatively mandated warning provided in section 1333 of the Act, the answers of Liggett Group, Philip Morris, and Lorillard each included a defense based on the preemptive effect of the Act. The Cipollones responded by filing a motion to strike the preemption defenses. Lorillard, later joined by Philip Morris, then moved for judgment on the pleadings pursuant to Federal Rule Civil Procedure 12(c). Holding that the Act preempted none of the Cipollones' claims, the district court granted the Cipollones' motion to strike the defenses and denied the motion for judgment on the pleadings. Cipollone v. Liggett Group, Inc., 593 F. Supp. 1146, 1171 (D.N.J. 1984). On January 21, 1984, this court granted appellants Lorillard and Liggett Group permission to appeal. Because we disagree with the district court's conclusion concerning the preemptive effect of the Act, we will reverse the district court's grant of the motion to strike and will remand the case for further proceedings.

I.

A. The Complaint

In their complaint, Rose and Antonio Cipollone alleged that Mrs. Cipollone developed lung cancer as a result of smoking cigarettes manufactured and sold by appellants. The complaint, which was originally filed on August 1, 1983, further averred that Mrs. Cipollone began smoking in 1942 and developed lung cancer as a result of her smoking. Mrs. Cipollone died in October 1984, but her husband has continued prosecuting this action, individually and as executor of his wife's estate. Mr. Cipollone is therefore the sole appellee in this case.

As observed by the district court, the fourteen-count complaint sets forth claims based on strict liability (Counts 2, 3, and 9), negligence (Counts 4 and 5), breach of warranty (Count 7), and intentional tort (Counts 6 and 8). The Cipollones claimed that the defendants' cigarettes were unsafe and defective (Count 2) and that defendants are subject to liability for their failure to warn of the hazards of cigarette smoking on the basis of negligence (Count 4) or strict liability (Count 3). In addition, the Cipollones asserted, defendants negligently (Count 5) or intentionally (Count 6) advertised their products in a manner that neutralized the warnings actually provided, warnings made meaningless by the addiction created by cigarettes (Count 9). Finally, the complaint stated that the defendants ignored, failed to act upon, and conspired to deprive the public of medical and scientific data reflecting the dangers associated with cigarettes (Count 8).

B. The Federal Cigarette and Advertising Labeling Act

The Federal Cigarette Labeling and Advertising Act, originally enacted in 1965, was a response to a growing awareness among members of federal as well as state government that cigarette smoking posed a significant health threat to Americans. The original Act required the following warning label on cigarette packages: "Caution: Cigarette Smoking May Be Hazardous to Your Health." 15 U.S.C. § 1333 (1970). Congress changed this warning, by amendment to the Act in 1969, to the following: "Warning: The Surgeon General Has Determined That Cigarette Smoking Is Dangerous to Your Health." 15 U.S.C. § 1333 (1976). The Act, as amended in 1970, expressly stated the policy behind the required warning:

It is the policy of the Congress, and the purpose of this chapter, to establish a comprehensive Federal program to deal with cigarette labeling and advertising with respect to any relationship between smoking and health, whereby – the public may be adequately informed that cigarette smoking may be hazardous to health by inclusion of a warning to that effect on each package of cigarettes; and commerce and the national economy may be (A) protected to the maximum extent consistent with this declared policy and (B) not impeded by diverse, non-uniform, and confusing cigarette labeling and advertising regulations with respect to any relationship between smoking and health.

15 U.S.C. § 1331 (1982).

The Act also contains a preemption provision, which provides that:

> *No statement relating to smoking and health, other than the statement required by section 1333 of this title, shall be required on any cigarette package.*
>
> *No requirement or prohibition based on smoking and health shall be imposed under State law with respect to the advertising or promotion of any cigarettes the packages of which are labeled in conformity with the provisions of this chapter. 15 U.S.C. § 1334 (1982).*

Confronted with this provision, the district court did not question that the Act prohibits state legislatures from requiring a warning on cigarette packages that alters that provided in section 1333. Nevertheless, after a comprehensive analysis of the Act, the court concluded that section 1334 does not preempt state common law claims such as those that the Cipollones have asserted.

II.

C. Preemption Principles

The United States Supreme Court has identified several principles for ascertaining congressional intent to preempt state authority. To begin, Congress may preempt state law by express statement. Jones v. Rath Packing Co., 430 U.S. 519, 525, 51 L. Ed. 2d 604, 97 S. Ct. 1305 (1977). Without the aid of express language, a court may find intent to preempt in two general ways. Silkwood v. Kerr-McGee Corp., 464 U.S. 238, 104 S. Ct. 615, 621, 78 L. Ed. 2d 443 (1984). First, a court may determine that Congress intended "to occupy a field" in a given area because 'the scheme of federal regulation may be so pervasive as to make reasonable the inference that Congress left no room for the States to supplement it, ' because 'the Act of Congress may touch a field in which the federal interest is so dominant that the federal system will be assumed to preclude enforcement of state laws on the same subject, ' or because "the object sought to be obtained by the federal law and the character of obligations imposed by it may reveal the same purpose. "

Fidelity Federal Savings & Loan Association v. De la Cuesta, 458 U.S. 141, 153, 73 L. Ed. 2d 664, 102 S. Ct. 3014 (1982) (quoting Rice v. Santa Fe Elevator Corp., 331 U.S. 218, 230, 91 L. Ed. 1447, 67 S. Ct. 1146 (1947)). Second, in those instances where Congress has not wholly superceded state regulation in a specific area, state law is preempted "to the extent that it actually conflicts with federal law." Pacific Gas & Electric Co. v. Energy Resources Conservation & Development Commission, 461 U.S. 190, 204, 75 L. Ed. 2d 752, 103 S. Ct. 1713 (1982). The Court has stated that such conflict arises when "compliance with both federal and state regulations is a physical impossibility," Florida Lime & Avocado Growers, Inc. v. Paul, 373 U.S. 132, 142-43, 10 L. Ed. 2d 248, 83 S. Ct. 1210 (1963), or where state law "stands as an obstacle to the accomplishment and execution of the full purposes and objectives of Congress." Hines v. Davidowitz, 312 U.S. 52, 67, 85 L. Ed. 581, 61 S. Ct. 399 (1941). Finally, in applying these principles, a court must be mindful of the overriding presumption that "Congress did not intend to displace state law." Maryland v. Louisiana, 451 U.S. 725, 746, 68 L. Ed. 2d 576, 101 S. Ct. 2114 (1981); see also Rice, 331 U.S. at 230.

B. Express Preemption

In applying these principles to the statutory scheme at issue here, we first express our agreement with the district court's conclusion that section 1334 does not provide for express preemption of the Cipollones' state common law claims. See Cipollone, 593 F. Supp. At 1154-55; accord Roysdon v. R.J. Reynolds Tobacco Co., 623 F. Supp. 1189, slip op. at 2 (E.D. Tenn. 1985); Roysdon v. R.J. Reynolds, No. 3-84-606, slip op. at 2 (E.D. Tenn. 1985). Because we are constrained by the presumption against preemption, we cannot say that the language of section 1334 clearly encompasses state common law. We find support for this determination in Congress's failure to include state common law explicitly within section 1334, as it has in numerous other statutes. Indeed, in the absence of a preemption provision encompassing state common law, the Supreme Court has relied generally on principles of implied preemption in evaluating whether a statutory scheme preempts state common law. See, e.g., Silkwood v. Kerr-McGee Corp., 464 U.S. 238, 104 S. Ct. 615, 78 L. Ed. 2d 443 (1984); Chicago & North Western Transportation Co. v. Kalo Brick & Tile Co., 450 U.S. 311, 67 L. Ed. 2d 258, 101 S. Ct. 1124 (1981). Accordingly, we turn to examining whether congressional intent to preempt the Cipollones' claims may be inferred under the two general principles of implied preemption.

C. Implied Preemption

In pressing their implied preemption arguments in this appeal, each side relies extensively on the legislative history of the Act. As is often the case with legislative history, both sides have succeeded in gleaning passages that bolster their contrary positions. Although we find the legislative history to the Act informative, no materials have come to our attention that we deem wholly dispositive of the issue before us. Even more important, we find the language of the statute itself a sufficiently clear expression of congressional intent without resort to the Act's legislative history. See Blum v. Stenson, 465 U.S. 886, 104 S. Ct. 1541, 1548, 79 L. Ed. 2d 891 (1984); Piper v. Chris-Craft Industries, Inc., 430 U.S. 1, 26, 51 L. Ed. 2d 124, 97 S. Ct. 926 (1977).

Under the principles of implied preemption, we must first determine whether Congress intended "to occupy the field" relating to cigarettes and health to the exclusion of state law product liability actions such as the Cipollones. Our examination of the Act leads us to agree with the district court's statements that "Congress . . . intended to occupy a field" and "indicated this intent as clearly as it knew how." Cipollone, 593 F. Supp. At 1164 (emphasis in original). Not only did Congress use sweeping language in describing the preemptive effect of the Act in section 1334, but it expressed its desire in section 1331 to establish "a comprehensive Federal program" in order to avoid "diverse, nonuniform, and confusing cigarette labeling and advertising regulations with respect to any relationship between smoking and health." See Palmer v. Liggett & Myers Tobacco, Inc., 635 F. Supp. 392 (D. Mass. 1984) (Congress has preempted field with respect to cigarette labeling).

In determining the scope of this field, we observe that the Cipollones' tort action concerns rights and remedies traditionally defined solely by state law. We therefore must adopt a restrained view in evaluating whether Congress intended to supercede entirely private rights of action such as those at issue here. See Rice, 331 U.S. at 230; Cipollone, 593 F. Supp. At 1165-66; see also Silkwood, 104 S. Ct. at 623-24; Florida Avocado Growers, 373 U.S. at 143-44. In light of this constraint, we cannot say that the scheme created by the Act is "so pervasive" or the federal interest involved "so dominant" as to eradicate all of the Cipollones' claims. Nor are we persuaded that the object of the Act and the character of obligations imposed by it reveal a purpose to exert exclusive control over every aspect of the relationship between cigarettes and health. See Banzhaf v. F.C.C., 132 U.S. App. D.C. 14, 405 F.2d 1082, 1089-91 (D.C. Cir. 1968), cert. denied, 396 U.S. 842, 90 S. Ct. 50, 24 L. Ed. 2d 93 (1969); see also Southern Railway Co. v. Railroad Commission of Indiana, 236 U.S. 439, 446-48, 59 L. Ed. 661, 35 S. Ct. 304 (1915). Thus, we look to the extent to which the Cipollones' state law claims "actually conflict" with the Act to ascertain whether they are preempted.

The test enunciated by this court for addressing a potential conflict between state and federal law requires us "to examine first the purposes of the federal law and second the effect of the operation of the state law on these purposes." Finberg v. Sullivan, 634 F.2d 50, 63 (3d Cir. 1980) (in banc) (citing Perez v. Campbell, 402 U.S. 637, 29 L. Ed. 2d 233, 91 S. Ct. 1704 (1971)). As mentioned above, Congress has provided us with an explicit statement of the Act's purposes in section 1331. That statement reveals that the Act represents a carefully drawn balance between the purposes of warning the public of the hazards of cigarette smoking and protecting the interests of national economy. See Banzhaf, 405 F.2d at 1090. Moreover, the preemption provision of section 1334, read together with section 1331, makes clear Congress's determination that this balance would be upset by either a requirement of a warning other than that prescribed in section 1333 or a requirement or prohibition based on smoking and health "with respect to the advertising or promotion" of cigarettes. See 15 U.S.C. § 1334.

Having identified the purposes of the Act, we now must evaluate the effect of the operation of state common law claims on these purposes. In so doing, we accept the appellants' assertion that the duties imposed through state common law damage actions have the effect of requirements that are capable of creating "an obstacle to the accomplishment and execution of the full purposes and objectives of Congress." See Hines, 312 U.S. at 67; see also Dawson v. Chrysler Corp., 630 F.2d 950, 962 (3d Cir. 1980) (liability under common law has the effect of imposing requirements), cert. denied, 450 U.S. 959, 101 S. Ct. 1418, 67 L. Ed. 2d 383 (1981). As the appellants point out, several

Supreme Court opinions reflect recognition of the regulatory effect of state law damage claims and their potential for frustrating congressional objectives. See, e.g., Fidelity, 458 U.S. at 156-59; Chicago & North Western Transportation Co., 450 U.S. at 324-25; San Diego Building Trades Council v. Garmon, 359 U.S. 236, 247, 3 L. Ed. 2d 775, 79 S. Ct. 773 (1959). Applying this principle, we conclude that claims relating to smoking and health that result in liability for noncompliance with warning, advertisement, and promotion obligations other than those prescribed in the Act have the effect of tipping the Act's balance of purposes and therefore actually conflict with the Act.

Based on the foregoing, we hold that the Act preempts those state law damage actions relating to smoking and health that challenge either the adequacy of the warning on cigarette packages or the propriety of a party's actions with respect to the advertising and promotion of cigarettes. We further hold that where the success of a state law damage claim necessarily depends on the assertion that a party bore the duty to provide a warning to consumers in addition to the warning Congress has required on cigarette packages, such claims are preempted as conflicting with the Act.

For the foregoing reasons, we will reverse the order of the district court to the extent that it granted the Cipollone's motion to strike the appellants' preemption defenses. We will also remand the case for further proceedings consistent with this opinion.

Questions

1. In *Wilkinson v. Bay Shore Lumber*, the plaintiff, a carpenter was building an outrigger on the roof of a house when he stepped on a board that broke due to internal dry rot, which was wholly concealed from view. Plaintiff sued under theories of negligence and strict liability.
2. Was the board an unavoidably dangerous product?
3. Is Bay Shore Lumber liable?
4. Is an airplane an unavoidably dangerous product? What are some circumstances where an airplane manufacturer could face a suit based on negligence?
5. In *Silkwood v. Kerr-McGee Corp.*, the daughter of the plaintiff worked as a laboratory technician for the defendant, Kerr-McGee Corp. Silkwood began investigating health and safety issues at the plant. In addition, she accused the company of falsifying inspection records. Shortly after, during a routine inspection, she was exposed to high amounts of plutonium. She blamed the company. On the way to a meeting with a journalist, she died in an unrelated car accident.
6. How could preemption come into play in this case?
7. Is Kerr-McGee Corp. liable?
8. What are some examples where negligence per se could apply? What are some specific statutes or administrative regulations that could apply?
9. Liggett Group Inc., the defendant, manufactures and sells cigarettes. The wife of the plaintiff, Mrs. Cipollone, developed lung cancer and died as a result of smoking the defendant's product. The plaintiff asserted that the defendant's cigarettes were unsafe and defective due to their failure to warn about the hazards of smoking. Additionally, the plaintiff claimed that the defendant negligently and intentionally advertised in a way that neutralized the warnings actually provided, rendering them inadequate and insufficient. Finally, the plaintiff brought up the point that the defendant deprived the public of medical data reflecting the dangers associated with the cigarettes. The defendants made the claim that federal statutes preempted the claims, specifically the Federal Cigarette Label & Advertising Act.
10. Does the Federal Cigarette Label & Advertising Act preempt any or all state common law claims? Is Liggett Group Inc. liable?

Appendix 4.1

THE DRUG DEVELOPMENT AND APPROVAL PROCESS

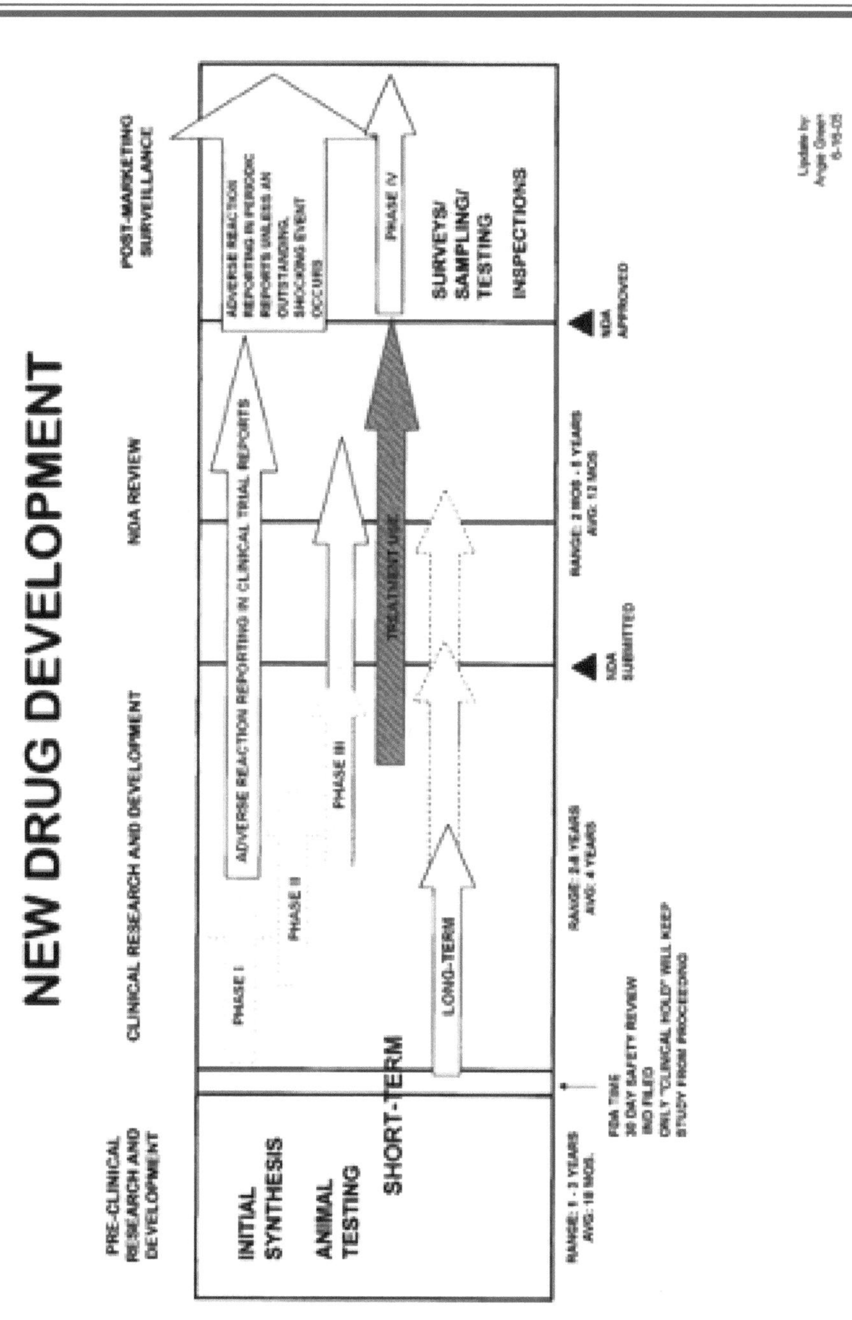

DRUG APPROVAL PROCESS

	Preclinical Testing			Phase I	Phase II	Phase III				FDA		Approval
YEARS	1	2	File IND	3	4	5	6	7	File NDA	8	9	⟶
Test Population	Laboratory and Animal Studies			20 to 100 Healthy Volunteers	100 to 300 Patient Volunteers	1000 to 10,000 Patient Volunteers				Review usually take about 12-18 months		Post-marketing safety monitoring
PURPOSE	Assess safety and biological activity			Determine safety and dosage	Evaluate effectiveness. Look for side effects	Verify Effectiveness, monitor adverse reactions from long-term use.						Large scale manufacturing
	30 days stability data required by FDA at IND filing			Build manufacturing plants in Phase I.	Expedited Review: Phase II and III can be combined to shorten approval process on new medicines for serious life-threatening diseases. Some compounds never get to Phase III when drug is deemed effective in Phase II. In this case, they skip to Phase IV.					FDA inspection usually 2 months after NDA filing		Distribution
	Manufacturing Stability Tests											Education

Updated by
Angie Green
6-15-05

Chapter Six

PRIVITY: A HISTORICAL PERSPECTIVE AND MODERN INTERPRETATION

PRIVITY

Consider this explanation from Gilliam, Products Liability in a Nutshell, 37 Or. L. Rev. 119, 131 (1958):

> *"When the consumer deals with the retailer rather than directly with the manufacturer, he establishes a contractual relationship with the retailer to which the manufacturer is not, legally speaking, a party. The manufacturer sells (directly or indirectly) to the retailer; the retailer sells to the consumer. The marketing process is a series of sales—a series of contracts. The parties to these contracts overlap in the middle of the marketing process, but not at the ends: there is an ultimate supplier and his customer, and so is the connecting link between them. The customer, however, makes no contract with... the manufacturer. These two do not deal with one another; typically they are strangers. In legal phraseology, there is no "privity of contract: between them."*

We begin this Chapter by taking a close look at the historical evolution of privity.

In the early 1800s, there were few sellers in the marketplace. As a result, cases alleging a product defect were decided on the basis of the theory of absolute liability against the manufacturer. As manufacturing capabilities increased, a negligence theory was adopted, but this led to enormous exposure on the part of the "new manufacturing class" developing in England during the Industrial Revolution. English courts developed a theory in tort cases, highly favorable to this "new manufacturing class" in the 1842 case of *Winterbottom v. Wright* that determined the scope of the manufacturer's duty. The court in *Winterbottom* held that a duty of a manufacturer to show reasonable care would only extend to the party with whom the manufacturer had actually dealt through its contract. Since a buyer rarely dealt with a manufacturer, no contractual relationship existed between the manufacturer and the buyer. Hence, the manufacturer had no duty of due or reasonable care to the buyer because no privity of contract existed.

On the other hand, since the buyer had dealt with the retailer in purchasing a chattel (the common law term for an item of personal property), could the buyer sue the retailer? As a factual matter, in most cases, the buyer had been injured by a defect in the product not caused by any negligence on the part of the retailer (the retailer had only passed on the manufacturer's product). So, the buyer was effectively barred from recovery against the retailer on a negligence theory and against the manufacturer on ground that the consumer was not in privity with the manufacturer. This was the origin of the doctrine termed caveat emptor, or "let the buyer beware!" which was the watch phrase of the emerging common law of the industrial age.

Two early exceptions were created by English courts. In 1852, a decade after *Winterbottom v. Wright*, an English court decided the case of *Thomas v. Winchester*, which determined that for products termed negligently labeled products (in this case, poisons), the manufacturer could not limit its liability through the defense of privity. Later in 1870, *Loop v. Litchfield* recognized the inherent unfairness and practical limiting nature of the doctrine of privity. The court extended the limitation on applying the privity doctrine to the range of imminently dangerous products such as poisons, explosives, deadly weapons, and the like.

The doctrine of privity was finally severely limited - some say obliterated - in Judge (later Justice) Cardozo's opinion in the case of *MacPherson v. Buick Motors*, a case arising in the Court of Appeals in New York. This case dealt with the issue of vertical privity; that is, from the Manufacturer to the Retailer to the Consumer or Buyer.

In *MacPherson*, the manufacturer was first found to be negligent on the basis that it could have discovered defects in the construction of wooden wheels by and through a reasonable inspection of the wheels which it had failed to do! The court noted that wooden wheels were not inherently dangerous products but that any product is likely to be dangerous if it is negligently made. The court then extended the duty of the manufacturer to those persons who would be foreseeable users within the vertical marketing chain, without a showing of privity, in the case of all products negligently constructed or made. Since it was foreseeable that others besides the retailer would use the product, the buyer (MacPherson) was a foreseeable party and should be permitted to bring suit on the basis of the theory of negligence.

MacPherson v. Buick Motor Company

Court of Appeals of N.Y., 217 N.Y.382, 111 N.E. 1050 (1916)

Cardozo, J . . . . The defendant is a manufacturer of automobiles. It sold an automobile to a retail dealer. The retail dealer resold to the plaintiff. While the plaintiff was in the car, it suddenly collapsed. He was thrown out and injured. One of the wheels was made of defective wood, and its spokes crumbled into fragments. The wheel was not made by the defendant; it was bought from another manufacturer. There is evidence, however, that its defects could have been discovered by reasonable inspection, and that inspection was missed. There is no claim that the defendant knew of the defect and willfully concealed it. The case, in other words, is not brought within the rule of Kuelling v. Lean Mfg. Co. * * *. The charge is one, not of fraud, but of negligence. The question to be determined is whether the defendant owed a duty of care and vigilance to any one but the immediate purchaser. The foundations of this branch of the law, at least in this state, were laid in Thomas v. Winchester * * *. A poison was falsely labeled. The sale was made to a druggist, who in turn sold to a customer. The customer recovered damages from the seller who affixed the label. The defendant's negligence,' it was said, put human life in imminent danger.' A poison falsely labeled is likely to injure any one who gets it. Because the danger is to be foreseen, there is a duty to avoid the injury. Cases were cited by way of illustration in which manufacturers were not subject to any duty irrespective of contract. The distinction was said to be that their conduct, though, negligent, was not likely to result in injury to any one except the purchaser. We are not required to say whether the chance of injury was always as remote as the distinction assumes. * * *

The defendant argues that things imminently dangerous to life are poisons, explosives, deadly weapons- things whose normal function it is to injure or destroy. But whatever the rule in Thomas v. Winchester may once have been, it has no longer that restricted meaning. A large coffee urn (Statler v. Ray Mfg. Co., supra) may have within itself, if negligently made, the potency of danger, yet no one thinks of it as an implement whose normal function is destruction. What is true of the coffee urn is equally true of bottles of aerated water (Torgeson v. Schultz, * * *).

We have mentioned only cases in this court. But the rule has received a like extension in our courts of intermediate appeal. In Burke v. Ireland, * * * it was applied to a builder who constructed a defective building; in Kahner v. Otis Elevator Co. * * * to the manufacturer of an elevator; in Davies v. Pelham Hod Elevating Co. * * *; affirmed in this court without opinion, (146 N.Y. 363) to a contractor who furnished a defective rope was to be used.

We are not required at this time either to approve or to disapprove the application of the rule that was made in these cases. It is enough that they help to characterize the trend of judicial thought. Devlin v. Smith was decided in 1882. A year later a very similar case came before the Court of Appeal in England (Heaven v. Pender, L.R. (11 Q.B.D.)503). We find in the opinion * * * the same conception of a duty, irrespective of contract, imposed upon the manufacturer by the law itself: Whenever one person supplies goods, or machinery, or the like, for the purpose of their being used by another person under such circumstances that every one of ordinary sense would, if he thought, recognize at once that unless he used ordinary care and skill with regard to the condition of the thing supplied or the mode of supplying it, there will be danger of injury to the person or property of him for whose use the thing is supplied, and who is to use it, a duty arises to use ordinary care and skill as the condition or manner of supplying such thing.' He then points out that for a neglect of such ordinary care or skill whereby injury happens, the appropriate remedy is an action for negligence. The right to enforce this liability is not to be confined to the immediate buyer. The right, he says, extends to the persons or class of persons for whose use the thing is supplied. It is enough that the goods would in all probability be used at once * * * before a reasonable opportunity for discovering any defect which might exist,' and that the thing supplied is of such a nature that a neglect of ordinary care or skill as to its condition or the manner of supplying it would probably cause danger to the person or property of the person for whose use it was supplied, and who was about to use it.'

On the other hand, he would exclude a case in which the goods are supplied under circumstances in which it would be a chance by whom they would be used or whether they would be used or not, or whether they would be before there would probably be means of observing any defect," or where the goods are of such a nature that a want of care or skill as to their condition or the manner of supplying them would not probably produce danger of injury to person or property." What was said by Lord Esher in that case did not command the full assent of his associates. His opinion has been criticized as requiring every man to take affirmative precautions to protect his neighbors as well as to refrain from injuring them'. * * * It may not be an accurate exposition of the law of England. Perhaps it may need some qualification even in our own state. Like most attempts at comprehensive definition, it may involve errors of inclusion and of exclusion. But its tests and standards, at least in their underlying principled, with whatever qualifications may be called for as they are applied to varying conditions, are the tests and standards of our law.

We hold, then, that the principle of Thomas v. Winchester is not limited to poisons, explosives, and things of like nature, to things which in their normal operation are implements of destruction. If the nature of a thing is such that it is reasonably certain to place and limb in peril when negligently made, it is then a thing of danger. Its nature gives warning of the consequences to be expected. If to the element of danger there is added knowledge that the thing will be used by persons other than the purchaser, and used without new tests then, irrespective of contract, the manufacturer of this thing of danger is under a duty to make it carefully. That is as far as we are required to go for the decision of this case. There must be knowledge of a danger, not merely possible, but probable. It is possible to use almost anything in a way that will make it dangerous if defective. That is not enough to charge the manufacturer with a duty independent of his contract. Whether a given thing is dangerous may be sometimes a question for the court and sometimes a question for the jury. There must also be knowledge that in the usual course of events the danger will be shared by others than the buyer. Such knowledge may often be inferred from the nature of the transaction. But it is possible that even knowledge of the danger and of the use will not always be enough.

The proximity or remoteness of the relation is a factor to be considered. We are dealing now with the liability of the manufacturer of the finished product, who puts it on the market to be used without inspection by his customers. If he is negligent, where danger is to be foreseen, a liability will follow. We are not required at this time to say that it is legitimate to go back of the manufacturer of the finished product and hold the manufacturers of the component parts. To make their negligence a cause of imminent danger, an independent cause must often intervene; the manufacturer of the finished product must also fail in his duty of inspection. It may be that in those circumstances the negligence of the earlier members of the series as too remote to constitute, as to the ultimate user, an actionable wrong * * * We leave that question open to you. We shall have to deal with it when it arises. The difficulty which it suggests is not present in this case. There is here no break in the chain of cause and effect. In such circumstances, the presence of a known danger, attendant upon a known use, makes vigilance a duty. We have put aside the notion that the duty to safeguard life and limb, when the consequences of negligence may be foreseen, grows out of contract and nothing else. We have put the source of the obligation where it ought not be. We have put its source in the law. From this survey of the decisions, there thus emerges a definition of the duty of a manufacturer which enables us to measure this defendant's liability.

Beyond all question, the nature of an automobile gives warning of probable danger if its construction is defective. This automobile was designed to go fifty miles an hour. Unless its wheels were sound and strong, injury was almost certain. It was as much a thing of danger as a defective engine for a railroad. The defendant knew the danger. It knew also that the care would be used by persons other than the buyer. This was apparent from its size; there were seats for three persons. It was apparent also from the fact that the buyer was a dealer in cars, who bought to resell. The maker of this car supplied it for the use of purchasers from the dealer just as plainly as the contractor in Devlin v. Smith supplied the scaffold for use by the servants of the owner. The dealer was indeed the one person of whom it might be said with some approach to certainly that by him the car would not be used. Yet the defendant would have us say that he was the one person whom it was under a legal duty to protect. The law does not lead us to so inconsequent a conclusion. Precedents drawn from the days of travel by stage coach do not fit the conditions of travel today. The principle that the danger must be imminent does not change, but the things subject to the principle do change. They are whatever the needs of life in a developing civilization require them to be. In reaching this conclusion, we do not ignore the decisions to the contrary in other jurisdictions. It was held in Cadillac M.C. Co. v. Johnson that an automobile is not within the rule of Thomas v. Winchester. * * * The earlier cases are * * * at first sight inconsistent with our conclusion, may be reconciled upon the ground that the negligence was too remote, and that another cause had intervened. But even when they cannot be reconciled, the difference is rather in the application of the principle than in the principle itself. Judge Sanborn says, for example, that the contractor who builds a bridge, or the manufacturer who builds a car, cannot ordinarily foresee injury to other persons than the owner as the probable result. * * * We take a different view. We think that injury to others is to be foreseen not merely as a possible, but as an almost inevitable result. * * * Indeed Judge Sanborn concedes that his view is not to be reconciled with our decision in Devlin v. Smith (supra). The doctrine of that decision has now become the settled law of this state, and we have no desire to depart form it. In England the limits of the rule are still unsettled. Winterbottom v. Wright * * * is often cited. The defendant undertook to provide a mail coach to carry the mail bags. The coach broke down from latent defects in its construction. The defendant, however, was not the manufacturer. The court held that he was not liable for injuries to a passenger. The case was decided on a demurrer to the declaration. * * *

* * * The court left it to the jury to say whether the defendant ought to have foreseen that the car, if negligently constructed, would become imminently dangerous.' Subtle distinctions are drawn by the defendant between things inherently dangerous and things imminently dangerous, but the case does not turn upon these verbal niceties. If danger was to be expected as reasonably certain, there was a duty of vigilance, and this whether you call the danger inherent or imminent. In varying forms that the court would not have been justified in ruling as a matter of law that the car was a dangerous thing. If there was any error, it was none of which the defendant can complain. We think the defendant was not absolved from a duty of inspection because it bought the wheels from a reputable manufacturer. It was not merely a dealer in automobiles. It was a manufacturer of automobiles. It was responsible for the finished product. It was not at liberty to put the finished product on the market without subjecting the component parts to ordinary and simple tests. * * * Under the charge of the trial judge nothing more was required of it. The obligation to inspect must vary with the nature of the thing to be inspected. The more probable the danger, the greater the need of caution. There is little analogy between this case and Carlson v. Phoenix Bridge Co., * * * where the defendant bought a tool for a servant's use. The making of tools was not the business on which the master was engaged. Reliance on the skill of the manufacturer was proper and almost inevitable. But that is not the defendant's situation. Both by its relation to the work and by the nature of its business, it is charged with a stricter duty. Other rulings complained of have been considered, but no error has been found on them.

The judgment should be affirmed.

The case of *Henningsen v. Bloomfield Motors* raised the issue of privity in a warranty action. The case involved both the issue of vertical privity (now settled in *MacPherson*) and horizontal privity, since it was Mrs. Henningsen who was seeking recovery for her personal injury and Mrs. Henningsen was not the purchaser of the automobile.

MANUFACTURER >>> RETAILER >>>

MR. KLAUS HENNINGSEN [PURCHASER] > HELEN HENNINGSEN [USER]

The manufacturer had argued that since it was not a party to the sale (contract) by the dealer to Mr. Henningsen, the absence of privity eliminated the existence of any warranty from the manufacturer to Mr. Henningsen, except that which was expressly given by the manufacturer. Based on *MacPherson*, however, the court rejected the requirement of privity and found that Mr. Henningsen was in fact covered by the implied warranty of merchantability - despite the lack of privity.

The court then turned its attention to the claims of Mrs. Helen Henningsen. Clearly, Mrs. Henningsen was not the purchaser of the automobile or a party to the contract. However, the court extended protection to Mrs. Henningsen (horizontally) by the following formulation, in effect, also extending the warranty of merchantability to all those persons who:

> *"Within the reasonable contemplation of the parties to the warranty might be expected to become a user of the automobile."*

The Henningsen rule of extended horizontal privity may be found in the original text of U.C.C. Section 2-318, Alternative A:

> *"A seller's warranty, whether express or implied, extends to any natural person who is in the family or household of his buyer or who is a guest in his home if it is reasonable to expect that such person may use, consume or be affected by the goods and who is injured in person by breach of the warranty. A seller may not exclude or limit the operation of this section."*

We will see later in our discussion of warranties under the UCC that Section 2-318 was extended to other parties as the law of warranties was further developed and extended.

Henningsen v. Bloomfield Motors, Inc.

Supreme Court of New Jersey, 32 N.J. 358, 161 A.2d 69 (1960)

FRANCIS, JUDGE

Mr. Henningsen purchased an automobile from defendant Bloomfield Motors and gave it to his wife as a gift. The automobile was manufactured by defendant Chrysler Corporation. Ten days after delivery of the car, Mrs. Henningsen was injured in an accident that resulted when the steering failed suddenly and without warning. Up to this time the car had functioned properly. Mrs. Henningsen sued both defendants for breach of express and implied warranties and for negligence. Her husband joined in the action seeking compensation for his consequential losses. The trial judge dismissed the negligence counts because of insufficient evidence. He gave the case to the jury on the implied warranty theory only. The jury rendered verdicts against both defendants in favor of the plaintiffs. Defendants appealed and plaintiffs cross-appealed, claiming that the negligence count should not have been dismissed.

The sales contract signed by Mr. Henningsen was a standard printed form. It contained the following language concerning the warranty. It was in fine print and located on the back of the form:

"7. It is expressly agreed that there are no warranties, express or implied, made by either the dealer or the manufacturer on the motor vehicle, chassis, of parts furnished hereunder except as follows." 'The manufacturer warrants each new motor vehicle (including original equipment placed thereon by the manufacturer except tires), chassis or parts manufactured by it to be free from defects in material or workmanship under normal use and service. Its obligation under this warranty being limited to making good at its factory any part or parts thereof which shall, within ninety (90) days after delivery of such vehicle to the original purchaser or before such vehicle has been driven 4,000 miles, whichever event shall first occur, be returned to it with transportation charges prepaid and which its examination shall disclose to its satisfaction to have been thus defective; this warranty being expressly in lieu of all other warranties expressed or implied, and all other obligation or liabilities on its part, and it neither assumes nor authorizes any other person to assume for it any other liability in connection with the sale of its vehicles. * * *.' " (Emphasis added.)

I. THE CLAIM OF IMPLIED WARRANTY AGAINST THE MANUFACTURER

In the ordinary case of sale of goods by description an implied warranty of merchantability is an integral part of the transaction. * * * If the buyer, expressly or by implication, makes known to the seller the particular purpose for which the article is required and it appears that he has relied on the seller's skill or judgment, an implied warranty arises of reasonable fitness for that purpose. * * * The former type of warranty simply means that the thing sold is reasonably fit for the general purpose for which it is manufactured and sold. * * * As Judge (later Justice) Cardozo remarked in Ryan, supra, the distinction between a warranty of fitness for a particular purpose and of merchantability in many instances is practically meaningless. In the particular case he was concerned with food for human consumption in a sealed container. Perhaps no more apt illustration of the notion can be thought of than the instance of the ordinary purchaser who informs the automobile dealer that he desires a car for the purpose of business and pleasure driving on the public highway.* * *

Of course such sales, whether oral or written, may be accompanied by an express warranty. Under the broad terms of the Uniform Sale of Goods Law any affirmation of fact relating to the goods is an express warranty if the natural tendency of the statement is to induce the buyer to make the purchase. * * * [The act] preserves and continues any permissible implied warranty, despite an express warranty, unless the two are inconsistent. * * * The uniform act codified, extended and liberalized the common law of sales. The motivation in part was to ameliorate the harsh doctrine of caveat emptor and in some measure to impose a reciprocal obligation on the seller to beware. The transcendent value of the legislation, particularly with respect to implied warranties, rests in the fact that obligations on the part of the seller were imposed by operation of law, and did not depend for their existence upon express agreement of the parties. And of tremendous significance in a rapidly expanding commercial society was the recognition of the right to recover damages on account of personal injuries arising from a breach of warranty. * * * The particular importance of this advance resides in the fact that under such circumstances strict liability is imposed upon the maker or seller of the product. Recovery of damages does not depend upon proof of negligence or know edge of the defect. * * *

As the Sales Act and its liberal interpretation by the courts threw this protective cloak about the buyer, the decisions in various jurisdictions revealed beyond doubt that many manufacturers took steps to avoid these ever increasing warranty obligations. Realizing that the act governed the relationship of buyer and seller, they undertook to withdraw from actual and direct contractual contact with the buyer. They ceased selling products to the consuming public through their own employees and making contracts of sale in their own names. Instead, a system of independent dealers was established; their products were sold to dealers who in turn dealt with the buying public, ostensibly solely in their own personal capacity as sellers. In the past in many instances, manufacturers were able to transfer to the dealers burdens imposed by the act and thus achieved a large measure of immunity for themselves. * * *

The terms of the warranty are a sad commentary upon the automobile manufacturers, marketing practices. Warranties developed in the law in the interest of and to protect the ordinary consumer who cannot be expected to have the knowledge or capacity or even the opportunity to make adequate inspection of mechanical instrumentalities, like automobiles, and to decide for himself whether they are reasonably fit for the designed purpose. * * * But the ingenuity of the Automobile Manufacturers Association, by means of its standardized form, has metamorphosed the warranty into a device to limit the maker's liability. * * *

Putting aside for the time being the problem of the efficacy of the disclaimer provisions contained in the express warranty, a question of first importance to be decided is whether an implied warranty of merchantability by Chrysler Corporation accompanied the sale of the automobile to Claus Henningsen.

Preliminarily, it may be said that the express warranty against defective parts and workmanship is not inconsistent with an implied warranty of merchantability. Such warranty cannot be excluded for that reason. * * *

Chrysler points out that an implied warranty of merchantability is an incident of a contract of sale. It concedes, of course, the making of the original sale to Bloomfield Motors, Inc., but maintains that this transaction marked the terminal point of its contractual connection with the car. Then Chrysler urges that since it was not a party to the sale by the dealer to Henningsen, there is no privity of contract between it and the plaintiffs, and the absence of this privity eliminates any such implied warranty.

There is no doubt that under early common-law concepts of contractual liability only those persons who were parties to the bargain could sue for a breach of it. In more recent times a noticeable disposition has appeared in a number of jurisdictions to break through the narrow barrier of privity when dealing with sales of goods in order to give realistic recognition to a universally accepted fact. The fact is that the dealer and the ordinary buyer do not, and are not expected to, buy goods, whether they be foodstuffs or automobiles, exclusively for their own consumption or use. Makers and manufacturers know this and advertise and market their products on that assumption; witness, the "family," car, the baby foods, etc. The limitations of privity in contracts for the sale of goods developed their place in the law when marketing conditions were simple, when maker and buyer frequently met face to face on an equal bargaining plane and when many of the products were relatively uncomplicated and conducive to inspection by a buyer competent to evaluate their quality. * * * With the advent of mass marketing, the manufacturer became remote from the purchaser, sales were accomplished through intermediaries, and the demand for the product was created by advertising media. In such an economy it became obvious that the consumer was the person being cultivated.

Manifestly, the connotation of "consumer" was broader than that of "buyer." He signified such a person who, in the reasonable contemplation of the parties to the sale, might be expected to use the product. Thus, where the commodities sold are such that if defectively manufactured they will be dangerous to life or limb, then society's interests can only be protected by eliminating the requirement of privity between the maker and his dealers and the reasonably expected ultimate consumer. In that way the burden of losses consequent upon use of defective articles is borne by those who are in a position to either control the danger or make an equitable distribution of the losses when they do occur. As Harper & James put it, "The interest in consumer protection calls for warranties by the maker that do run With the goods, to reach all who are likely to be hurt by the use of the unfit commodity for a purpose ordinarily to be expected." * * *

Although only a minority of jurisdictions have thus far departed from the requirement of privity, the movement in that direction is most certainly gathering momentum. Liability to the ultimate consumer in the absence of direct contractual connection has been predicated upon a variety of theories. Some courts hold that the warranty runs with the article like a covenant running with land; others recognize a third-party beneficiary thesis; still others rest their decision on the ground that public policy requires recognition of a warranty made directly to the consumer. * * *

Most of the cases where lack of privity has not been permitted to interfere with recovery have involved food and drugs. * * * In fact, the rule as to such products has been characterized as an exception to the general doctrine. But more recently courts, sensing the inequity of such limitation, have moved into broader fields: home permanent wave set, * * *

We see no rational doctrinal basis for differentiating between a fly in a bottle of beverage and a defective automobile. The unwholesome beverage may bring illness to one person, the defective car, with its great potentiality for harm to the driver, occupants, and others, demands even less adherence to the narrow barrier of privity. * * *

Under modern conditions the ordinary layman, on responding to the importuning of colorful advertising, has neither the opportunity nor the capacity to inspect or to determine the fitness of an automobile for use; he must rely on the manufacturer who has control of its construction, and to some degree on the dealer who, to the limited extent called for by the manufacturer's instructions, inspects and services it before delivery. In such a marketing milieu his remedies and those of persons who properly claim through him should not depend "upon the intricacies of the law of sales. The obligation of the manufacturer should not be based alone on privity of contract. It should rest, as was once said, upon 'the demands of social justice.' " Masetti v. Armour & Co., 75 Wash. 622, 135 P. 633, 635, 48 L.R.A., N.S., 213 (Sup.Ct. 1913). "If privity of contract is required," then, under the circumstances of modern merchandising, "privity of contract exists in the consciousness and understanding of all right-thinking persons., Madouros v. Kansas City Coca-Cola Bottling Co., [90 S.W.2d 445, 450 (Mo.App. 1936).

Accordingly, we hold that under modern marketing conditions, when a manufacturer puts a new automobile in the stream of trade and promotes its purchase by the public, an implied warranty that it is reasonably suitable for use as such accompanies it into the hands of the ultimate purchaser. Absence of agency between the manufacturer and the dealer who makes the ultimate sale is immaterial.

II. THE EFFECT OF THE DISCLAIMER AND LIMITATION OF LIABILITY CLAUSES ON THE IMPLIED WARRANTY OF MERCHANTABILITY

* * *

In view of the cases in various jurisdictions suggesting at the conclusion which we have now reached with respect to the implied warranty of merchantability, it becomes apparent that manufacturers who enter into promotional activities to stimulate consumer buying may incur warranty obligations of either or both the express or implied character. These developments in the law inevitably suggest the inference that the form of express warranty made part of the Henningsen purchase contract was devised for general use in the automobile industry as a possible means of avoiding the consequences of the growing judicial acceptance of the thesis that the described express or implied warranties run directly to the consumer.

In the light of these matters, what effect should be given to the express warranty in question which seeks to limit the manufacturer's liability to replacement of defective parts, and which disclaims all other warranties, express or implied? In assessing its significance we must keep in mind the general principle that, in the absence of fraud, one who does not choose to read a contract before signing it, cannot later relieve himself of its burdens.

* * * And in applying that principle, the basic tenet of freedom of competent parties to contract is a factor of importance. But in the framework of modern commercial life and business practices, such rules cannot be applied on a strict, doctrinal basis. The conflicting interests of the buyer and seller must be evaluated realistically and justly, giving due weight to the social policy evinced by the Uniform Sales Act, the progressive decisions of the courts engaged in administering it, the mass production methods of manufacture and distribution to the public, and the bargaining position occupied by the ordinary consumer in such an economy. This history of the law shows that legal doctrines, as first expounded, often prove to be inadequate under the impact of later experience. In such case, the need for justice has stimulated the necessary qualifications or adjustments. * * *

It is apparent that the public has an interest not only in the safe manufacture of automobiles, but also, as shown by the Sales Act, in protecting the rights and remedies of purchasers, so far as it can be accomplished consistently with our system of free enterprise. In a society such as ours, where the automobile is a common and necessary adjunct of daily life, and where its use is so fraught with danger to the driver, passengers and the public, the manufacturer is under a special obligation in connection with the construction, promotion and sale of his cars. Consequently, the courts must examine purchase agreements closely to see if consumer and public interests are treated fairly.

* * * As we have said, warranties originated in the law to safeguard the buyer and not to limit the liability of the seller or manufacturer. It seems obvious in this instance that the motive was to avoid the warranty obligations which are normally incidental to such sales. The language gave little and withdrew much. In return for the delusive remedy of replacement of defective parts at the factory, the buyer is said to have accepted the exclusion of the maker's liability for personal injuries arising from the breach of the warranty, and to have agreed to the elimination of any other express or implied warranty. An instinctively felt sense of justice cries out against such a sharp bargain. But does the doctrine that a person is bound by his signed agreement, in the absence of fraud, stand in the way of any relief?

In the modern consideration of problems such as this, Corbin suggests that practically all judges are "chancellors" and cannot fail to be influenced by any equitable doctrines that are available. And he opines that "there is sufficient flexibility in the concepts of fraud, duress, misrepresentation and undue influence, not to mention differences in economic bargaining power" to enable the courts to avoid enforcement of unconscionable provisions in long printed standardized contracts. * * * Freedom of contract is not such an immutable doctrine as to admit of no qualification in the area in which we are concerned. * * *

The traditional contract is the result of free bargaining of parties who are brought together by the play of the market, and who meet each other on a footing of approximate economic equality. In such a society there is no danger that freedom of contract will be a threat to the social order as a whole. But in present-day commercial life the standardized mass contract has appeared. It is used primarily by enterprises with strong bargaining power and position. "The weaker party, in need of the goods or services, is frequently not in a position to shop around for better terms, either because the author of the standard contract has a monopoly (natural or artificial) or because all competitors use the same clauses. His contractual intention is but a subjection more or less voluntary to terms dictated by the stronger party, terms whose consequences are often understood in a vague way, if at all." * * *

The warranty before us is a standardized form designed for mass use. It is imposed upon the automobile consumer. He takes it or leaves it, and he must take it to buy an automobile. No bargaining is engaged in with respect to it. In fact, the dealer through whom it comes to the buyer is without authority to alter it; his function is ministerial -- simply to deliver it. The form warranty is not only standard with Chrysler but, as mentioned above, it is the uniform warranty of the Automobile Manufacturers Association. * * *

* * *

The task of the judiciary is to administer the spirit as well as the letter of the law. On issues such as the present one, part of that burden is to protect the ordinary man against the loss of important rights through what, in effect, is the unilateral act of the manufacturer. The status of the automobile industry is unique. Manufacturers are few in number and strong in bargaining position. In the matter of warranties on the sale of their products, the Automotive Manufacturers Association has enabled them to present a united front. From the standpoint of the purchaser, there can be no arms length negotiating on the subject. Because his capacity for bargaining is so grossly unequal, the inexorable conclusion which follows is that he is not permitted to bargain at all. He must take or leave the automobile on the warranty terms dictated by the maker. He cannot turn to a competitor for better security. Public policy at a given time finds expression in the Constitution, the statutory law and in judicial decisions. In the area of sale of goods, the legislative will has imposed an implied warranty of merchantability as a general incident of sale of an automobile by description. The warranty does not depend upon the affirmative intention of the parties. It is a child of the law; it annexes itself to the contract because of the very nature of the transaction. Minneapolis Steel & Machinery Co. v. Casey Land Agency, 51 N.D. 832, 201 N.W. 172 (Sup.Ct. 1924). The judicial process has recognized a right to recover damages for personal injuries arising from a breach of that warranty. The disclaimer of the implied warranty and exclusion of all obligations except those specifically assumed by the express warranty signify a studied effort to frustrate that protection. True, the Sales Act authorizes agreements between buyer and seller qualifying the warranty obligations. But quite obviously the legislature contemplated lawful stipulations (which are determined by the circumstances of a particular case) arrived at freely by parties of relatively equal bargaining strength. The lawmakers did not authorize the automobile manufacturer to use its grossly disproportionate bargaining power to relieve itself from liability and to impose on the ordinary buyer, who in effect has no real freedom of choice, the grave danger of injury to himself and others that attends the sale of such a dangerous instrumentality as a defectively made automobile. In the framework of this case, illuminated as it is by the facts and the many decisions noted, we are of the opinion that Chrysler's attempted disclaimer of an implied warranty of merchantability and of the obligations arising therefrom is so inimical to the public good as to compel an adjudication of its invalidity. * *

IV. PROOF OF BREACH OF THE IMPLIED WARRANTY OF MERCHANTABILITY

Both defendants argue that the proof adduced by plaintiffs as to the happening of the accident was not sufficient to demonstrate a breach of warranty. Consequently, they claim that their motion for judgment should have been granted by the trial court. We cannot agree. In our view, the total effect of the circumstances shown from purchase to accident is adequate to raise an inference that the car was defective and that such condition was causally related to the mishap. See, Yormack v. Farmers, Coop. Ass'n of N.J., 11 N.J. Super. 416, 78 A.2d 421 (App. Div. 1951) * * *. Thus, determination by the jury was required.

The proof adduced by the plaintiffs disclosed that after servicing and delivery of the car, it operated normally during the succeeding ten days, so far as the Henningsens could tell. They had no difficulty or mishap of any kind, and it neither had nor required any servicing. It was driven by them alone. The owner's service certificate provided for return for further servicing at the end of the first 1,000 miles--less than half of which had been covered at the time of Mrs. Henningsen's injury.

The facts, detailed above, show that on the day of the accident, ten days after delivery, Mrs. Henningsen was driving in a normal fashion, on a smooth highway, when unexpectedly the steering wheel and the front wheels of the car went into the bizarre action described. Can it reasonably be said that the circumstances do not warrant an inference of unsuitability for ordinary use against the manufacturer and the dealer? Obviously there is nothing in the proof to indicate in the slightest that the most unusual action of the steering wheel was caused by Mrs. Henningsen's operation of the automobile on this day, or by the use of the car between delivery and the happening of the incident. Nor is there anything to suggest that any external force or condition, unrelated to the manufacturing or servicing of the car operated as an inducing or even concurring factor.

* * *

[T]he question of breach of warranty * * * was properly placed in the hands of the jury. In our judgment, the evidence shown, as a matter of preponderance of probabilities, would justify the conclusion by the ultimate triers of the facts that the accident was caused by a failure of the steering mechanism of the car and that such failure constituted a breach of the warranty of both defendants.

* * *

V. THE DEFENSE OF LACK OF PRIVITY AGAINST MRS. HENNINGSEN

Both defendants contend that since there was no privity of contract between them and Mrs. Henningsen, she cannot recover for breach of any warranty made by either of them. On the facts, as they were developed, we agree that she was not a party to the purchase agreement. * * * Her right to maintain the action, therefore, depends upon whether she occupies such legal status thereunder as to permit her to take advantage of a breach of defendants' implied warranties.

For the most part the cases that have been considered dealt with the right of the buyer or consumer to maintain an action against the manufacturer where the contract of sale was with a dealer and the buyer had no contractual relationship with the manufacturer. In the present matter, the basic contractual relationship is between Claus Henningsen, Chrysler, and Bloomfield Motors, Inc. The precise issue presented is whether Mrs. Henningsen, who is not a party to their respective warranties, may claim under them. In our judgment, the principles of those cases and the supporting texts are just as proximately applicable to her situation. We are convinced that the cause of justice in this area of the law can be served only by recognizing that she is such a person whom in the reasonable contemplation of the parties to the warranty, might be expected to become a user of the automobile. Accordingly, her lack of privity does not stand in the way of prosecution of the injury suit against the defendant Chrysler.

* * *

[I]t cannot be overlooked that historically actions on warranties were in tort also, sounding in deceit. * * * The contract theory gradually emerged, although the tort idea has continued to lurk in the background, making the warranty "a curious hybrid of tort and contract." Prosser, supra, 83. An awareness of this evolution makes for ready acceptance of the relaxation of rigid concepts of privity when third persons, who in the reasonable contemplation of the parties to a warranty might be expected to use or consume the product sold, are injured by its unwholesome or defective state.

* * *

Under all of the circumstances outlined above, the judgments in favor of the plaintiffs and against the defendants are affirmed.

In *Henningsen*, the hybrid nature of a warranty, arising both under contract and tort theories, led the court to reject the rigid privity requirement of contract and instead to adopt a more consumer friendly foreseeability standard associated with tort liability, especially in negligence cases.

Questions

1. The plaintiff, Winterbottom, had been contracted by the postmaster general to drive a mail coach. The defendant, Wright, had been contracted by the postmaster to maintain the coach. While Winterbottom was driving, the coach collapsed and he sustained injuries. Winterbottom brought suit asserting that Wright was negligent and disregarded his contract.

   a. How did the ruling constrain the law's stance on negligence?

   b. Is Wright liable?

2. How did Thomas v. Winchester determine that manufacturers could not limit liability through the defense of privity.

3. How did Loop v. Litchfield uncover the flaw of the doctrine of privity?

4. Buick Motor Company, the defendant, is a manufacturer of automobiles. It sold one of its automobiles to a retail dealer that proceeded to resell to MacPherson, the plaintiff. While driving, the car collapsed because one of the wheels was made from defective wood. Consequently, the plaintiff was thrown out of the car and sustained injuries. Furthermore, the wheel was not made by the defendant, but bought from another manufacturer. However, its defects could have been discovered by reasonable inspection. The plaintiff sued for negligence.

   a. Does the doctrine of vertical privity apply? If so, how?

   b. Is Buick Motor Company liable?

5. Mr. Henningsen purchased an automobile from defendant, Bloomfield Motors Inc., as a gift for his wife. The automobile was manufactured by Chrysler Corporation. Ten days after delivery, Mrs. Henningsen was injured in an accident when the steering suddenly failed. Mrs. Henningsen brought suit against Bloomfield Motors Inc. and Chrysler Corporation for breach of express and implied warranties and additionally for negligence.

   a. How was horizontal privity extended in this case?

   b. Is Chrysler liable? Is Bloomfield Motors Inc. liable?

Chapter Seven

Negligence, Causation and Res Ipsa Loquitur

"A manufacturer's duty to produce a safe product, with appropriate warnings and instructions where necessary, rests initially on the responsibility each of us bears to exercise care to avoid unreasonable risks of harm to others." (Hall v. E.I. DuPont)

"Negligence is the omission or failure to do something which a reasonable man would do or doing something which a reasonable and prudent man would not do under the same or similar circumstances." (see Restatement, 2d Torts)

A classic case from the common law provides an insight on the issue of the reasonable man.

Case Study: Cordas v. Peerless Transportation Co.

Procedural Posture

Plaintiffs brought an action for damages in the City Court of New York, (New York) against defendant cab company in an action alleging negligence.

Overview

A chauffeur driving a cab owned by defendant cab company abandoned his vehicle while it was in motion after he was threatened by his passenger, a thief with a pistol who was fleeing from the scene of a crime. The passenger also abandoned the vehicle and then, the unattended cab injured plaintiffs, a mother and her two children. Plaintiffs filed a negligence action against defendant cab company. The court found in favor of defendant. It said that defendant was suddenly faced with patent danger, not of its own making, and the court presumed defendant abandoned the vehicle involuntarily. It said that the law does not hold one in an emergency to the exercise of that mature judgment required of him under circumstances where he has an opportunity for deliberate action. It found defendant's actions reasonable under the circumstances.

Outcome

The court found for defendant cab company in an action for negligence where it said that defendant could not be found negligent when it was suddenly faced with patent danger, not of its own making, and the court presumed defendant's response was done involuntarily.

Negligence

In general, negligence involves proof of unreasonable conduct, which is the cause in fact, and proximate or legal cause of injury to the plaintiff. The plaintiff must both plead and prove that specific acts or omissions of the defendant were negligent. The traditional elements of proving negligence are a proof of a duty of due care; breach of that duty; causation; and damages.

Negligence can arise in numerous ways and standard principles of negligence now apply fully and clearly to individuals who design, manufacture, and sell products. These areas include inspection, processing, packaging, warning, designing, or marketing of products, or of the service portion of a transaction involving a product.

At the end of trial, judges are required to charge a jury relating to the law on negligence. For example, the jury instructions found in the case of *Garnes v. Gulf & Western Manufacturing Co.* provide:

> *"You are instructed that it is the law that the manufacturer of a machine has a nondelagable duty to make a machine that includes necessary safety devices. You are instructed that it is the law that the manufacturer has a duty to produce a safe product with warnings and instructions where necessary."*

Courts will employ the standard of the reasonable man or the reasonable person in the position of the manufacturer, or designer, or marketer. *Wilson v. Piper Aircraft* reminds us that in product cases, expert testimony or evidence will be required in most cases—and absolutely in any case involving medical malpractice, or medical negligence—where an expert would be expected to testify what a reasonable medical practitioner in the same or similar community under the same or similar circumstances would or would not do. The court concluded:

> *"We conclude that the plaintiff had the burden to prove by expert medical evidence what a reasonable medical practitioner of the same school and same or similar community under the same or similar circumstances would have disclosed to his patient about the*

risks incident to a proposed diagnosis or treatment, that the physician departed from that standard, causation, and damages."

The standard for a manufacturer in a design case is straightforward: Did the manufacturer exercise all reasonable skill and knowledge concerning the design of the product as would other designers under the same or similar circumstances? A manufacturer must keep abreast of recent scientific and technological developments, and may be required to conduct tests or research to learn about any inherent dangers in their products. *Taylor v. Wyeth Labs* indicates that a manufacturer will be held accountable under a standard of professional skill and knowledge:

> *"A manufacturer is held to such reasonable skill, knowledge, and diligence as that of the experts in the filed to design and produce a product that is reasonably safe for its intended and foreseeable use. Ignorance of risks which were scientifically knowable or known at the time of sale or manufacture, or design; and failure to act is no defense and may, in itself, constitute negligence as an omission."*

The Restatement, Section 395, and Comment F embody this principle:

> *"A manufacturer who fails to exercise reasonable care in the manufacture of a chattel which, unless carefully made, he should recognize as involving an unreasonable risk of causing physical harm to those who use it for a purpose for which the manufacturer should expect it to be used and those whom he should expect to be endangered by its probable use, is subject to liability for physical harm caused to them by its lawful use in a manner and for a purpose for which it is supplied."*

> *"The particulars are (1) the adoption of a formula or plan which, if properly followed, will produce an article safe for the use for which it is sold, (2) the selection of material and parts to be incorporated in the finished article, (3) the fabrication of the article by every member of the operative staff no matter how high or low his position, (4) the making of such inspections and tests during the course of manufacturer and after the article is completed as the manufacturer should recognize as reasonably necessary to secure the production of a safe article, and (5) the packing of the article so as to be safe for those who must be expected to unpack it."*

FORMULA OR PLAN = DESIGN

FABRICATION = MANUFACTURE

What about the negligence of a manufacturer in cases involving a duty to warn? Generally, as we have seen, there is no duty to warn in a case of a patent or obvious danger. However, a case of a latent defect, a duty to warn arises. This dichotomy goes back to the consumer expectations test that we have previously discussed: If the defect or danger is patent or obvious, a manufacturer will not be required to issue a warning because the consumer has no expectation of receiving a warning and the consumer would not really receive anything of value or importance in the warning that he does not already know.

The issue of "to whom is the duty owed" was discussed in the famous *Palsgraf* case. Judge (later Justice) Cardozo adopted a restrictive view of duty in his foreseeability formation. In contrast, Judge Andrews, who served on the New York State Court of Appeals with Judge Cardozo, viewed the matter as one of causation and not duty and adopted what has been termed as the direct connection test, with "practical limitations in both time and space." According to Judge Cardozo, this issue is one for the court to decide as a matter of law; according to Judge Andrews, the issue is always one for the jury!

Palsgraf v. Long Island R.R. Co.

248 N.Y. 339, 162 N.E. 99 (1928)

CARDOZO, C. J. . . . Plaintiff was standing on a platform of defendant's railroad after buying a ticket to go to Rockaway Beach. A train stopped at the station, bound for another place. Two men ran forward to catch it. One of the men reached the platform of the car without mishap, though the train was already moving. The other man, carrying a package, jumped aboard the car, but seemed unsteady as if about to fall. A guard on the car, who had held the door open, reached forward help him in, and another guard on the platform pushed him from behind. In this act, the package was dislodged, and fell upon the rails. It was a package of small size, about fifteen inches long, and was covered by a newspaper. In fact it contained fireworks, but there was nothing in its appearance to give notice of its contents. The fireworks when they fell exploded. The shock of the explosion threw down some scales at the other end of the platform many feet away. The scales struck the plaintiff, causing injuries for which she sues.

The conduct of the defendant's guard, if a wrong in its relation to the holder of the package, was not a wrong in its relation to the plaintiff, standing far away. Relatively to her it was not negligence at all. Nothing in the situation gave notice that the falling package had in it the potency of peril to persons thus removed. Negligence is not actionable unless it involves the invasion of a legally protected interest, the violation of a right. Proof of negligence in the air, so to speak, will not do.' * * * Negligence is the absence of care, according to the circumstances.' * * * The plaintiff, as she stood upon the platform of the station, might claim to be protected against intentional invasion of her bodily security. Such invasion is not charged. She might claim to be protected against unintentional invasion by conduct involving in the thought of reasonable men an unreasonable hazard that such invasion would ensue. These, from the point of view of the law, were the bounds of her immunity, with perhaps some rare exceptions, survivals for the most part of ancient forms of liability, where conduct is held to be at the peril of the actor. * * * If no hazard was apparent to the eye of ordinary vigilance, an act innocent and harmless, at least to outward seeming, with reference to her, did not take to itself the quality of a tort because it happened to be a wrong, though apparently not one involving the risk of bodily insecurity, with reference to some one else.

This does not mean, of course, that one who launches a destructive force is always relieved of liability, if the force, though known to be destructive, pursues an unexpected path. It was not necessary that the defendant should have had notice of the particular method in which an accident would occur, if the possibility of an accident was clear to the ordinarily prudent eye.' * * * Some acts, such as shooting are so imminently dangerous to any one who may come within reach of the missile however unexpectedly, as to impose a duty of prevision not far from that of an insurer. * * * Even to-day, and much oftener in earlier stages of the law, one acts sometimes at one's peril. Under this head, it may be, fall certain cases of what is known as transferred intent, an act willfully dangerous to A. resulting by misadventure in injury to B. * * * These cases aside, wrong is defined in terms of the natural or probable, at least when unintentional. * * * The range of reasonable apprehension is at times a question for the court, and at times, if varying inferences are possible, a question for the jury. Here, by concession, there was nothing in the situation to suggest to the most cautious mind that the parcel wrapped in newspaper would spread wreckage through the station. If the guard had thrown it down knowingly and willfully, he would not have threatened the plaintiff's safety, so far as appearances could warn him. His conduct would not have involved, even then, an unreasonable probability of invasion of her bodily security. Liability can be no greater where the act is inadvertent.

The law of causation, remote or proximate, is thus foreign to the case before us. The question of liability is always anterior to the question of the measure of the consequences that go with liability. If there is no tort to be redressed, there is no occasion to consider what damage might be recovered if there were a finding of a tort. We may assume, without deciding, that negligence, not at large or in the abstract, but in relation to the plaintiff, would entail liability for any and all consequences, however novel or extraordinary. * * * There is room for argument that a distinction is to be drawn according to the diversity of interests invaded by the act, as where conduct negligent in that it threatens an insignificant invasion of an interest in property results in an unforeseeable invasion of an interest of another order, as, e. g., one of bodily security. Perhaps other distinctions may be necessary. We do not go into the question now. The consequences to be followed must first be rooted in a wrong.

The judgment of the Appellate Division and that of the Trial Term should be reversed, and the complaint dismissed, with costs in all courts.

ANDREWS, J. (dissenting).

Assisting a passenger to board a train, the defendant's servant negligently knocked a package from his arms. It fell between the platform and the cars. Of its contents the servant knew and could know nothing. A violent explosion followed. The concussion broke some scales standing a considerable distance away. In falling, they injured the plaintiff, an intending passenger. Upon these facts, may she recover the damages she has suffered in an action brought against the master? The result we shall reach depends upon our theory

> as to the nature of negligence. Is it a relative concept--the breach of some duty owing to a particular person or to particular persons? Or, where there is an act which unreasonably threatens the safety of others, is the doer liable for all its proximate consequences, even where they result in injury to one who would generally be thought to be outside the radius of danger? This is not a mere dispute as to words. We might not believe that to the average mind the dropping of the bundle would seem to involve the probability of harm to the plaintiff standing many feet away whatever might be the case as to the owner or to one so near as to be likely to be struck by its fall. If, however, we adopt the second hypothesis, we have to inquire only as to the relation between cause and effect. We deal in terms of proximate cause, not of negligence.

Res Ipsa Loquitur

"Res Ipsa Loquitur", as translated from the Latin, means "The thing speaks for itself." This doctrine arises when the plaintiff attempts to prove negligence through circumstantial evidence, because the plaintiff is unable to show any specific acts of negligence on the part of a defendant. The application of res ipsa loquitur permits the court to shift the burden of proof to the defendant to explain his/her conduct in an attempt to avoid the imposition of liability.

The *Escola* case (an exploding bottle case) discusses the issue of the application of res ipsa loquitur. In order to apply the doctrine, two conditions must be met:

- The defendant must have exclusive control over the thing causing injury (in the case of a product, at least at the time it was made);
- The injury is of such a nature that it would not ordinarily occur in the absence of some negligence.
- The plaintiff was not contributorily negligent.

The plaintiff must prove that the condition of the instrumentality had not been changed after it left the defendant's possession and that the plaintiff him/herself had exercised reasonable care. At this point, the burden of proof is shifted to the defendant to show that he/she was not negligent, since the defendant has superior knowledge so as to make it reasonable for him to come forward with the required proof. Pay special notice to the concurring opinion of Justice Traynor in *Escola* alluding to absolute liability, a theory not formally adopted until 1963. Because of the influence of Justice Traynor, it has been said that strict liability may be based on the same inferences as is res ipsa loquitur!

The doctrine of res ipsa loquitur cannot ordinarily be applied in cases where there is direct evidence of the cause of the injury.

Escola v. Coca Cola Bottling Co. Of Fresno

24 Cal.2d 453, 150 P.2d 436 (1944)

GIBSON, Chief Justice. . . . Plaintiff, a waitress in a restaurant, was injured when a bottle of Coca Cola broke in her hand. She alleged that defendant company, which had bottled and delivered the alleged defective bottle to her employer, was negligent in selling bottles containing said beverage which on account of excessive pressure of gas or by reason of some defect in the bottle was dangerous * * * and likely to explode.' This appeal is from a judgment upon a jury verdict in favor of plaintiff.

Many authorities state that the happening of the accident does not speak for itself where it took place some time after defendant had relinquished control of the instrumentality causing the injury. Under the more logical view, however, the doctrine may be applied upon the theory that defendant had control at the time of the alleged negligent act, although not at the time of the accident, provided plaintiff first proves that the condition of the instrumentality had not been changed after it left the defendant's possession.

Upon an examination of the record, the evidence appears sufficient to support a reasonable inference that the bottle here involved was not damaged by any extraneous force after delivery to the restaurant by defendant. It follows, therefore, that the bottle was in some manner defective at the time defendant relinquished control, because sound and properly prepared bottles of carbonated liquids do not ordinarily explode when carefully handled.

The next question, then, is whether plaintiff may rely upon the doctrine of res ipsa loquitur to supply an inference that defendant's negligence was responsible for the defective condition of the bottle at the time it was delivered to the restaurant.

An explosion such as took place here might have been caused by an excessive internal pressure in a sound bottle, by a defect in the glass of a bottle containing a safe pressure, or by a combination of these two possible causes. The question is whether under the evidence there was a probability that defendant was negligent in anyaof these respects. If so, the doctrine of res ipsa loquitur applies.

Although it is not clear in this case whether the explosion was caused by an excessive charge or a defect in the glass there is a sufficient showing that neither cause would ordinarily have been present if due care had been used. Further, defendant had exclusive control over both the charging and inspection of the bottles. Accordingly, all the requirements necessary to entitle plaintiff to rely on the doctrine of res ipsa loquitur to supply an inference of negligence are present.

It is true that defendant presented evidence tending to show that it exercised considerable precaution by carefully regulating and checking the pressure in the bottles and by making visual inspections for defects in the glass at several stages during the bottling process. It is well settled, however, that when a defendant produces evidence to rebut the inference of negligence which arises upon application of the doctrine of res ipsa loquitur, it is ordinarily a question of fact for the jury to determine whether the inference has been dispelled. * * *

The judgment is affirmed.

SHENK, CURTIS, CARTER, and SCHAUER, JJ., concurred.

TRAYNOR, Justice.

I concur in the judgment, but I believe the manufacturer's negligence should no longer be singled out as the basis of a plaintiff's right to recover in cases like the present one. In my opinion it should now be recognized that a manufacturer incurs an absolute liability when an article that he has placed on the market, knowing that it is to be used without inspection, proves to have a defect that causes injury to human beings. MacPherson v. Buick Motor Co., * * * established the principle, recognized by this court, that irrespective of privity of contract, the manufacturer is responsible for an injury caused by such an article to any person who comes in lawful contact with it. * * * In these cases the source of the manufacturer's liability was his negligence in the manufacturing process or in the inspection of component parts supplied by others. Even if there is no negligence, however, public policy demands that responsibility be fixed wherever it will most effectively reduce the hazards to life and health inherent in defective products that reach the market. It is evident that the manufacturer can anticipate some hazards and guard against the recurrence of others, as the public cannot. Those who suffer injury from defective products are unprepared to meet its consequences. The cost of an injury and the loss of time or health may be an overwhelming misfortune to the person injured, and a needless one, for the risk of injury can be insured by the manufacturer and distributed among the public as a cost of doing business. It is to the public interest to discourage the marketing of products having defects that are a menace to the public. If such products nevertheless find their way into the market it is to the public interest to place the responsibility for whatever injury they may cause upon the manufacturer, who, even if he is not negligent in the manufacture of the product, is responsible for its reaching the market. However intermittently such injuries may occur and however haphazardly they may strike, the risk of their occurrence is a constant risk and a general one. Against such a risk there should be general and constant protection and the manufacturer is best situated to afford such protection. The retailer, even though not equipped to test a product, is under an absolute liability to his customer, for the implied warranties of fitness for proposed use and merchantable quality include a warranty of safety of the product. * * * This warranty is not necessarily a contractual one * * * for public policy requires that the buyer be insured at the seller's expense against injury. * * * The courts recognize, however, that the retailer cannot bear the burden of this warranty, and allow him to recoup any losses by means of the warranty of safety attending the wholesaler's or manufacturer's sale to him. Much would be gained if the injured person could base his action directly on the manufacturer's warranty.

In the food products cases the courts have resorted to various fictions to rationalize the extension of the manufacturer's warranty to the consumer: that a warranty runs with the chattel; that the cause of action of the dealer is assigned to the consumer; that the consumer is a third party beneficiary of the manufacturer's contract with the dealer. They have also held the manufacturer liable on a mere fiction of negligence: 'Practically he must know it [the product] is fit, or take the consequences, if it proves destructive.' * * * Such fictions are not necessary to fix the manufacturer's liability under a warranty if the warranty is severed from the contract of sale between the dealer and the consumer and based on the law of torts * * * Warranties are not necessarily rights arising under a contract. * * * And it is still generally possible where a distinction of procedure is observed between actions of tort and of contract to frame the declaration for breach of warranty in tort. * * * On the basis of the tort character of an action on a warranty, recovery has been allowed for wrongful death as it could not be in an action for breach of contract. * * * As the court said in Greco v. S. S. Kresge Co., 'Though the action may be brought solely for the breach of the implied warranty, the breach is a wrongful act, a default, and, in its essential nature, a tort.' Even a seller's express warranty can arise from a noncontractual affirmation inducing a person to purchase the goods. Chamberlain Co. v. Allis-Chalmers, etc., Co., * * * 'As an actual agreement to contract is not essential, the obligation of a seller in such a case is one imposed by law as distinguished from one voluntarily assumed. It may be called an obligation either on a quasi-contract or quasi-tort, because remedies appropriate to contract and also to tort are applicable.' * * * As handicrafts have been replaced by mass production with its great markets and transportation facilities, the close relationship between the producer and consumer of a product has been altered. Manufacturing processes, frequently valuable secrets, are ordinarily either inaccessible to or beyond the ken of the general public. The consumer no longer has means or skill enough to investigate for himself the soundness of a product, even when it is not contained in a sealed package, and his erstwhile vigilance has been lulled by the steady efforts of manufacturers to build up confidence by advertising and marketing devices such as trade-marks. * * * Consumers no longer approach products warily but accept them on faith, relying on the reputation of the manufacturer or the trade mark. * * * Manufacturers have sought to justify that faith by increasingly high standards of inspection and a readiness to make good on defective products by way of replacements and refunds. * * * The manufacturer's obligation to the consumer must keep pace with the changing relationship between them; it cannot be escaped because the marketing of a product has become so complicated as to require one or more intermediaries. Certainly there is greater reason to impose liability on the manufacturer than on the retailer who is but a conduit of a product that he is not himself able to test. * * *

The manufacturer's liability should, of course, be defined in terms of the safety of the product in normal and proper use, and should not extend to injuries that cannot be traced to the product as it reached the market.

Section 328D of the Restatement of Torts

Section 328D sets forth the following elements of proof of res ipsa loquitur:

> *"It may be inferred that harm suffered by the plaintiff is caused by negligence of the defendant when a) the event is of a kind which ordinarily does not occur in the absence of negligence; b) other responsible causes, including the conduct of the plaintiff and third person, are sufficiently eliminated by the evidence; and c) the indicated negligence is within the scope of the defendant's duty."*

Causation

In both strict liability and negligence cases, the plaintiff must prove that the defect was a cause in fact of the injury. The issue of causation (causation in fact or legal cause) may be especially problematic in negligence cases. Under Section 431 of the Restatement, the plaintiff must prove that the negligent conduct is the legal cause of the harm to another. This is determined by showing:

- The defendant's conduct is a substantial factor in bringing about the harm, and
- There is no rule of law or legal excuse relieving the actor from liability (i.e., no defense exists).

In addition,the plaintiff must show that the cause was proximate. Lord Bacon described proximate cause as follows: "In jure, non remota causa sed proxima spectator," which may be translated as "In law, the near cause is looked to, not the remote one."

There are two traditional formulations of the proximate cause test:

- But for, or *sine qua non*, is the basic, common sense test, still used by most courts. The plaintiff must prove that the injury would not have occurred had there not been the negligent act or omission of the defendant, or if the defect had not existed. This is essentially a negative test: The defendant's conduct is not a cause of the event if the event would have occurred without it.
- If two or more factors exist (two or more possible causes), then courts use the "substantial factor" test to determine if both parties have caused the injury. This test is sometimes used where there are concurrent causes—where two or more factors come together to cause an injury. In *DeLuryea v. Winthrop Laboratories*, an inadequate warnings case, the court used the term proximate cause and stated that each cause may contribute to the plaintiff's harm.

One of the causes need not be the sole cause of the injury - just that it has contributed as a substantial factor to the plaintiff's injury. In a case where a court has found concurrent causes of a plaintiff's injury, both parties are jointly and severally liable for any injury. What this means is that the plaintiff may look to both defendants jointly for the damage (joint liability). In some states, a jury may decide to apportion damages to reflect each party's percentage of liability or fault. The rule of joint and several liability also permits a plaintiff to seek recovery from one defendant, in effect, holding that one party responsible for paying the entire judgment (several liability), leaving it to a defendant to seek contribution from a joint tortfeasor.

One final note… might an intervening cause that occurs after the initial negligent act serve to cut off the liability of the original negligent actor or tortfeasor? This aspect of causation involves foreseeing the normal consequences created by an actor's negligent conduct. Several events are generally considered to be within the area of foreseeable conduct and thus would not terminate the responsibility of the original actor for their consequences.

Rescue Cases

Suppose that a rescuer is injured coming to the aid of an individual who has been injured as a result of a defective product? A little background is in order. First, there was a strange anomaly regarding certain rescuers under the common law. Under the common law of most states, so-called lay (nonprofessional/volunteer) rescuers who were themselves injured by the same defective product as the person whom they were intending to rescue are considered as foreseeable plaintiffs, and thus the rescuer could bring a suit in products liability against the manufacturer of the product that was defective. However, a majority of courts denied recovery to a professional rescuer under these circumstances, simply on policy grounds. Concerning the issue of injury to either a lay or professional rescuer by the negligent act of a third party during the rescue, it appears today that such an injury is foreseeable as to both professional and non-professional rescuers and the negligent act would not be considered as an intervening cause. The party creating the defective product could be found liable for all of these injuries.

Subsequent Injury or Illness

A subsequent injury or illness to a plaintiff caused by the plaintiff's weakened condition has been held to be foreseeable.

Efforts to Avert Harm

Efforts by the plaintiff to avert harm are seen as reasonably foreseeable.

Negligent Medical Treatment

Even subsequent negligent medical treatment by a third party has been held to be foreseeable and thus not intervening.

Contribution and Indemnity

In looking at the issue of joint and several liability raised in the discussion of proximate cause, a comparison must be made with the concept of contribution. Contribution is a rule that distributes the loss among the various tortfeasors by requiring each to pay his/her proportional share, based on their percentage of liability? Contribution is accomplished through a process called impleading, seeking to force a party to pay their rightful share of any judgment.

Indemnity is a legal principle that shifts the loss from one tortfeasor who has been compelled to pay despite the lack of any fault to another who should bear it instead. This may be accomplished by a contractual provision providing for indemnity or through operation of law.

Questions

1. A chauffeur working for the defendant, Peerless Transportation Co. abandoned his vehicle while it was in motion because he was being threatened by his passenger, a thief wielding a pistol. Subsequently, the unattended cab ran up onto a sidewalk and injured the plaintiff, Cordas. Cordas filed action under the theory of negligence.

   a. Is Peerless Transportation Co. liable?

2. The plaintiff, Palsgraf, was standing on a platform of Long Island R.R. Co. after buying a ticket. A man with a package was trying to catch a train. To get on, he was pulled on by one guard in the train and pushed off the platform by another guard. However, he lost his package during this effort. The package fell onto the track where it was struck by the train prompting it to explode because it was filled with fireworks. The shock of the explosion caused some scales to hit and injure the plaintiff. Palsgraf filed a suit against Long Island R.R. Co. for negligence.

   a. Does negligence apply? If so, how?

   b. Does proximate cause apply? If so, how?

   c. Is the Long Island R.R. Co. liable? Upon what theory?

3. Escola, the plaintiff, was waitressing in a restaurant and suffered injuries when a bottle of Coca Cola broke in her hand. She claimed that the defendant, Coca Cola Bottle Co. of Fresno, provided her employer with a defective product due to its excessive gas or some other defect, which caused it to explode.

   a. Does the doctrine of Res Ipsa Loquitur apply? If so, how?

   b. Was Coca Cola Bottle Co. of Fresno negligent?

   c. Is the product defective?

   d. Is Coca Cola Bottle Co. of Fresno liable?

4. Find a case that features either contribution or indemnity. Prove it using their definitions and formulations.

5. Suppose a defective platform at a train station causes a waiting passenger to fall on the track and become injured. Subsequently, a Good Samaritan rescues the passenger from an oncoming train but also sustains injuries in the process. Can the Samaritan bring action for negligence against the manufacturer of the defective platform?

Notes

Chapter Eight

Misrepresentation and Fraud

Misrepresentation and Fraud

A basic distinction between misrepresentation and fraud lies in the presence or absence of *scienter*, or the intent to deceive. A misrepresentation without proof of scienter is sometimes termed as an innocent misrepresentation - but only to distinguish it from actionable fraud. A second distinction lies in the fact that if a plaintiff can prove actionable fraud (as opposed to mere misrepresentation), then the plaintiff can collect punitive damages in order to punish the defendant for his intentional conduct. In a normal case, damages may be awarded which reflect the difference between the value of the item as received and the value of the item as represented (so-called benefit of the bargain damages). In the alternative, a party may choose to simply rescind the contract; or may decide to rescind the contract and seek damages under the remedy of cover (going into the market place to purchase a reasonable substitute good).

The causes of action for misrepresentation and fraud were essentially a hybrid of both contract and tort, which evolved into a contract action for a buyer who was dissatisfied with the bargain that he or she had entered into. To establish a common law action in fraud, a plaintiff must prove four elements:

1. That the defendant made a false representation or statement of a material fact; [through words, actions (known as concealment), or through silence, where there is a duty to speak];
2. That the defendant knew the statement was false (knowledge of falsity), or had no knowledge of its truth or falsity (reckless disregard of the truth), or that he did not have as strong a basis for his statement as he implied; [this is the scienter requirement]
3. That the defendant intended the plaintiff to rely on the statement and that the plaintiff justifiably relied on the statement; and

4. That the plaintiff suffered damage.

Generally, there is no duty to speak in a traditional arms length business transaction. Thus, silence will not form the basis of fraud. However, a duty to speak will be found in the following circumstances:

- In the sale of a home or other real property, many courts (most especially California and Colorado) require full disclosure of all material defects or important facts known by the defendant;
- In a fiduciary relationship [a relationship of trust and confidence between the parties such as broker-client, partners in a business, etc.] there is a duty of full disclosure of all important financial facts or information that might impact on an individual's decision to enter into a contract;
- To correct a prior misstatement or where a party gives a false impression by revealing some facts and withholding others (*Bergeron v. DuPont*).

Bergeron v. Dupont

359 A.2D 627 (1976)

BACKGROUND AND FACTS

The plaintiff purchased a mobile home park from the defendant. Subsequent to the transfer of title, plaintiff brought this action to recover damages allegedly sustained as a result of fraudulent misrepresentations by the defendant, Lawrence Dupont, Jr., through his agent.

On January 25, 1973, the plaintiff and defendant executed a purchase and sale agreement which specified a sale price of $89,999. In the course of negotiations, the agent represented that the septic system in the park was satisfactory, requiring only an occasional pumping out for proper functioning.

Subsequent to the signing of the agreement but prior to the closing, complaints were lodged by park residents in February, 1973, with the water supply and pollution control commission to the effect that effluent from some of the systems was emerging above ground. Tests by the State in February were inconclusive because of weather conditions, but on March 13 and 14, tests disclosed that three of the systems had failed. The Defendant was informed by a sanitary engineer from Concord sometime during this period that they were testing the system because of the emergence of the effluent. The title was transferred on March 14, 1973, and shortly thereafter the plaintiffs were informed that three of the septic systems had failed. The plaintiff replaced them and the cost of replacement was the basis for the verdict.

The master found on the issue of defendant's fraud as follows: At no time did the defendant reveal to the plaintiff that the state was investigating a complaint from tenants.

The defendant's representations to the plaintiff regarding the conditions of the septic tank and systems were a material factor in persuading the plaintiff to buy the mobile home park. When the defendant acquired new knowledge regarding the conditions of the septic systems, he came under the duty to disclose this additional information to the plaintiff since it was at variance with the representations previously made.

The Master correctly ruled that a representation which was true when made could be fraudulent if the maker failed to disclose subsequent information which made the original representation false. While it is true that one who makes a representation believing it to be true and does not disclose its falsity until after the transaction has been consummated has committed no fraud, both parties herein treat March 14, the date of the closing, as the time at which the rights of the parties became fixed.

AFFIRMED.

Discussion: Differentiating Between Facts and Opinions

To be actionable, a representation or statement must be one of fact rather than of opinion. Statements merely of quality or value (or other common forms of sales talk) constitute sales puffing and are generally not actionable. Exceptions occur where commendations or opinions are made by a party with "superior knowledge" (an expert's opinion, as was found in Vokes v. Arthur Murray), or where the parties "were not on equal footing" (as in *Sellers v. Looper* - where statements made by a real estate agent included the phrase "a good well"). Predictions of future events or opinions as to future contingencies are generally not actionable, unless the speaker purports to have special or unique knowledge.

Vokes v. Arthur Murray, Inc.

District Court Of Appeal Of Florida, 2D District (1968), 212 SO. 2D 906

BACKGROUND AND FACTS

The defendant, Arthur Murray, Inc., operated dancing schools throughout the nation through local franchised operators, one of whom was the defendant. The plaintiff, Audrey E. Vokes, a widow without family, wished to become "an accomplished dancer" to find "a new interest in life." In 1961 she was invited to attend a "dance party" at J. P. Davenport's "School of Dancing." Vokes went to the school and received elaborate praise from her instructor for her grace, poise, and potential as "an excellent dancer." The instructor sold her eight half hour dance lessons for $14.50 each, to be utilized within one calendar month.

Subsequently, over a period of less than sixteen months, Vokes bought a total of fourteen dance courses, which amounted to 2,302 hours of dancing lessons for a total cash outlay of $31,090.45, all at Davenport's school.

PIERCE, Judge

These dance lesson contracts and the monetary consideration therefore of over $31,000 were procured from her by means and methods of Davenport and his associates which went beyond the unsavory, yet legally permissible, parameter of "sales puffing" and intruded well into the forbidden area of undue influence, the suggestion of falsehood, the suppression of truth, and the free exercise of rational judgment, if what plaintiff alleged in her complaint was true. From the time of her first contact with the dancing school in February, 1961, she was influenced unwittingly by a constant and continuous barrage of flattery, false praise, excessive compliments, and panegyric encomiums, to such extent that it would be not only inequitable, but unconscionable, for a Court exercising inherent chancery power to allow such contracts to stand.

She was incessantly subjected to overreaching blandishment and cajolery. She was assured she had "grace and poise"; that she was "rapidly improving and developing in her dancing skill"; that the additional lessons would "make her a beautiful dancer, capable of dancing with the most accomplished dancers"; that she was "rapidly progressing in the development of her dancing skill and gracefulness", etc., etc. She was given "dance aptitude tests" for the ostensible purpose of "determining" the number of remaining hours of instructions would be needed by her from time to time.

At one point she was sold 545 additional hours of dancing lessons to be entitled to award of the "Bronze Medal" signifying that she had reached "the Bronze Standard," a supposed designation of dance achievement by students of Arthur Murray, Inc.

Later she was sold an additional 926 hours in order to gain the "Silver Medal," indicating she had reached "the Silver Standard," at a cost of $12,501.35.

At one point, while she still had to her credit about 900 unused hours of instructions, she was induced to purchase an additional 24 hours of lessons to participate¨ in a trip to Miami at her own expense, where she would be "given the opportunity to dance with members of the Miami Studio.

She was induced at another point to purchase an additional 126 hours of lessons in order to be not only eligible for the Miami trip but also to become "a life member of the Arthur Murray Studio," carrying with it certain dubious emoluments, at a further cost of $1,752.¨30.

At another point, while she still had over 1,000 unused hours of instruction she was induced to buy 151 additional hours at a cost of $2,049.00 to be eligible for a "Student Trip to Trinidad," at her own expense as she later learned.

Also, when she still had 1100 unused hours to her credit, she was prevailed upon to purchase an additional 347 hours at a cost of $4,235.74, to qualify her to receive a "Gold Medal" for achievement, indicating she had advanced to "the Gold Standard."

On another occasion, while she still had over 1200 unused hours, she was induced to buy an additional 175 hours of instruction at a cost of $2,472.75 to be eligible "to take a trip to Mexico."

Finally, sandwiched in between other lesser sales promotions, she was influenced to buy an additional 481 hours of instruction at a cost of $6,523.81 in order to "be classified as a Gold Bar Member, the ultimate achievement of the dancing studio."

All the foregoing sales promotions, illustrative of the entire fourteen separate contracts, were procured by defendant Davenport and Arthur Murray, Inc., by false representations to her that she was improving in her dancing ability, that she had excellent potential, that she was responding to instructions in dancing grace, and that they were developing her into a beautiful dancer, whereas in truth and in fact she did not develop in her dancing ability, she had no "dance aptitude," and in fact had difficulty in "hearing the musical beat." The complaint alleged that such representations to her "were in fact false and known by the defendant to be false and contrary to the plaintiff's true ability, the truth of plaintiff's ability being fully known to the defendants, but withheld from the plaintiff for the sole and specific intent to deceive and defraud the plaintiff and to induce her in the purchasing of additional hours of dance lessons." It was averred that the lessons were sold to her "in total disregard to the true physical, rhythm, and mental ability of the plaintiff". In other words, while she first exulted that she was entering the "spring of her life", she finally was awakened to the fact there was "spring" neither in her life nor in her feet.

It is true that "generally a misrepresentation, to be actionable, must be one of fact rather than of opinion". But this rule has significant qualifications, applicable here. It does not apply where there is a fiduciary relationship between the parties, or where there has been some artifice or trick employed by the representor, or where the parties do not in general deal at "arm's length" as we understand the phrase, or where the representee does not have equal opportunity to become apprised of the truth or falsity of the fact represented.

" * * * A statement of a party having * * * superior knowledge may be regarded as a statement of fact although it would be considered as opinion if the parties were dealing on equal terms."

It could be reasonably supposed here that defendants had "superior knowledge" as to whether plaintiff had "dance potential" and as to whether she was noticeably improving in the art of terpsichore. And it would be a reasonable inference from the untended averments of the complaint that the flowery eulogists heaped upon her by defendants as a prelude to her contracting for 1944 additional hours of instruction in order to attain the rank of the Bronze Standard, thence to the bracket of the Silver Standard, thence to the class of the Gold Bar Standard, and finally to the crowning plateau of a Life Member of the Studio, proceeded as much or more from the urge to "ring the cash register" as from any honest or realistic appraisal of her dancing prowess or a factual representation of her progress.

" * * * (W)hat is plainly injurious to good faith ought to be considered as a fraud sufficient to impeach a contract," and that an improvident agreement may be avoided" * * * because of surprise, or mistake, want of freedom, undue influence, the suggestion of falsehood, or the suppression of truth." (Emphasis supplied.)

Judgment and Remedy.

Here is a case involving a commendation or the use of certain adjectival words.

Sellers v. Looper

Supreme Court Of Oregon, 264 Ore. 13; 503 P.2d 692 (1972)

BACKGROUND AND FACTS

This is an action for damages based upon fraudulent misrepresentation pertaining to a well on property the plaintiffs purchased from defendants. The trial court found for plaintiffs. On motion, the trial court found JNOV and plaintiffs appealed.

Defendants argue here that the plaintiff had not submitted evidence sufficient to establish fraudulent representations to induce plaintiffs to enter into the contract to purchase the property.

The plaintiffs contend: Statements regarding quality, value or the like may be considered misrepresentations of fact where the parties are not on equal footing and do not have equal knowledge or means of knowledge "and the decision of whether a representation is of fact or of opinion is always left to the jury" and therefore the order setting aside the jury's verdict should not have been entered.

* * * Defendant's argue that the representation of a "good well" was a mere inclusion of adjectival words of commendation or opinion and therefore, not actionable.

In Holland v. Lentz, we held:

* * * It is recognized that statements of opinion regarding quality, value or the like, may be considered as misrepresentations of fact, that is, of the speaker's state of mind, if a fiduciary relationship exists between the parties, as for example, representations of value of a real estate broker to his principal; or where the parties are not on equal footing and do not have equal knowledge or means of knowledge.

Prosser stated: * * * misrepresentation will not lie for misstatements of opinion as distinguished from those of fact * * *

The evidence discloses that defendants owned a house and acreage located in Illinois

Valley near the city of Cave Junction, Oregon. In May of 1969, defendants executed a listing agreement to sell the property with Mrs. McLean, a real estate broker. This agreement included information given by the defendants to Mrs. McLean. Mrs. McLean testified:

> *I asked the Loopers: Do you have a good well * * * and the comment came back, "Yes, we have a good well * * *."*
>
> *On May 28, 1969, plaintiffs contacted Mrs. McLean.*
>
> *Q: At the time you told them that there was a good well on the property, did you tell them that for the purpose of inducing them to buy the Looper's property?*
>
> *A: A good well on any property is a tremendous inducement. If you have a good well, that's a selling point...*
>
> *Q: At the time you told them that there was quote, a good well on the property, what did you mean to convey by that, what meaning did you mean to get across to the prospective buyers?*
>
> *A: * * * that it was an adequate well, there was plenty of water * * **
>
> *Q: Plenty of water for what?*
>
> *A: Adequate for household, and usually that includes a modest garden.*

In the early evening of July 28, 1969, the parties met and inspected the house and "looked at the well and pumphouse." No specifications as to the depth of the well or how many gallons it would pump per hour were given the plaintiffs and the realtor did not have this information. The sale was later consummated.

On August 15, 1969, plaintiffs moved onto the property and on August 22, 1969, the well went dry. Plaintiffs drilled two additional wells but found no water.

We conclude that there was sufficient evidence to submit the case to the jury. A reasonable person could believe that a "good well" meant a well with adequate water for family household use and the plaintiffs relied on this representation.

The evidence shows that defendants knew the water in the well got low in the Fall of the year and they had to be careful in flushing the indoor toilet or the well would probably go dry. The plaintiffs were not on equal footing with the defendants and did not have equal knowledge of the adequacy or lack of adequacy of the water in the well. The jury returned a verdict for the plaintiffs and "These matters are ordinarily for the determination of the jury."

* * *"

Reversed With Instructions to Reinstate the Jury's Verdict.

Statements regarding matters of law were generally held to be opinions rather than facts (*Puckett Paving v. Carrier Leasing,* where under the common law, "everyone is presumed to know the law"), with the following exceptions:

- When they are intended to be statements of fact and are understood as such;
- When a special relationship of trust and confidence exists between two parties (lawyer-client, accountant-client) and the statement is made in the context of that relationship;
- When the defendant represents himself to have special knowledge of the law (professionals such as estate planners, insurance salesmen, tax professionals, etc.).

In cases of a presumed misrepresentation of a matter of law, it is now settled or good law that "statements made by a professional in a professional setting as to a matter of law are generally held to be actionable" under the precedent of *Yorke v. Taylor*.

Puckett Paving v. Carrier Leasing Corp.

Supreme Court Of Georgia, 236 GA. 891; 225 S.E.2D 910 (1976)

BACKGROUND AND FACTS

Carrier brought an action to recover four heavy-duty trucks from Puckett. The pleadings and the evidence show that Puckett was in possession of the vehicles under the terms of two certain leases providing for monthly payments in stated sums for 44 months.

Puckett had an option to purchase same for a stated price after all monthly payments had been made; that Puckett had made all monthly payments but refused to purchase the vehicles or to return them. Carrier elected to recover the vehicles rather than damages.

Puckett filed an answer and cross claim alleging that the contracts were induced by fraud in that an agent of Carrier "assured defendant that the lease agreements entered into would be considered a lease by the IRS" but that the IRS considered the same to be a sale and not a lease, resulting in damage to Puckett. The trial Court ordered Puckett to return the vehicles.

We affirm. Assuming such statements were made by an agent of Carrier to Puckett, they could only have been expressions of an opinion as to how the IRS had treated such agreements or would treat them in the future.

"Where no fiduciary relationship exists, misrepresentations as to a question of law will not constitute remedial fraud, since everyone is presumed to know the law and therefore cannot in legal contemplation be deceived by erroneous statements of law, and such representations are ordinarily regarded as mere expressions of opinion."

Affirmed.

To be actionable, a representation or statement of fact must be material. The test of materiality is whether the statement would be important to a reasonable person—an objective standard. This requirement of materiality is designed to prevent a party from using a trivial misrepresentation as an excuse to set aside a bargain that appears to be unwise or bad in retrospect!

In a products case, a statement is material if it significantly affects the manner in which the plaintiff used the product, thereby potentially increasing its danger. A statement concerning safety, for example, would normally be a material assertion.

Justifiable reliance would not lie where the plaintiff knows the truth of a statement, or in the case of goods, where a reasonable inspection would have turned up the falsity of any assertion or statement, the plaintiff had the opportunity to conduct an inspection, and fails to do so. In the case of an inspection, a plaintiff would not be required to engage in an inspection if the inspection would prove to be unduly burdensome or costly.

The element of justifiable reliance creates the anomaly of Joe Isuzu, an over-the-top TV pitchman of a by-gone era who intentionally exaggerated just about every aspect of the product he was touting. Sometimes the more a person lies (misrepresents) the least likely a court would find justifiable reliance on the part of the plaintiff!

Section 402B of the Restatement of Torts

Section 402B provides the second basis of recovery in tort:

> *"One engaged in the business of selling chattels, who, by advertising, or otherwise, makes to the public a misrepresentation of a material fact concerning the character or quality of a chattel sold by him is subject to liability for physical harm to a consumer of the chattel caused by justifiable reliance upon the misrepresentation...."*

Under Section 402B, the seller must be a merchant (one engaged in the business of selling chattels) and not one who engages in a casual sale. Section 402B would apply to all suppliers of chattels who have either:

- Made the representation; or
- Adopted a representation made by another.

Comment I to Section 402B provides that an employee or family member of the purchaser who uses the product is also a consumer of that product, as is "anyone who makes use of the chattel in the manner which a purchaser may be expected to use it."

Section 402B of the Restatement will provide an additional cause of action where a consumer has experienced physical harm. A calculation of the harm has included lost wages or profits as well as damages for personal injury.

As in common law actions for fraud or misrepresentation, the plaintiff under Section 402B must prove justifiable reliance. Justifiable reliance will not lie "where the misrepresentation is not known, or there is indifference to it, or it does not influence the purchase or a party's subsequent conduct." (Comment j) The same standards apply under Section 402B as do in the case of the contractual remedy; that is, if a person is aware of the truth of any misstatement, that person cannot recover. Likewise, many courts have held that if a reasonably prudent person would have been aware of the facts or would have investigated further, that person cannot recover. Any statement, however, does not have to be the sole inducement to purchase but only that the statement is a substantial factor in the inducement. This issue is generally a question of fact for a jury to determine.

Questions

1. What is the difference between misrepresentation and fraud?
2. Find a modern day example of fraud. Prove it is fraud by making reference to the four elements of fraud.
3. What is the significance of the *Sellers v. Looper* case in relation to misrepresentation?
4. What is the significance of *Puckett Paving v. Carrier Leasing* in relation to misrepresentation?
5. The plaintiff, *Volks*, chose to become a professional dancer. The defendant, Arthur Murray was the franchisor of Arthur Murray dance schools. Vokes claimed the defendant's employees used flattery, cajolery, and awards to trick her into believing there was a real possibility of her becoming a professional dancer. Subsequently, the defendant persuaded the plaintiff to sign up for $31,000 worth of dance classes. Plaintiff asserted she had not developed any skill and consequently brought suit against Arthur Murray.
   a. Does the doctrine of misrepresentation apply to this case? If so, how?
   b. What is the relationship of Arthur Murray to the J.P. Davenport Dance Studio?
   c. Is Arthur Murray liable? Upon what basis?

Notes

Chapter Nine

WARRANTY ACTIONS

Warranty actions may arise in two ways: where a plaintiff suffered personal injury from a defective product or where the product is defective but caused no personal injury and the plaintiff suffers only purely economic damage. There are three aspects of warranties that can be traced back to early tort and contract roots:

- Warranties can arise as a matter of law (i.e., can be implied) regardless of whether the parties intended to create them;
- Because of its contractual nature, parties may disclaim warranties under certain circumstances or limit the remedies available for breach of a warranty;
- The plaintiff is required to give prompt notice of breach of warranty to the seller (this was later termed the "booby trap for the unwary" by Justice Traynor—which was one of the factors that led to the creation of strict liability in tort).

Common law recognized three separate types of sales warranties: the express warranty, the implied warranty of merchantability, and the implied warranty of fitness for a particular purpose. These warranties were codified first into the Uniform Sales Act (1906) and later into Article 2 of the Uniform Commercial Code (1961), which all states have now adopted. In the development of the warranty aspects of the UCC, no case could have been more important than *Henningsen v. Bloomfield Motors*, in which the court gave the victim of an automobile accident a remedy against the defendant-manufacturer even though she was not in privity of contract with the defendant-manufacturer. The court also refused to enforce the disclaimer and remedy limitation in the "standard form" (boilerplate) contract on the grounds that the limitation would be unconscionable under UCC Section 2-302.

The warranty provisions of Article 2 of the UCC apply only to the sale of goods. Section 2-106(1), defines a sale as "the passing of title from the seller to the buyer for a price." Goods are defined in Section 2-105 as all "things movable and tangible…." Consequently, transactions in "goods" other than sales (leases and bailments) were not governed by the original Article 2 warranty provisions. That coverage was specifically added in the addendum to Article 2, relating to bailments. In addition to Article 2 coverage, warranties may, however, be governed by strict liability in tort or by common law warranties that still survive under state law. This Chapter looks at the warranty provisions under Article 2 of the UCC.

Types of Warranties

Express Warranty (Section 2-313)

"Express warranties by the seller are created as follows:

1. Any affirmation [statement] of fact or promise made by the seller to the buyer which relates to the goods and becomes part of the basis of the bargain creates an express warranty that the goods shall conform to the affirmation or promise.
2. Any description of the goods which is made part of the basis of the bargain creates an express warranty that the goods shall conform to the description.
3. Any sample or model which is made part of the basis of the bargain creates an express warranty that the whole of the goods shall conform to the sample or model."

As to any specific language required under the Code to create an express warranty:

> *"It is not necessary to the creation of an express warranty that the seller use words such as warrant or guarantee or that he have a specific intention to make a warranty, but an affirmation merely of the value of the goods or a statement purportedly to be merely the seller's opinion or commendation of the goods does not create a warranty."*

Notes on Express Warranties

A sample is actually drawn from the bulk of goods which is the subject matter of the sale; a model is not drawn from the bulk of goods but is offered for inspection by a seller or salesperson when the subject matter is not at hand.

The affirmation of fact or promise or a description of goods is usually made in words; however, they can also be made by pictures or other forms of communication (such as advertisements on radio and TV or those found in a variety of magazines, newspapers, or trade publications).

Courts generally use the prior analysis under misrepresentation and fraud to determine the distinctions between fact and opinion, fact and commendation, etc. relating to any statements made by the defendant.

A promise or affirmation of fact must relate to the goods. Promises unrelated to the goods ("This car will make you popular with the Snookie crowd") do not create express warranties.

Once an affirmation of fact or promise is made, or a description given, or sample or model shown, the presumption is that such affirmation, promise, description, sample, or model is intended to be a basis of the bargain.

Unlike an action for misrepresentation or fraud, no particular reliance is required in order to create a warranty; likewise, no particular intention is required to create the warranty. We focus, instead, on the words or actions of the seller in creating an express warranty.

Comment 7 to Section 2-313 provides that "post-sale" representations may be considered as part of the basis of the bargain—especially those concerning safety—where such statements would give the buyer a false sense of security or might cause the buyer not to be vigilant or decide not to return goods. This is a public policy consideration.

Section 2-313 does not require that an express warranty be in writing; however, express warranties are subject to the parol evidence rule of Section 2-202 (if there is a writing that was intended to be the final expression of agreement between the parties, the express warranty could not "contradict" the writing but could "explain or supplement" any such writing with a "consistent additional term.") The Statute of Frauds (Section 2-201) may also apply if the contract was for sale of goods for the purchase price of $500.00 or more and may require that a warranty be in writing.

The express warranty is applicable to all sellers—merchants and non-merchants alike!

However, the warranty is only applicable to the one who makes the statement. Thus, a retailer is not automatically liable for a manufacturer's express warranty. If a retailer repeats the manufacturer's warranty as a part of a sales promotion, the retailer now becomes liable for the express warranty as well.

Werner v. Montana

Supreme Court of New Hampshire, 117 N.H. 721 (1977)

OPINION BY: LAMPRON, JUDGE

This is an action brought by plaintiff seeking to rescind his purchase from defendant of a Friendship Sloop known as the White Eagle.... Defendant purchased the Friendship Sloop known as the White Eagle in 1955. Sometime in 1971 defendant decided to sell the sloop and on or about September 1, 1971, plaintiff and defendant began discussing its sale. On October 17, 1971, the parties signed an "Intent to Purchase and Sell," with an agreed price of $13,500 for the sloop. The price was later reduced by $250 and on January 1, 1972, the parties signed a bill of sale for the White Eagle with a sale price of $13,250.

At the end of June 1972, plaintiff put the White Eagle into the water. After allowing ordinarily sufficient time for the planking to swell, or "make up," to form a watertight hull, plaintiff found that the White Eagle still leaked and could not be sailed. Plaintiff then discovered that there was extensive dry rot in the hull and that the cost of repairs would be substantial. After some discussions with defendant in the course of the summer concerning the problem, on September 8, 1972, plaintiff wrote defendant a letter complaining about the dry rot and unseaworthiness of the White Eagle and demanding that defendant take back the White Eagle and refund the purchase price. Defendant refused and plaintiff brought this action.

The basis for plaintiff's action is that there was a breach of an express warranty. RSA 382-A:2-313. Plaintiff alleged that defendant, in the course of negotiations prior to sale, made certain statements to the effect that the White Eagle would "make up" when placed in the water and become watertight, and that such statements amounted to an express warranty as to the sloop's condition. Defendant argues that any statements made by defendant prior to sale could not be admitted or considered as constituting an express warranty by virtue of RSA 382-A:2-202 (Parol or Extrinsic Evidence Rule)...

Under the Uniform Commercial Code an express warranty may be created by a seller who makes "any affirmation of fact or promise... to the buyer which relates to the goods and becomes part of the basis of the bargain." RSA 382-A:2-313(1)(a). In addition, "any description of the goods which is made part of the basis of the bargain creates an express warranty that the goods shall conform to the description." RSA 382-A:2-313(1)(b).

In general, affirmations of fact made by a seller about the goods being sold are considered a part of the description of the goods and are regarded as forming a part of the sales agreement. Uniform Laws Comment 3 to RSA 382-A:2-313; 1 R. Anderson, Uniform Commercial Code § 2-313:45 (2d ed. 1970). There was evidence that during the course of negotiations the parties had discussed the ship's watertightness and that defendant had told plaintiff that the White Eagle would become watertight once placed in water and allowed sufficient time to "make up." Considering the negotiations of the parties as a whole, particularly plaintiff's concern with whether the White Eagle was watertight, and considering the importance of watertightness for a ship, these assurances by defendant regarding the condition of the White Eagle could properly be considered as making part of the basis of the bargain. See 1 R. Anderson, supra § 2-313:7. Therefore, unless the master was otherwise precluded from considering these statements by defendant, the master did not err in granting plaintiff's request for findings and rulings that these affirmations or descriptions of the White Eagle by defendant created an express warranty under both RSA 382-A:2-313(1)(a) and (b). See Fargo Machine & Tool Co. v. Kearney & Trecker Corp.,428 F.Supp. 364(E.D.)

RSA 382-A:2-202 excludes evidence of any additional oral agreement or terms when a written agreement is intended by the parties to be a final expression of their agreement. However, unless the writing was intended as a complete and exclusive statement of the terms of the agreement, evidence of consistent additional terms is admissible. RSA 382-A:2-202(b). There was no evidence that the writings in this case, the notice of intent to purchase, the bill of sale, and the advertisement incorporated therein by reference, were intended by the parties as constituting a complete and exclusive statement of the terms of their agreement. The master therefore could properly find defendant's statements regarding the White Eagle's watertightness as being an express warranty which was a consistent additional term of the agreement...1 R. Anderson, Uniform Commercial Code § 2-313:22; R. Nordstrom, Sales § 53 (1970).

* * * Defendant argues that plaintiff failed to prove a breach of warranty because the evidence did not establish that the leaking of the White Eagle was caused by the dry rot, or by any other cause, and therefore did not establish that the leaking constituted a breach of the alleged warranty. It is true that the master found there was no evidence to connect the leaking with the dry rot in the hull. However, the master did not find that defendant had made any warranty that the White Eagle was free from any dry rot. Rather, the master found that defendant had told plaintiff that the White Eagle was suitable for sailing, and that defendant's statements, which created the warranty were to the effect that the White Eagle had not leaked and would not leak after a sufficient swelling period was allowed. The master found that the White Eagle's "inability to `make up'" created a breach of this warranty. While it is true that there was no evidence to establish the cause of the leaking, such evidence was not necessary. The plaintiff was required only to establish the existence of an express warranty and to establish that the White Eagle was defective in that its condition did not comply with the condition warranted by defendant...The evidence was undisputed that the White Eagle continued to leak and was not seaworthy despite being allowed to soak for over six weeks. Plaintiff therefore met his burden establishing the boat's defective condition.

Defendant also argues that any warranty made related only to the condition of the White Eagle at the time of sale and that plaintiff failed to prove that the White Eagle was not as warranted at that time. While an express warranty generally related only to the condition of the goods at the time of sale, a warranty may relate to another point in time if so specified. 1 R. Anderson, supra § 2-313:12. The warranty found by the master to have been made by defendant was that the White Eagle would not leak; that it would be tight after a two-week swelling period. The discussions between the parties prior to sale occurred after September 1, 1971, and the bill of sale was dated January 1, 1972. It would not be until the following spring or summer that plaintiff would have the first occasion to put the White Eagle in the water and allow for the swelling defendant indicated would occur. The warranty as to tightness therefore did not relate simply to the condition of the White Eagle as of the date of sale, but necessarily related to the time when the boat would be put in the water and prepared for sailing. Under these circumstances defendant's statement amounted to an express warranty.

Although reliance on the part of the buyer is not necessary for the creation of an express warranty, the master properly found that plaintiff did in fact rely on defendant's affirmation that the boat would not leak and it became part of the bargain...

Judgment affirmed.

Implied Warranty of Merchantability (Section 2-314)

This is perhaps the most important of all the warranty protections!

> *"Unless excluded or modified, a warranty that the goods shall be merchantable is implied in a contract for their sale if the seller is a merchant with respect to goods of that kind. Under this section, serving for value food or drink to be consumed either on the premises or elsewhere is a sale."*

"Goods to be merchantable at least must:

- Pass without objection in the trade under the contract description; and
- In the case of fungible goods, are of fair average quality within the description; and
- Are fit for the ordinary purpose for which such goods are used; and
- Run, within the variations permitted by the agreement, of even kind, quality and quantity within each unit and among all units involved; and
- Are adequately contained, packaged, and labeled as the agreement may require; and
- Conform to the promises or affirmations of fact made on the container or label if any."

Coffer v. Standard Brands, Inc. deals with a familiar issue, as the plaintiff was injured when he bit down on an unshelled nut from a bottle of otherwise shelled, mixed nuts. The *Coffer* court held that since the impurity complained of "was a natural incident of the goods in question," there was no breach of the implied warranty of merchantability. Recall the foreign-natural test discussed earlier to determine if such a product was defective!

Notes on the Implied Warranty of Merchantability

Merchantability is not equated with perfection, and thus is not a strict liability standard, in that sense. However, it is not normally a defense to a claim of breach of the warranty of merchantability that the seller could not have done anything to detect or prevent the defect.

Fair average quality is a term appropriate to agricultural bulk products and means goods centering on the middle belt of quality, not the least or the worst. A fair percentage of the least (as determined by the trade usage, course of dealings, etc.) is permissible, but the goods are not of fair average quality if they all are of the least or worst quality possible.

Fitness for the ordinary purposes for which goods of the type are used is the fundamental concept of the warranty of merchantability. A determination of a product's ordinary purpose depends on the circumstances of each case.

The goal of subsection (f) is that goods must conform to the representations found on their labels. Even if a consumer failed to read the label (and hence, there could be no express warranty), a violation of the implied warranty of merchantability might still obtain.

Comment 3 provides that "a contract for secondhand [used] goods…involves only such obligation as is appropriate to such goods." Thus, while a warranty of merchantability is possible, the extent of that warranty would probably be one for a jury.

The definition of merchant is a narrow one and the warranty of merchantability is applicable only to a person who, in a professional status, sells a particular kind of goods giving rise to the warranty. (UCC Section 2-104 and *Siemen v. Alden*). A person making an isolated sale of goods is not a merchant.

There is a split of decisions regarding whether or not a farmer is or is not a merchant with respect to Section 2-104 and thus Section 2-314 as a matter of law. This determination is left to a case-by-case basis.

Implied Warranty of Fitness for a Particular Purpose (Section 2-315)

"Where the seller at the time of contracting has reason to know any particular purpose for which the goods are required and that the buyer is relying on the seller's skill or judgment to select or furnish suitable goods, there is unless excluded or modified under the next section an implied warranty that the goods shall be fit for such purposes."

Notes on the Warranty of Fitness

There are two requirements for this warranty:

- The seller has reason to know of the use for which the goods are purchased;
- The buyer must rely on the seller's expertise in supplying the proper product. (*Lewis v. Mobil Oil*). This is a question of fact to be determined by looking at the circumstances of the transaction and the specific requests or words used by the parties.

The warranty of fitness applies to merchants and non-merchants alike. However, it only applies to a person who originated or created the warranty and not to all suppliers within the marketing chain.

The specificity with which the buyer ordered the goods is also a factor in determining whether the buyer relied on the seller's expertise. A buyer's claim is weakened if the buyer has control over the detailed specifications of the goods. Likewise, if the buyer examined the goods, he is less likely to have relied on the seller's judgment in furnishing the goods.

PERSONS TO BE PROTECTED: THE NEW PRIVITY

SECTION 2-318: THIRD PARTY BENEFICIARIES OF WARRANTIES (EXTENSION OF HORIZONTAL PRIVITY)

> *"Alternative A: A seller's warranty whether express or implied extends to any natural person who is in the family or household of his buyer or who is a guest in his home if it is reasonable to expect such a person may use, consume or be affected by the goods and who is injured in person by breach of the warranty. A seller may not exclude or limit the operation of this section."*
>
> *"Alternative B: ...extends to any natural person who may be reasonably expected to use, consume or be affected by the goods and who is injured in person by breach of the warranty. A seller may not exclude or limit the operation of this section."*
>
> *"Alternative C: ...extends to any person who may reasonably be expected to use, consume or be affected by the goods and who is injured by the breach of the warranty. A seller may not exclude or limit the operation of this section with respect to injury to the person of an individual to whom the warranty extends."*

NOTES ON THE EXTENSION OF HORIZONTAL PRIVITY

The last sentence of each alternative forbids the exclusion of liability to the persons to whom the warranties are made under each section.

Alternative A is the *Henningsen* principle and is by far the most popular of the alternatives.

> *"Accordingly, we hold that under modern marketing conditions, when a manufacturer puts a new automobile in the stream of trade and promotes its purchase to the public, an implied warranty that it is reasonably suitable for use as such accompanies it into the hands of the ultimate purchaser...We are convinced that he cause of justice in this area of law can be served only be recognizing that she (Mrs. Henningsen) is such a person who, in the reasonable contemplation of the parties to the warranty, might be expected to become a user of the automobile. Accordingly, her lack of privity does not stand in the way of prosecution of the injury suit against the defendant Chrysler."*

Most states are still quite strict in requiring vertical privity regarding express warranties since an express warranty is based upon the express words or statements made by a particular party. The same is true of the warranty of fitness. Some states have, however, abolished the requirement of vertical privity in any actions for breach of warranties—including the express warranty or the warranty of fitness for a particular purpose. (*Salvador v. Atlantic Steel Boiler Co.*) - but this is not the majority view.

Alternatives B and C have been applied to bystanders. Alternative C has been held to cover monetary damages sustained by a corporation.

However, Alternative A is by far the most popular of the warranty provisions.

KLEIN V. SEARS ROEBUCK AND CO.

United States Court of Appeals, Fourth Circuit, 773 F.2d 1421 (1985)

OPINION BY: SPROUSE, Circuit Judge:

Sears, Roebuck and Co. appeal from a judgment entered in this diversity case after a jury verdict awarding Steven B. Klein $633,000 compensatory damages and his wife Claudia Klein $104,000 for lost consortium due to Steven's injuries received in a riding lawn mower accident. Klein, a jeweler, received extensive and severe injuries to his right hand when the mower overturned while he was cutting grass on a 19% incline slope and his hand came into contact with the rotating mowing blade. The issues were submitted to the jury on theories of express and implied warranties of fitness for a particular purpose and negligent misrepresentation.

Sears contends that the court erred in not granting a directed verdict or judgment n.o.v. because there was not sufficient evidence to sustain the verdict; in allowing evidence of the lack of a safety device; in failing to instruct on proximate cause; and in failing to set aside both awards as excessive. The Kleins cross-appeal contesting the denial of leave to file an amendment to their complaint to assert a claim against Sears for punitive damages. Finding no reversible error except that relating to the issue of consortium, we affirm the award of compensatory damages to Steven Klein. We reverse the award of damages for lost consortium, however, finding insufficient evidence to support it. We also affirm the district court's denial of leave to amend the complaint.

Steven and Claudia Klein were married in the fall of 1979...Steven's parents came for a visit in May, 1980 and decided to buy a riding mower as a gift for Steven and Claudia. Claudia and Steven's parents went to a local Sears store where they consulted with a Sears salesman about the intended purchase.

The three of them informed the salesman that they had no experience with lawnmowers and that the property on which the mower was to be used was a 3/4 acre tract containing numerous hills. The salesman recommended a Sears Craftsman, eight horsepower electric start rear engine riding mower with a 30-inch cutting deck. The sale, however, was conditioned on an inspection of the Kleins' property, to be conducted at the time of delivery of the mower.

A few days later, the Sears salesman delivered the mower to the Kleins' residence. At this time, the salesman conducted an inspection of the property and pronounced the mower suitable for mowing the property, although he warned that the mower should be driven vertically up and down the hills.

Steven used the mower without incident from late May throughout the summer and early fall of 1980. On April 18, 1981, the first day that Steven mowed that year, he was mowing vertically up a 19 ° slope on the property when the mower tipped over backwards and Steven's hand came in contact with the rotating mower blade. His right thumb and part of his right index finger were severed, all of his fingers were fractured, and he suffered extensive lacerations and nerve damage to his right hand. At trial, the orthopedic surgeon who treated Steven testified that Steven had suffered an 80% permanent impairment of his entire right arm, including his right hand. The doctor also testified that Steven had undergone nine surgical procedures.

At the time of the accident, Steven was employed as a jeweler — a talent that he had developed over many years. The injuries to his right hand, however, rendered continued employment in this capacity an impossibility…

Sufficiency of Evidence

Although the complaint alleged other grounds for relief, including negligent design and strict liability, the case was submitted to the jury only on the theories of express and implied warranties and negligent misrepresentation. The jury found for Sears on the negligent misrepresentation question, so the issues on appeal relate only to express and implied warranties.

Under Maryland law, recovery for breach of warranty requires proof of three elements: (1) the existence of a warranty, (2) a breach of the warranty, and (3) harm proximately caused by the breach…

An express warranty is created by "[a]ny affirmation of fact or promise made by the seller to the buyer which relates to the goods and becomes part of the basis of the bargain." Md.Com.Law Code Ann. § 2-313(1)(a) (1975). Sears contends that the statements made by their salesman, both at the store and at the Klein's residence, were insufficient to constitute express warranties because they were statements of opinion or commendation. See Md.Com.Law Code Ann. § 2-313(2) (1975). Sears also urges that the sale was completed at the Sears store and thus any later statements were necessarily not part of express warranties…

The implied warranty of fitness for a particular purpose arises "[w]here the seller at the time of contracting has reason to know any particular purpose for which the goods are required and that the buyer is relying on the seller's skill or judgment to select or furnish suitable goods."Md.Com. Law Code Ann. § 2-315(1) (1975). Sears fails to advance any argument that no implied warranty emerged from the facts of this case.

If express or implied warranties did arise, Sears argues that they were limited to include only a warranty that the mower was fit to cut grass safely when used properly…Sears also contends that the fact that Steven used the mower during the first mowing season without mishap prevents the Klein's from satisfying the requirement that the mower did not conform to the representations of the warranty at the time it left their control…

Finally, Sears maintains that the evidence fails to support a finding that the alleged breach was the proximate cause of Steven's injury, arguing that because Steven was operating the mower on a slope in excess of 15 degrees, contrary to the instructions contained in the Owner's Manual, it was Steven's intervening activities that caused the unfortunate accident.

In testing the sufficiency of the evidence, we must view the evidence in the light most favorable to the jury's verdict and afford the prevailing party the benefit of all reasonable inferences which can be drawn from the evidence...Applying this standard, we believe that there is ample evidence to support the jury's conclusion that Sears made and breached express and implied warranties and that the breach was the proximate cause of Steven's injury.

Claudia Klein testified that she and Steven's parents told the Sears salesman of the intended use of the mower and that the salesman responded by suggesting that they purchase the specific model involved here. She also testified that although payment was made at the Sears store, the sale was contingent upon an inspection of the Kleins' property by the salesman and was not finalized until the salesman pronounced the mower safe for use on the Kleins' property. The salesman essentially corroborated Claudia's testimony. We believe it was reasonable for the jury to find, under these circumstances, that an express warranty was created.

There was also ample evidence presented that Claudia and Steven's parents relied on the Sears salesman to recommend a suitable mower and that the salesman had reason to know of both their reliance and the particular purpose for which the mower was being purchased. This was sufficient to constitute an implied warranty of fitness for a particular purpose.

We also find adequate evidence to support the finding that Sears breached the warranties. Assuming the accuracy of Sears' assertion that it only promised that the mower was fit to cut grass safely when used properly, there was ample evidence that Steven was operating the mower in a manner consistent with the representations made by Sears' salesmen, i.e. vertically on a slope that was pronounced safe.

Likewise, Sears' assertions regarding proximate cause involve factual issues properly resolved by the jury. Throughout the trial, Sears contended that Steven's misuse of the mower was the proximate cause of the accident while the Kleins countered that the mower was unsuitable for its intended use. While there was evidence presented on both sides of this issue, the jury obviously was convinced that the accident was caused by the failure of the machine to conform to the express and implied warranties.

Evidence of Lack of Safety Device

Sears next contends that the court erred in permitting the introduction of evidence showing that there was no "deadman's switch" on the riding mower. It argues that such evidence was not relevant to the warranty issues and improperly injected into the trial considerations of negligent design and strict product liability.

The absence of a "deadman's switch" was adverted to in the Kleins' opening statement. Additionally, two of the Kleins' witnesses, an expert in safety analysis and a mechanical engineer, also referred to the absence of the device. The "deadman's switch" issue also arose during cross-examination of Sears' engineer and in the rebuttal portion of the Kleins' closing argument.

Sears argues that, because the Kleins limited the issues to breach of warranty and negligent misrepresentation, the evidence concerning the absence of a "deadman's switch" was wholly irrelevant and served only to inflame and prejudice the jury. We disagree.

The evidence was relevant to the Kleins' breach of express warranty claim. The jury could have inferred that the warranty created by the salesman's statement at the Kleins' residence contemplated that the mower would operate safely on their lawn, would not overturn in mowing the existing slopes, and, if it did overturn, would not injure the operator. Thus, the evidence regarding the instability of the mower was relevant to the accident, while the evidence regarding the failure to incorporate the "deadman's switch" was relevant to the injury.

Nonetheless, Sears contends that even if the "deadman's device" was admissible, the trial judge was required to give an immediate limiting instruction, citing United States v. McClain. Sears' reliance is misplaced.

In the first place, McClain involved the admission into evidence of prior violent acts at a trial for second degree murder — a criminal case. Further, the principle enunciated 1426*1426 in McClain has been modified considerably in subsequent cases, United States v. Lewis. The more modern approach is to defer to the trial court's discretion as to the timing of the limiting instruction even in criminal trials.

During the course of the trial, the district judge expressed some doubt as to the propriety of admitting evidence on this issue and stated that he intended to give a limiting instruction to the jury. He later instructed the jury:

During the course of the trial there has been considerable testimony about what has been referred to as a deadman's control. This is not, however, a design product — or product design case and most of that testimony is irrelevant and whether or not that control was present is basically an irrelevant matter to you. It has been admitted for certain limited purposes, but as I say, again, this is not a product design case and therefore, much of that testimony has no relevance in this case.

Sears maintains that this instruction was wholly inadequate and mandates reversal.

We first note that Sears, although given the opportunity, failed to object to the limiting instruction pursuant to Fed.R.Civ.P. 51, and Sears did not offer limiting instructions of its own. Such failure insulates the instruction from reversal unless the instruction given amounts to plain error affecting substantial rights of the parties...Beyond that, it appears that the jury was adequately instructed. We agree that the limiting instruction should have been more specific but reviewing all of the instructions as a whole, we are convinced that from them the jury should have understood the limited purpose for which they could consider the evidence relating to the deadman's switch.

Court's Proximate Cause Instructions

Sears maintains that the issue of proximate cause was not clearly presented to the jury by either the court's instructions or special verdict form. Sears submitted a "Verdict Form, Including Special Interrogatories for the Jury" that included, among other things, three proposed questions:

1. How do you find on the breach of express warranty claim?
2. How do you find on the breach of implied warranty of fitness for a particular purpose claim?
3. How do you find on the negligent misrepresentation claim?

The special verdict form ultimately submitted to the jury included:

1. Did the defendant make and breach an express warranty of fitness for a particular purpose?
2. Did the defendant breach an implied warranty of fitness for a particular purpose?
3. Did the defendant make a negligent misrepresentation?

Sears argues that the verdict form used by the court erroneously omitted the element of proximate cause and that this error was compounded by the court's inadequate jury instructions on this issue. It is settled in this jurisdiction that the formulation of issues and the form of interrogatories is committed to the sound discretion of the trial judge... In considering the adequacy of the verdict form, we consider several factors, including whether the interrogatories adequately presented the contested issues to the jury when read as a whole and in conjunction with the general charge, whether submission of the issues to the jury was fair, and whether the ultimate questions of fact were clearly submitted to the jury. Tights, Inc., 541 F.2d at 1060. Of almost prescient relevance is the statement of this court in Cunningham v. M-G Transport Services, Inc:

The drafting of special interrogatories is largely a matter of common sense and local practice, for example, proximate causation might be submitted as a separate issue if thought appropriate. They may be as detailed as counsel and the district court wish to make them, and the particular verbiage used is of no great consequence so long as the questions were framed so that the jury knows what it is deciding.

We feel that the instructions given by the trial judge were sufficient to apprise the jury of the need for a finding that Steven's injuries were proximately caused by the failure of the mower to conform to the relevant warranties. In instructing the jury on the breach of warranty theory, the court instructed that "[a] Seller, Sears, for example, is responsible to a person who sustains an injury only if the injury proximately results from the failure of the product to conform to a statement that constitutes a warranty." The instruction on negligent misrepresentation included the element "that the Plaintiffs suffered damages proximately caused by the Defendant's negligence." In its general instructions to the jury, the court, after explaining the plaintiffs' theories, stated:

The Defendant, on the contrary, maintained that there were no warranties created with regard to the area where the accident occurred, and that even if the warranties were created, that the accident occurred not because the lawn mower was unsafe for the lawn where it was being used, but rather because Steven Klein, who was operating the lawn mower, was misusing the machine when the accident occurred.

The court's instructions paralleled the evidence presented on this issue and together they clearly defined for the jury the question of proximate cause. Aside from the issue of whether the Sears salesman had warranted the lawnmower as alleged, the keystone of Sears' defense was whether Steven Klein had been mowing his yard in accordance with the instructions given by the salesman — i.e., whether the proximate cause of the accident was the unsuitability of the mower or operator misuse. As Sears' counsel stated in his opening argument:

The case really is going to come down to, when it gets down to it, I am convinced of it, one really significant question, was it an error in the operation of that particular mower on that day that caused it to flip over or was it unfit for use, an improper mower and that is why it flipped over.

Further, during closing argument, counsel for Sears stated, "I remain of the view that the fundamental issue in this case, was it operator error or was that mower unfit for use on that slope ... when the accident occurred? It was a fundamental issue when the case began, it remains a fundamental issue here today." The Kleins and Sears each submitted evidence supporting their version of the facts bearing on these issues and the jury, adequately instructed, reviewed a verdict form substantially in the form submitted by Sears but in any event sufficiently adapted to the issues and facts that we cannot say that the court abused its discretion.

Viewing all of the instructions and the evidence, we find no abuse of discretion in the selection of the verdict form or in the jury's instruction.

JUDGMENT AFFIRMED IN PART, REVERSED IN PART WITH INSTRUCTIONS.

Limitations on Liability

Section 2-316: Exclusion or Modification of Warranties

> *"Words or conduct relevant to the creation of an express warranty or words or conduct tending to negate or limit a warranty shall be construed wherever reasonable as consistent with each other; but subject to the provisions of this Article on parol or extrinsic evidence, negation or limitation is inoperative to the extent that such construction is unreasonable."*
>
> *"Subject to subsection (3), to exclude or modify the implied warranty of merchantability or any part of it, the language must mention merchantability and in the case of a writing must be conspicuous, and to exclude or modify any implied warranty of fitness, the exclusion must be by a writing and conspicuous. Language to exclude all implied warranties of fitness is sufficient if it states, for example, that "There are no warranties which extend beyond the description of the face hereof.""*

"Notwithstanding subsection (2),

1. Unless the circumstances indicate otherwise, all implied warranties are excluded by expressions like as is, with all faults, or other language which in common understanding calls the buyer's attention to the exclusion of warranties and makes plain that there is no implied warranty; and
2. When the buyer before entering into the contract has examined the goods or the sample or model as fully as he desired or has refused to examine the goods, there is no implied warranty with regard to defects which an examination ought in the circumstances to have revealed to him; and
3. An implied warranty can also be excluded or modified by course of dealings or course of performance or usage of trade.
4. Remedies for breach of warranty can be limited in accordance with the provisions of this Article on liquidation or limitation [repair, replacement, return of the article] of damages and on contractual modification of remedy."

Notes on Limitations of Warranties

Many states now require that the exclusion of a warranty must be in writing and that the writing must be conspicuous.

Conspicuous is defined in Section 1-201(10) as:

> *"A term or clause is conspicuous when it is so written that a reasonable person against whom it is to operate ought to have noticed it. Language in the body of a form is conspicuous if it is in larger or other contrasting type or color. But in a telegram any stated term is conspicuous. Whether a term or clause is conspicuous or not is for decision by the court."*

There is a split as to whether "as is" disclaimers must likewise be conspicuous.

A fire sale or an unclaimed freight sale might be an example where a warranty might be excluded because of trade usage.

A post-sale disclaimer would be difficult to uphold because it is illogical to think that a buyer would agree to be bound by a post-sale disclaimer that would limit his/her chances of recovery.

As a general rule, it is almost impossible to orally disclaim an express warranty once it has been offered. Such an oral disclaimer would almost always be subject to the parol evidence rule and would be excluded because the oral disclaimer would plainly contradict the express warranty.

Contractual Modification or Limitation of Remedy (Section 2-719)

> *"Subject to the provisions of subsection 2 and 3 of this section and of the proceeding section on liquidation and limitation of damages,*
>
> *The agreement may provide for remedies in addition to or in substitution for those provided in this Article and may limit or alter the measure of damages recoverable under this article, as by limiting the buyer's remedies to return of the goods and repayment of the price or to repair and replacement of nonconforming goods or parts; and*
>
> *Resort to a remedy as provided is optional unless the remedy is expressly agreed to be exclusive, in which case it is the sole remedy.*
>
> *Where circumstances cause an exclusive or limited remedy to fail of its essential purpose, remedy may be had as provided in this act.*
>
> *Consequential damages [for lost profits or personal injury] may be limited or excluded unless the limitation or exclusion is unconscionable. Limitation of consequential damages for injury to the person in the case of consumer goods [goods purchased for "personal, family, or household use"] is prima facie unconscionable but limitation of damages where the loss is commercial [for producer goods or for injury to property] is not."*

Notes on Contractual Limitations

In a case where a consumer good causes personal injury, a limitation to "repair only" would "fail the essential purpose" of the Act and would not be enforced. (*Soo Line R.R. Co. v. Fruehauf Corp.*)

Warranties can be limited in terms of time provided that the period is deemed reasonable. Think about the range of time limitations in automobile warranties.

Subsection 2-607 (23) (a) provides that the buyer must "within a reasonable time after he discovers or should have discovered any breach notify the seller of breach or be barred from any remedy." This is usually no more than three months.

The notice requirement of Subsection 2-607 (23) is not the same as the Statute of Limitations requirement. Under Section 2-725, the Statute of Limitations may never be reduced to a period less than one year and may extend to a period of four years. In general, the Statute of Limitations for filing a suit for a breach of warranty begins from the date of the breach of warranty. The contractual warranty period begins when the tender of delivery is made.

Notwithstanding the above, a few courts have marked the statute of limitations from the date of discovery of an injury or from the date when the injury should have been discovered as a matter of public policy. Individual state law should be consulted as to this issue.

Several states have adopted statutes of repose of ten or twenty years as an absolute period of time after which a seller/manufacturer may not be held liable, but their application is highly speculative in light of the discussion above. Statutes of repose have been sought vigorously by the airplane-manufacturing sector, which has lobbied for an absolute 20-year statute of repose in the sale or resale of airplanes.

In practical terms, there is a two step process for determining warranty protections: you must first determine if a warranty provision is applicable to a particular plaintiff by consulting which of the Alternatives found in UCC Section 2-316 is applicable. Secondly, you must then determine whether the sale involves either a producer or a consumer good.

If a warranty provision extends to an employee or to another party under Alternative B of Section 2-316, for example, it would be difficult to prove that a disclaimer should apply to that party without express agreement of that party, which rarely could be shown.

Questions

1. What was the significance of *Henningsen v.. Bloomfield Motors Inc.* in relation to warranty actions?
2. Research *Coffer v. Standard Brands Inc.*
    a. Was there a breach of implied warranty?
    b. How does the foreign/natural test apply?
    c. Was Standards Brands Inc. liable?
3. What is the significance of *Siemen v. Alden* in relation to the implied warranty of merchantability?
4. What was the significance of *Soo Line R.R. Co. v. Fruehauf Corp.* in relation to contractual limitations?
5. Lewis, the plaintiff, is a saw mill operator. In order to face competition, the plaintiff converted his power equipment to hydraulic equipment. After installation, the plaintiff sought the proper fluid to run his hydraulic equipment. On the recommendation of Frank Rowe, a Mobil Oil dealer, the plaintiff purchased Ambrex 810, which is straight mineral oil with no additives. After the use of Ambrex 810, his machine equipment broke down. Plaintiff claimed that Mobil Oil supplied him with oil that was claimed to be warranted fit for use in his hydraulic system. Consequently, he brought suit against Mobil Oil.
    a. Is Mobil Oil liable for breach of warranty of fitness?

Appendix 9.1

The Magnuson-Moss Warranty Act

On January 4, 1975, President Ford signed into law the Magnuson-Moss Warranty Act, Title 1, ..101-112, 15 U.S.C. ..2301 et seq. This act, effective July 4, 1975, is designed to "improve the adequacy of information available to consumers, prevent deception, and improve competition in the marketing of consumer products. . . ." The Magnuson-Moss Warranty Act applies only to consumer products, which are defined as "any tangible personal property which is distributed in commerce and which is normally used for personal, family, or household purposes (including any such property intended to be attached to or installed in any real property without regard to whether it is so attached or installed)." Under Section 103 of the Act, if a warrantor sells a consumer product costing more than $15 under written warranty, the writing must state the warranty in readily understandable language as determined by standards set forth by the Federal Trade Commission. There is, however, no requirement that a warranty be given nor that any product be warranted for any length of time. Thus the Act only requires that when there is a written warranty, the warrantor clearly disclose the nature of his warranty obligation prior to the sale of the product. The consumer may then compare warranty protection, thus shopping for the "best buy." To further protect the consumer from deception, the Act requires that any written warranty must be labeled as either a "full" or a "limited" warranty. Only warranties that meet the standards of the Act may be labeled as "full." One of the most important provisions of the Act prohibits a warrantor from disclaiming or modifying any implied warranty whenever any written warranty is given or service contract entered into. Implied warranties may, however, be limited in duration if the limitation is reasonable, conscionable, and set forth in clear and unmistakable language prominently displayed on the face of the warranty. A consumer damaged by breach of warranty, or noncompliance with the act, may sue in either state or federal district court. Access to federal court, however, is severely limited by the Act's provision that no claim may be brought in federal court if: (a) The amount in controversy of any individual claim is less than $25,000; (b) the amount in controversy is less than the sum or value of $50,000 computed on the basis of all claims in the suit; or (c) a class action is brought, and the number of named plaintiffs is less than 100. In light of these requirements it is likely that most suits will be brought in state court. If the consumer prevails, he is awarded costs and attorneys' fees. Nothing in the Act invalidates any right or remedy available under state law, and most suits should proceed on claims based on both the Code and the Act.

Understanding the Magnuson-Moss Warranty Act

The Magnuson-Moss Warranty Act is the federal law that governs consumer product warranties. Passed by Congress in 1975, the Act requires manufacturers and sellers of consumer products to provide consumers with detailed information about warranty coverage. In addition, it affects both the rights of consumers and the obligations of warrantors under written warranties.

To understand the Act, it is useful to be aware of Congress' intentions in passing it. First, Congress wanted to ensure that consumers could get complete information about warranty terms and conditions. By providing consumers with a way of learning what warranty coverage is offered on a product before they buy, the Act gives consumers a way to know what to expect if something goes wrong, and thus helps to increase customer satisfaction.

Second, Congress wanted to ensure that consumers could compare warranty coverage before buying. By comparing, consumers can choose a product with the best combination of price, features, and warranty coverage to meet their individual needs.

Third, Congress intended to promote competition on the basis of warranty coverage. By assuring that consumers can get warranty information, the Act encourages sales promotion on the basis of warranty coverage and competition among companies to meet consumer preferences through various levels of warranty coverage.

Finally, Congress wanted to strengthen existing incentives for companies to perform their warranty obligations in a timely and thorough manner and to resolve any disputes with a minimum of delay and expense to consumers. Thus, the Act makes it easier for consumers to pursue a remedy for breach of warranty in the courts, but it also creates a framework for companies to set up procedures for resolving disputes inexpensively and informally, without litigation.

What the Magnuson-Moss Act Does Not Require

In order to understand how the Act affects you as a business person, it is important first to understand what the Act does not require.

First, the Act does not require any business to provide a written warranty. The Act allows businesses to determine whether to warrant their products in writing. However, once a business decides to offer a written warranty on a consumer product, it must comply with the Act.

Second, the Act does not apply to oral warranties. Only written warranties are covered.

Third, the Act does not apply to warranties on services. Only warranties on goods are covered. However, if your warranty covers both the parts provided for a repair and the workmanship in making that repair, the Act does apply to you.

Finally, the Act does not apply to warranties on products sold for resale or for commercial purposes. The Act covers only warranties on consumer products. This means that only warranties on tangible property normally used for personal, family, or household purposes are covered. (This includes property attached to or installed on real property.) Note that applicability of the Act to a particular product does not, however, depend upon how an individual buyer will use it.

The following section of this manual summarizes what the Magnuson-Moss Warranty Act requires warrantors to do, what it prohibits them from doing, and how it affects warranty disputes.

What the Magnuson-Moss Act Requires

In passing the Magnuson-Moss Warranty Act, Congress specified a number of requirements that warrantors must meet. Congress also directed the FTC to adopt rules to cover other requirements. The FTC adopted three Rules under the Act, the Rule on Disclosure of Written Consumer Product Warranty Terms and Conditions (the Disclosure Rule), the Rule on Pre-Sale Availability of Written Warranty Terms (the Pre-Sale Availability Rule), and the Rule on Informal Dispute Settlement Procedures (the Dispute Resolution Rule). In addition, the FTC has issued an interpretive rule that clarifies certain terms and explains some of the provisions of the Act. This section summarizes all the requirements under the Act and the Rules.

The Act and the Rules establish three basic requirements that may apply to you, either as a warrantor or a seller.

- As a warrantor, you must designate, or title, your written warranty as either "full" or "limited."
- As a warrantor, you must state certain specified information about the coverage of your warranty in a single, clear, and easy-to-read document.
- As a warrantor or a seller, you must ensure that warranties are available where your warranted consumer products are sold so that consumers can read them before buying.

The titling requirement, established by the Act, applies to all written warranties on consumer products costing more than $10. However, the disclosure and pre-sale availability requirements, established by FTC Rules, apply to all written warranties on consumer products costing more than $15. Each of these three general requirements is explained in greater detail in the following chapters.

What the Magnuson-Moss Act Does Not Allow

There are three prohibitions under the Magnuson-Moss Act. They involve implied warranties, so-called "tie-in sales" provisions, and deceptive or misleading warranty terms.

Disclaimer or Modification of Implied Warranties

The Act prohibits anyone who offers a written warranty from disclaiming or modifying implied warranties. This means that no matter how broad or narrow your written warranty is, your customers always will receive the basic protection of the implied warranty of merchantability.

There is one permissible modification of implied warranties, however. If you offer a "limited" written warranty, the law allows you to include a provision that restricts the duration of implied warranties to the duration of your limited warranty. For example, if you offer a two-year limited warranty, you can limit implied warranties to two years. However, if you offer a "full" written warranty, you cannot limit the duration of implied warranties.

If you sell a consumer product with a written warranty from the product manufacturer, but you do not warrant the product in writing, you can disclaim your implied warranties. (These are the implied warranties under which the seller, not the manufacturer, would otherwise be responsible.) But, regardless of whether you warrant the products you sell, as a seller, you must give your customers copies of any written warranties from product manufacturers.

"Tie-In Sales" Provisions

Generally, tie-in sales provisions are not allowed. Such a provision would require a purchaser of the warranted product to buy an item or service from a particular company to use with the warranted product in order to be eligible to receive a remedy under the warranty. The following are examples of prohibited tie-in sales provisions.

In order to keep your new Plenum Brand Vacuum Cleaner warranty in effect, you must use genuine Plenum Brand Filter Bags. Failure to have scheduled maintenance performed, at your expense, by the Great American Maintenance Company, Inc., voids this warranty.

While you cannot use a tie-in sales provision, your warranty need not cover use of replacement parts, repairs, or maintenance that is inappropriate for your product. The following is an example of a permissible provision that excludes coverage of such things.

While necessary maintenance or repairs on your AudioMundo Stereo System can be performed by any company, we recommend that you use only authorized AudioMundo dealers. Improper or incorrectly performed maintenance or repair voids this warranty.

Although tie-in sales provisions generally are not allowed, you can include such a provision in your warranty if you can demonstrate to the satisfaction of the FTC that your product will not work properly without a specified item or service. If you believe that this is the case, you should contact the warranty staff of the FTC's Bureau of Consumer Protection for information on how to apply for a waiver of the tie-in sales prohibition.

Deceptive Warranty Terms

Obviously, warranties must not contain deceptive or misleading terms. You cannot offer a warranty that appears to provide coverage but, in fact, provides none. For example, a warranty covering only "moving parts" on an electronic product that has no moving parts would be deceptive and unlawful. Similarly, a warranty that promised service that the warrantor had no intention of providing or could not provide would be deceptive and unlawful.

How the Magnuson Moss Act May Affect Warranty Disputes

Two other features of the Magnuson-Moss Warranty Act are also important to warrantors. First, the Act makes it easier for consumers to take an unresolved warranty problem to court. Second, it encourages companies to use a less formal, and therefore less costly, alternative to legal proceedings. Such alternatives, known as dispute resolution mechanisms, often can be used to settle warranty complaints before they reach litigation.

Consumer Lawsuits

The Act makes it easier for purchasers to sue for breach of warranty by making breach of warranty a violation of federal law, and by allowing consumers to recover court costs and reasonable attorneys' fees. This means that if you lose a lawsuit for breach of either a written or an implied warranty, you may have to pay the customer's costs for bringing the suit, including lawyer's fees.

Because of the stringent federal jurisdictional requirements under the Act, most Magnuson-Moss lawsuits are brought in state court. However, major cases involving many consumers can be brought in federal court as class action suits under the Act.

Although the consumer lawsuit provisions may have little effect on your warranty or your business, they are important to remember if you are involved in warranty disputes.

Source: http://www.impalaclub.com (April 2012)

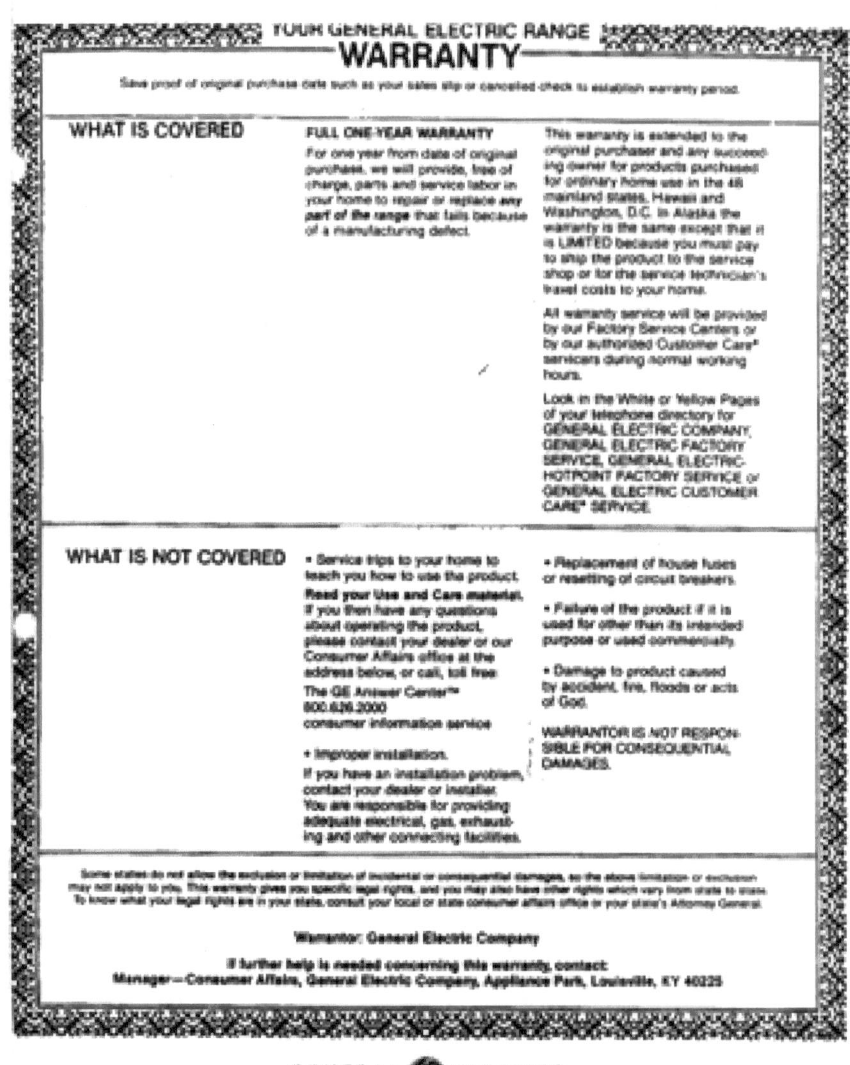

YOUR GENERAL ELECTRIC RANGE

WARRANTY

Save proof of original purchase date such as your sales slip or cancelled check to establish warranty period.

WHAT IS COVERED

FULL ONE-YEAR WARRANTY

For one year from date of original purchase, we will provide, free of charge, parts and service labor in your home to repair or replace ***any part of the range*** that fails because of a manufacturing defect.

This warranty is extended to the original purchaser and any succeeding owner for products purchased for ordinary home use in the 48 mainland states, Hawaii and Washington, D.C. In Alaska the warranty is the same except that it is LIMITED because you must pay to ship the product to the service shop or for the service technician's travel costs to your home.

All warranty service will be provided by our Factory Service Centers or by our authorized Customer Care® servicers during normal working hours.

Look in the White or Yellow Pages of your telephone directory for GENERAL ELECTRIC COMPANY, GENERAL ELECTRIC FACTORY SERVICE, GENERAL ELECTRIC-HOTPOINT FACTORY SERVICE or GENERAL ELECTRIC CUSTOMER CARE® SERVICE.

WHAT IS NOT COVERED

- Service trips to your home to teach you how to use the product.

Read your Use and Care material. If you then have any questions about operating the product, please contact your dealer or our Consumer Affairs office at the address below, or call, toll free:

The GE Answer Center™
800.626.2000
consumer information service

- Improper installation.

If you have an installation problem, contact your dealer or installer. You are responsible for providing adequate electrical, gas, exhausting and other connecting facilities.

- Replacement of house fuses or resetting of circuit breakers.
- Failure of the product if it is used for other than its intended purpose or used commercially.
- Damage to product caused by accident, fire, floods or acts of God.

WARRANTOR IS NOT RESPONSIBLE FOR CONSEQUENTIAL DAMAGES.

Some states do not allow the exclusion or limitation of incidental or consequential damages, so the above limitation or exclusion may not apply to you. This warranty gives you specific legal rights, and you may also have other rights which vary from state to state. To know what your legal rights are in your state, consult your local or state consumer affairs office or your state's Attorney General.

Warrantor: General Electric Company

If further help is needed concerning this warranty, contact:
Manager—Consumer Affairs, General Electric Company, Appliance Park, Louisville, KY 40225

GENERAL ELECTRIC

...rt No. 862A725 P141
Pub. No. 49-4633

Full Two-Year Warranty

Black & Decker (U.S.) Inc. warrants this product against any defects that are due to faulty material or workmanship for a two-year period after the original date of consumer purchase or receipt as a gift. This warranty does not include damage to the product resulting from accident or misuse.

If the product should become defective within the warranty period, we will repair it or elect to replace it free of charge. We will return your product, transportation charges prepaid, provided it is delivered prepaid to any Black & Decker (U.S.) Inc. Household Appliance Company-Owned or Authorized Service Center.

This warranty gives you specific legal rights, and you may also have other rights which vary from state to state.

Answers to any questions regarding warranty service/locations may be obtained by writing to:

Consumer Assistance and Information
Black & Decker (U.S.) Inc.
6 Armstrong Road
Shelton, CT 06484

Limited Warranty

Mr. Coffee, inc. warrants to the consumer that Mr. Coffee® Automatic Coffee Brewer, Model Series SR (except for cord set and glass parts) are free from manufacturer defects in material or workmanship for a period of one year from the date of original purchase when used in compliance with directions as outlined in the manufacturer's instructions, which will constitute reasonable and necessary maintenance by the consumer.

In case of manufacturer defects in material or workmanship, Mr. Coffee, inc. agrees to repair (remedy) a defective coffee brewer without charge.

To be covered under this warranty, repairs must be made by the *authorized* Mr. Coffee Service Center most convenient to the consumer. A list of *authorized* Mr. Coffee Service Centers is enclosed. As the consumer, you assume all cost incurred in transporting your Mr. Coffee machine to the Authorized Mr. Coffee Service Center.

This warranty gives you specific legal rights, and you may also have other rights which vary from state to state. Any implied warranty is limited in duration to the one year provided in this, the only, expressed warranty. Some states do not allow limitations on how long an implied warranty lasts, so the above limitations may not apply to you.

No responsibility is assumed for incidental or consequential damages; nor damage due to misuse or the use of any unauthorized attachment; nor assumption of responsibility for damage by use of an unspecified electrical circuit. Some states do not allow the exclusion or limitation of incidental or consequential damages, so the above limitation or exclusion may not apply to you.

Warranty is void:

- If unit is subjected to service by anyone other than a service center appearing on the enclosed Authorized Mr. Coffee Service Center list

REMINGTON PRODUCTS-SHAVERS

■■■■■■■ IMPORTANT! IMPORTANT! ■■■■■■■

PLEASE FILL OUT AND RETURN WITHIN THE NEXT 10 DAYS.

REMINGTON LIMITED WARRANTY

ONE (1) YEAR LIMITED WARRANTY

Blender

WARRANTY LIMITATIONS

EXCEPT AS EXPRESSLY STATED HEREIN, ACER MAKES NO WARRANTIES EXPRESSED OR IMPLIED, BY OPERATION OF LAW OR OTHERWISE INCLUDING ANY WARRANTY OF MERCHANTABILITY OR FITNESS FOR A PARTICULAR PURPOSE. IN NO EVENT SHALL ACER BE LIABLE FOR ANY INCIDENTAL, SPECIAL OR CONSEQUENTIAL DAMAGES INCLUDING, BUT NOT LIMITED TO LOST PROFITS OR LOSS OF USE HOWEVER CAUSED, WHETHER FOR BREACH OF WARRANTY, STRICT LIABILITY, NEGLIGENCE, BREACH OF CONTRACT OR OTHERWISE.

Chapter Ten

STRICT LIABILITY IN TORT

"A manufacturer is strictly liable in tort when an article he places on the market, knowing that it to be used without inspection for defects, proves to have a defect that causes injury to a human being."

"Although...strict liability has usually been based on the theory of an express or implied warranty running from the manufacturer to the plaintiff, the abandonment of the requirement between them, the recognition that the liability is not assumed by agreement but imposed by law...and the refusal to permit the manufacturer to define the scope of his own responsibility for defective products...make clear that the liability is not one governed by the law of contract warranties but by the law of strict liability in tort."

"The purpose of such liability is to insure that the costs of injuries resulting from defective products are borne by the manufacturers that put such products on the market rather than by the injured persons who are powerless to protect themselves."

"To establish the manufacturer's liability it was sufficient that plaintiff proved that he was injured while using the Shopsmith in a way it was intended to be used as a result of a defect in design and manufacture of which plaintiff was not aware that made the Shopsmith unsafe for its intended use." (Excerpts from Greenman v. Yuba Power)

THE HISTORICAL DEVELOPMENT OF THE THEORY OF STRICT LIABILITY IN TORT

Before the *Greenman* decision in 1963, a plaintiff in a products liability case had to rely on the theories of negligence, breach of warranty, or misrepresentation or fraud for recovery. These theories were not specific to products cases and presented plaintiffs with certain formidable obstacles.

To review... negligence requires that a plaintiff normally prove a specific act or omission on the part of a defendant. A claim of negligence was subject to the harsh defense of contributory negligence, often an absolute bar to recovery and to a lack of privity. Warranties required a plaintiff to contend with the issues of privity, notice, and disclaimers. Under the theories of misrepresentation and fraud, a plaintiff had to plead and prove justifiable reliance on specific assertions or statements of the defendant and had to prove intent or scienter.

In 1944, in *Escola v. Coca Cola Bottling* (a res ipsa loquitur case), Justice Traynor argued in his concurring opinion that these traditional theories were inadequate and that the court should adopt a new and special theory for product cases. "In my opinion, it should now be recognized that a manufacturer incurs an absolute liability when an article he has placed on the market, knowing that it is to be used without inspection, proves to have a defect that causes injury to human beings." Justice Traynor pointed out that a type of strict liability is already imposed on products sellers under the law of warranty, i.e., merchantability. The privity requirement, however, rendered the remedy inadequate because most consumers could not, at that pre-*Henningsen* time (1960), sue the manufacturer of the defective product because they were not in privity of contract with the manufacturer.

Greenman v. Yuba Power Products, Inc.

Supreme Court of California , 59 Cal.2d 57, 27 Cal. Rptr. 697, 377 P.2d 897 (1963)

TRAYNOR, JUSTICE.

Plaintiff brought this action for damages against the retailer and the manufacturer of a Shopsmith, a combination power tool that could be used as a saw, drill, and wood lathe. He saw a Shopsmith demonstrated by the retailer and studied a brochure prepared by the manufacturer. He decided he wanted a Shopsmith for his home workshop, and his wife bought and gave him one for Christmas in 1955. In 1957 he bought the necessary attachments to use the Shopsmith as a lathe for turning a large piece of wood he wished to make into a chalice.

After he had worked on the piece of wood several times without difficulty, it suddenly flew out of the machine and struck him on the forehead, inflicting serious injuries. About ten and a half months later, he gave the retailer and the manufacturer written notice of claimed breaches of warranties and filed a complaint against them alleging such breaches and negligence. After a trial before a jury, the court ruled that there was no evidence that the retailer was negligent or had breached any express warranty and that the manufacturer was not liable for the breach of any implied warranty. Accordingly, it submitted to the jury only the cause of action alleging breach of implied warranties against the retailer and the causes of action alleging negligence and breach of express warranties against the manufacturer. The jury returned a verdict for the retailer against plaintiff and for plaintiff against the manufacturer in the amount of $65,000. The trial court denied the manufacturer's motion for a new trial and entered judgment on the verdict. The manufacturer and plaintiff appeal.

Plaintiff seeks a reversal of the part of the judgment in favor of the retailer, however, only in the event that the part of the judgment against the manufacturer is reversed. Plaintiff introduced substantial evidence that his injuries were caused by defective design and construction of the Shopsmith. His expert witnesses testified that inadequate set screws were used to hold parts of the machine together so that normal vibration caused the tailstock of the lathe to move away from the piece of wood being turned permitting it to fly out of the lathe. They also testified that there were other more positive ways of fastening the parts of the machine together, the use of which would have prevented the accident. The jury could therefore reasonably have concluded that the manufacturer negligently constructed the Shopsmith. The jury could also reasonably have concluded that statements in the manufacturer's brochure were untrue, that they constituted express warranties, and that plaintiff's injuries were caused by their breach.

The manufacturer contends, however, that plaintiff did not give it notice of breach of warranty within a reasonable time and that therefore his cause of action for breach of warranty is barred by section 1769 of the Civil Code. Since it cannot be determined whether the verdict against it was based on the negligence or warranty cause of action or both, the manufacturer concludes that the error in presenting the warranty cause of action to the jury was prejudicial.

Section 1769 of the Civil Code provides: "In the absence of express or implied agreement of the parties, acceptance of the goods by the buyer shall not discharge the seller from liability in damages or other legal remedy for breach of any promise or warranty in the contract to sell or the sale. But, if, after acceptance of the goods, the buyer fails to give notice to the seller of the breach of any promise or warranty within a reasonable time after the buyer knows, or ought to know of such breach, the seller shall not be liable therefore."

Like other provisions of the uniform sales act (Civ. Code, §§ 1721-1800), section 1769 deals with the rights of the parties to a contract of sale or a sale. It does not provide that notice must be given of the breach of a warranty that arises independently of a contract of sale between the parties. Such warranties are not imposed by the sales act, but are the product of common-law decisions that have recognized them in a variety of situations. * * * It is true that in many of these situations the court has invoked the sales act definitions of warranties (Civ. Code, §§ 1732, 1735) in defining the defendant's liability, but it has done so, not because the statutes so required, but because they provided appropriate standards for the court to adopt under the circumstances presented. * * *

The notice requirement of section 1769, however, is not an appropriate one for the court to adopt in actions by injured consumers against manufacturers with whom they have not dealt. (La Hue v. Coca-Cola Bottling, 50 Wash.2d 645, 314 P.2d 421, 422; Chapman v. Brown, D.C., 198 F.Supp. 78, 85, affd. Brown v. Chapman, 9 Cir., 304 F.2d 149.) "As between the immediate parties to the sale [the notice requirement] is a sound commercial rule, designed to protect the seller against unduly delayed claims for damages. As applied to personal injuries, and notice to a remote seller, it becomes a booby-trap for the unwary. The injured consumer is seldom "steeped in the business practice which justifies the rule,' [James, Product Liability, 34 Texas L. Rev. 44, 192, 197] and at least until he has had legal advice it will not occur to him to give notice to one with whom he has had no dealings." (Prosser, Strict Liability to the Consumer, 69 Yale L.J. 1099, 1130, footnotes omitted.) * * * We conclude, therefore, that even if plaintiff did not give timely notice of breach of warranty to the manufacturer, his cause of action based on the representations contained in the brochure was not barred.

Moreover, to impose strict liability on the manufacturer under the circumstances of this case, it was not necessary for plaintiff to establish an express warranty as defined in section 1732 of the Civil Code. A manufacturer is strictly liable in tort when an article he places on the market, knowing that it is to be used without inspection for defects, proves to have a defect that causes injury to a human being. Recognized first in the case of unwholesome food products, such liability has now been extended to a variety of other products that create as great or greater hazards if defective. * * *

Although in these cases strict liability has usually been based on the theory of an express or implied warranty running from the manufacturer to the plaintiff, the abandonment of the requirement of a contract between them, the recognition that the liability is not assumed by agreement but imposed by law * * * and the refusal to permit the manufacturer to define the scope of its own responsibility for defective products * * * make clear that the liability is not one governed by the law of contract warranties but by the law of strict liability in tort. Accordingly, rules defining and governing warranties that were developed to meet the needs of commercial transactions cannot properly be invoked to govern the manufacturer's liability to those injured by their defective products unless those rules also serve the purposes for which such liability is imposed.

We need not recanvass the reasons for imposing strict liability on the manufacturer. They have been fully articulated in the cases cited above. (See also 2 Harper and James, Torts, ?? 28.15-28.16, pp. 1569-1574; Prosser, Strict Liability to the Consumer, 69 Yale L.J. 1099; Escola v. Coca Cola Bottling Co., 24 Cal.2d 453, 461, 150 P.2d 436, concurring opinion.) The purpose of such liability is to insure that the costs of injuries resulting from defective products are borne by the manufacturers that put such products on the market rather than by the injured persons who are powerless to protect themselves.

Sales warranties serve this purpose fitfully at best. (See Prosser, Strict Liability to the Consumer, 69 Yale L.J. 1099, 1124-1134.) In the present case, for example, plaintiff was able to plead and prove an express warranty only because he read and relied on the representations of the Shopsmith's ruggedness contained in the manufacturer's brochure. Implicit in the machine's presence on the market, however, was a representation that it would safely do the jobs for which it was built. Under these circumstances, it should not be controlling whether plaintiff selected the machine because of the statements in the brochure, or because of the machine's own appearance of excellence that belied the defect lurking beneath the surface, or because he merely assumed that it would safely do the jobs it was built to do. It should not be controlling whether the details of the sales from manufacturer to retailer and from retailer to plaintiff's wife were such that one or more of the implied warranties of the sales act arose. (Civ.Code, 1735.) "The remedies of injured consumers ought not to be made to depend upon the intricacies of the law of sales." (Ketterer v. Armour & Co., D.C., 200 F. 322, 323; Klein v. Duchess Sandwich Co., 14 Cal.2d 272, 282, 93 P.2d 799.) To establish the manufacturer's liability it was sufficient that plaintiff proved that he was injured while using the Shopsmith in a way it was intended to be used as a result of a defect in design and manufacture of which plaintiff was not aware that made the Shopsmith unsafe for its intended use.

THE JUDGMENT IS AFFIRMED.

Courts are continuing to work out the details of strict liability, by addressing such issues as defenses (misuse, extension of contributory negligence, assumption of risk, etc.) causation, scope of duty, and the applicability and extension of strict tort liability to particular products, sellers, and situations.

In 1965, the American Law Institute embraced the *Greenman* principle in Section 402A of the Restatement (Second) of Torts. The text of Section 402A:

1. One who sells any product in a defective condition unreasonably dangerous to the user or consumer or to his property is subject to liability for physical harm thereby caused to the ultimate user or consumer, or to his property, if
    a. The seller is engaged in the business of selling such a product, and
    b. Is expected to and does reach the user or consumer without substantial change in the condition in which it is sold.

The rule applies although:

a. The seller has exercised all possible care in the preparation and sale of his product, and
b. The user or consumer has not bought the product from or entered into any contractual relation with the seller.

The *Greenman* decision, coupled with Section 402A (originally thought to apply only to food and drink cases), provided the intellectual basis for the transition from warranty to strict liability in tort and represented the beginning of modern products liability law. A great many developments have taken place since 1965 and, as a result, many courts have departed substantially from the original Restatement rule. Each state is free to interpret Section 402A and to expand this important concept on a case-by-case basis. There is no national product liability law at this time! Do you think there should be?

The philosophy articulated by Justice Traynor in the *Greenman* decision has been followed in the Restatement version of strict liability. Subsection (2) is clearly intended to place responsibility for safe products on the seller or manufacturer rather than on an unknowing user or consumer. Further, Section 402A continues to remove the requirement of proof of fault as did Greenman. However, Section 402A adds the condition that the product be unreasonably dangerous. This addition has generated some significant controversy and has led a variety of jurisdictions to adopt the Greenman standard rather than purely Section 402A. Barker v. Lull Engineering is illustrative of this disagreement.

As a general rule, the basic elements of strict products liability cases may be expressed as follows:

- The defendant was in the business of producing or selling the product [status as a merchant];
- The product was expected to and did reach the purchaser without substantial change in the condition in which it was sold;
- The product was defective [in design, manufacture, or warnings] when it left the defendant's control;
- The harm resulted when the product was being used in a reasonable foreseeable manner;
- The person harmed was foreseeable [later expanded to include a bystander]; and
- The defect was the cause in fact and proximate cause [legal cause] of physical harm to the plaintiff's person or property.

Policies Underlying Strict Liability

Courts, commentators, scholars, and even professors have advanced a variety of policy justifications for the imposition of strict tort liability. The following are the most prevalent and are summarized briefly for your consideration.

Loss Spreading

It is fair to shift losses from an individual to all consumers of a product by imposing strict liability on manufacturers, in order to spread potential losses among all purchasers through appropriate pricing policies or the purchase of product liability insurance.

Deterrence / Incentive

Imposing strict liability on manufacturers provides them with an incentive to market safer products. Strict liability induces manufacturers to go beyond traditional negligence standards of a reasonable person, especially if the cost of the added safety measures is less than the potential cost of liability for failure to take them (cost/benefit, risk/utility analysis)—most especially if the cost of any change or modification is minimal.

Strict liability should be based upon reasonable concepts of risk/utility, recognizing that there is some risk in all areas of human activity. Imposition of strict liability will encourage manufacturers to produce useful products even if there is some risk involved. At its core, a plaintiff will not be compensated simply because he has been injured; rather, a plaintiff will still need to prove that a product is defective, thus holding out to the manufacturer that proper conduct will not be punished. (However, see Chapter 15!)

In *First National Bank v. Nor-Am Agricultural Products, Inc.*, Mr. Huckleby, unbeknownst to him, fed his hogs grain that had been treated with a disinfectant containing mercury, manufactured by the defendant. His children ate one of the hogs infected with the chemical and suffered blindness and paralysis as a result of mercury poisoning. In an action based on the failure to warn, the trial court granted the defendant's motion for a summary judgment.

The appellate court reversed and held that "The public interest in human life, health and safety requires that the law give consumers maximum protection against dangerous product defects." The court continued:

> *"The marketing of dangerously defective products can have tragic consequences. Allowing injured plaintiffs to proceed on this theory of manufacturing liability, without the necessity of proving negligence, will cause manufacturers to take cautionary steps to prevent the marketing of dangerously defective products. Such preventive measures may have [averted] tragedies as befell the Huckleby family, and thereby save our system the cost of lawsuits such as this one."*

The court added:

> *"When a defendant's product is adjudged by a jury to be dangerously defective, imposition of liability on the manufacturer will cause him to take some steps or at least make calculations to improve this product.... we suspect that, in the final analysis, the imposition of liability has a beneficial effect on manufacturers of defective products both in the care they take and in the warning they give."*

Proof Problems

Modern complexities in manufacturing have made it very difficult to establish negligence in many cases, especially since a manufacturer is usually at a relative advantage in terms of access to expertise, information, and resources. Strict liability will eliminate a plaintiff's need to prove negligence, or may even eliminate proof of the identity of a specific defendant through the imposition of enterprise liability which will be discussed in Chapter 15.

Protection of Consumer Expectations

Since modern advertising and marketing techniques induce consumers to rely on manufacturers to provide them with safe, high-quality products, consumers should likewise expect protection from unknown dangers in products, best exemplified through the imposition of strict liability.

Cost Internalization

Forcing manufacturers to compensate victims of defective products through the purchase of appropriate products liability insurance or by making a decision to essentially self- insure will lead to a more efficient allocation of resources and pricing of products to include all of their true costs, including the costs associated with damages caused by defective products. If funds are already available from which injured parties can be compensated, manufacturers will be more apt to admit liability rather than stonewall in handling complaints of product defects.

Are there any negative aspects to these justifications?

Questions

1. How did the *Escola v. Coca Cola Bottling Co. of Fresno* case shape the development of product cases?

2. Greenman, the plaintiff, brought action against the retailer and manufacturer of a 'Shopsmith,' which is a combination power tool. Plaintiff's wife bought the product as a gift for him on Christmas. Subsequently, he bought attachments to use the 'Shopsmith' as a lathe. During its use, the wood he was working on flew out and struck his forehead.

   a. Does the doctrine of strict liability apply? If so, how?

   b. Is the retailer liable? Is the manufacturer liable?

3. Was Mr. Greenman in privity of contract with the manufacturer? Did that matter?

4. How did the *Greenman* decision shape product cases in terms of strict liability? How were cases handled prior to the decision?

5. How does *Barker v. Lull Engineering* illustrate the difference between the *Greenman* standard and section 402A of the Restatement of Torts?

6. Find examples of the following in relation to strict liability:

   a. Loss spreading

   b. Deterrence/incentive

   c. Encouraging useful conduct

   d. Proof problems

   e. Protection of consumer expectations

   f. Cost internalization

Notes

Chapter Eleven

Scope of Liability

Let's first review the formulation of the definition of strict liability:

> *"A manufacturer is strictly liable in tort when an article he places on the market, knowing it is to be used without inspection for defects, proves to have a defect that causes injury to a human being." (Greenman v. Yuba Power - 1963)*

Today, most courts uniformly apply strict liability to both sale and to lease transactions, holding that there is little difference in supplying products to the public in either a sale or a lease transaction. But that was not always the case!

Sales

A sale is defined as the "passing of title between a buyer and a seller." Section 402A of the Restatement, setting forth the requirements for the imposition of strict liability, would certainly apply to a sale ("one who sells a product....") Likewise, an action based on warranty (either express or implied—especially one involving the warranty of merchantability) would apply in the case of a sale. However, the question remains: Can areas be expanded or is a sale strictly required for liability to be applied?

Case Study: Martin v. Ryder Truck Rental, Inc.

Procedural Posture

Plaintiff appealed an order from the Superior Court (Delaware) in which the court granted summary judgment in defendant's favor on plaintiff's complaint for strict liability.

Overview

Plaintiff brought suit against defendant, based upon the doctrine of strict tort liability, when a commercial truck owned by defendant and leased to a third-party collided with plaintiff's vehicle due to a failure of the braking system. Defendant moved for summary judgment. The lower court granted judgment in defendant's favor. On appeal, the court reversed. The court held that a bailment-lease of a motor vehicle, entered into in the regular course of a truck rental business, was subject to application of the doctrine of strict tort liability in favor of an injured bystander. Accordingly, defendant could be held strictly liable in tort, without proof of negligence, if the truck it placed in circulation proved to have a defect that proximately caused personal injury or property damage to plaintiff.

Outcome

The court reversed the lower court's judgment for defendant truck rental company, holding that a bailment-lease of a motor vehicle, entered into the regular course of a truck rental business, was subject to application of the doctrine of strict tort liability in favor of the plaintiff injured bystander.

Martin makes an important point and notes "the common law must grow to fulfill the requirements of justice as dictated by changing times and conditions." Thus, liability has been expanded to a variety of other transactions, depending on the specific facts developed in each case. It should also be noted that strict liability has been applied recently in product demonstration cases, supplying free samples, or even in the case of a gift where the product was defective.

Leases

In recent years, it is clear that most courts will apply strict liability to a lease of a chattel or of a product (as in *Dewberry v. Lafollette*), but only if the lessor is "in the business of leasing products of this kind," and where the product itself has been "introduced into the stream of commerce" through the lease "in the regular course of the rental business." (*Martin v. Ryder Truck Rental, Inc.*).

A bailment for hire or mutual benefit bailment is a special type of product lease that involves the temporary surrender of an item of personal property from the bailor (lessor) to the bailee (lessee) with a provision for its return in which the bailor is compensated in some way. In such a case, if the property is defective (through a defect in production, design, or warnings), the bailor/lessor may be held liable.

In other cases, there are major difficulties in imposing strict liability and proof of negligence is usually required. What this means is that a plaintiff may still be compensated for the harm caused by a defective product - but under a theory other than strict liability.

Two questions must be resolved. First, should principles associated with product liability law be applied in these circumstances? Second, what would be the best theory (negligence, warranty, fraud, or strict liability) to press such a claim?

Franchising

The court imposed liability for breach of an implied warranty on 7-Up because 7-Up, as the franchiser, had exercised control over the "type, style, size, and design" of the carton under its "quality control" obligation. With knowledge of its design, 7-Up consented to the entry of this product "into the stream of commerce," and thus should be held liable for breach of warranty.

Kosters v. Seven-Up Company

United States Court Of Appeals, Sixth Circuit, 595 F.2d 347 (1979)

OPINION BY: MERRITT, JUDGE

During the past two decades, franchising has become a common means of marketing products and services, but our legal system has not yet settled the principles that define the liabilities of franchisors for injuries sustained by customers of their franchisees. This diversity case requires us to interpret the theories of tort and contract liability which Michigan law allows a jury to consider when deciding whether an injured purchaser is entitled to recover against the franchisor of a product.

I. STATEMENT OF THE CASE

The defendant, the Seven-Up Company, appeals from a $ 150,000 jury verdict awarded for injuries caused by an exploding 7-Up bottle. The plaintiff removed a cardboard carton containing six bottles of 7-Up from a grocery shelf, put it under her arm and headed for the check-out counter of the grocery store. She was blinded in one eye when a bottle slipped out of the carton, fell on the floor and exploded, causing a piece of glass to strike her eye as she looked down. The 7-Up carton was a so-called "over-the-crown" or "neck-thru" carton designed to be held from the top and made without a strip on the sides of the carton which would prevent a bottle from slipping out if held underneath.

The carton was designed and manufactured by Olinkraft, Inc. Olinkraft sold it to the Brooks Bottling Company, a franchisee of the defendant, Seven-Up Company. Seven-Up retains the right to approve the design of articles used by the bottler, including cartons. The franchise agreement between Seven-Up and the Brooks Bottling Company requires that "cases, bottles, and crowns used for 7-Up will be of a type . . . and design approved by the 7-Up Company," and "any advertising . . . material . . . must be approved by the 7-Up Company before its use by the bottler."

Using an extract provided by Seven-Up, Brooks produced the beverage and poured it into bottles. After securing Seven-Up's approval of the design under the franchise agreement, Brooks packaged the bottles in cartons selected and purchased by Brooks from various carton manufacturers, including Olinkraft. Brooks then sold cartons of 7-Up to stores in some 52 Michigan counties, including Meijers Thrifty Acres Store in Holland, Michigan, where the plaintiff picked up the carton and carried it under her arm toward the checkout counter. Plaintiff settled her claims against the bottler, the carton manufacturer and the grocer for $ 30,000.

Seven-Up denied liability, insisting its approval of the cartons was only of the "graphics" and for the purpose of assuring that its trademark was properly displayed.

The District Judge submitted the case to the jury on five related theories of product liability a negligence theory, three strict liability theories and one contract theory:

We do not know which of these theories the jury accepted because it returned a general verdict. On appeal, Seven-Up argues that all of the theories are wrong except negligence. We begin our consideration of this diversity case by acknowledging that the views of an experienced District Judge on questions concerning the law of the state in which he sits are entitled to great respect.

II. THE LIABILITY ISSUES

Michigan appellate courts have not had the occasion to consider these principles in the context of franchising. It appears to be a new question not generally considered in other jurisdictions. The franchise system is a method of selling products and services identified by a particular trade name which may be associated with a patent, a trade secret, a particular product design or management expertise. The franchisee usually purchases some products from the franchisor in this case, the 7-Up syrup and makes royalty payments on the basis of units sold, in exchange for the right to offer products for sale under the trademark. The franchise agreement establishes the relationship between the parties and usually regulates the quality of the product, sales territory, the advertising and other details; and it usually requires that certain supplies be purchased from the franchisor.

Seven-Up Company concedes that a franchisor, like a manufacturer or supplier, may be liable to the consumer for its own negligence, without regard to privity, under the doctrine of MacPherson v. Buick Motor Co. Seven-Up contends, however, that it does not carry the liabilities of a supplier when it did not supply the product and that other theories of strict tort liability do not apply. Liability may not be laid on the basis of implied warranty, it says, when the franchisor did not manufacture, handle, design or require the use of the particular product. The precise question before us here is whether Michigan's principles of "strict accountability" for breach of implied warranty extend to a franchisor who retains the right of control over the product (the carton) and specifically consents to its distribution in the form sold but does not actually manufacture, sell, handle, ship or require the use of the product.

Different questions may arise in other franchising contexts. In some instances, the franchisor may not retain the right of control or may not actually approve the form of the product. The franchisee may sell a product contrary to the instructions or without the knowledge of the franchisor. The consumer may attempt to hold the franchisor liable for the conduct of the franchisee under the agency doctrines of Respondeat Superior or apparent authority. We do not deal with these questions here.

In this case, the Seven-Up Company not only floated its franchisee and the bottles of its carbonated soft drink into the so-called "stream of commerce." The Company also assumed and exercised a degree of control over the "type, style, size and design" of the carton in which its product was to be marketed. The carton was submitted to Seven-Up for inspection. With knowledge of its design, Seven-Up consented to the entry in commerce of the carton from which the bottle fell, causing the injury. The franchisor's sponsorship, management and control of the system for distributing 7-Up, plus its specific consent to the use of the carton, in our view, places the franchisor in the position of a supplier of the product for purposes of tort liability.

We are not saying that the Seven-Up Company is absolutely liable as an insurer of the safety of the carton under the theory of implied warranty, simply by virtue of its status as a franchisor. In the first place, under Michigan's theory of implied warranty of fitness, the carton must be found to be "defective," or as the District Judge more accurately put it, "not reasonably safe." It must be harmful or unsafe because something is wrong with it, and the jury must so find. Moreover, here the franchisor inspected the carton and approved it. Thus, we need not reach the question whether the franchisor would carry the liabilities of a supplier if it had not been made aware of the product and given the opportunity to assess the risks.

When a franchisor consents to the distribution of a defective product bearing its name, the obligation of the franchisor to compensate the injured consumer for breach of implied warranty, we think, arises from several factors in combination: (1) the risk created by approving for distribution an unsafe product likely to cause injury, (2) the franchisor's ability and opportunity to eliminate the unsafe character of the product and prevent the loss, (3) the consumer's lack of knowledge of the danger, and (4) the consumer's reliance on the trade name which gives the intended impression that the franchisor is responsible for and stands behind the product. Liability is based on the franchisor's control and the public's assumption, induced by the franchisor's conduct, that it does in fact control and vouch for the product.

These are factors Michigan courts have relied on in the past in determining who may be held liable for breach of implied warranty of fitness in other products liability situations. We believe Michigan courts would apply these principles in the franchising situation presented by this case, and we therefore conclude that the case was correctly submitted to the jury to assess liability for breach of implied warranty.

Publications

In the case of a publication, there is an additional consideration: The First Amendment and the guaranty of freedom of commercial speech (freedom to publish), found in the important case of *Gertz v. Welch*. The court said: "To hold those who perform this essential function liable, regardless of fault, when an injury results would severely restrict the flow of ideas they distribute." So, the plaintiff would have to show more than mere publication (under strict liability) and would have to prove some negligence (a positive act that is unreasonable or perhaps a negligent omission) or a failure to warn of a known danger on the part of the publisher or retailer.

However, liability under a negligence theory has been applied to certain other publications—most notably air and sea navigation charts—where the defect was as a result of either faulty surveying, or faulty printing.

There is also potential liability for certain parties called "product certifiers" (Good Housekeeping or United Laboratories) who must use "reasonable care" in their certification of products. If they fail to use "reasonable care," product certifiers may be held liable for their negligence for failing to carry out their responsibilities in an ordinary prudent manner. In sum, the warranty of merchantability is limited to the "physical properties" of the book itself and not to any of the material or ideas communicated in the book.

Case Study: Cardozo v. True

The "Cookbook" Case

Overview

Plaintiff purchased a cookbook from defendant retail book dealer. While preparing a meal from a recipe in the cookbook, plaintiff ate one of the ingredients. Plaintiff became violently ill and was hospitalized. The cookbook failed to mention that the ingredient was poisonous if not cooked. Plaintiffs, the wife and her husband, filed a suit against defendant that alleged among other things that that defendant had impliedly warranted that the book was reasonably fit for its intended use, and that it was not, due to inadequate instructions and warnings. In response to certified questions from the court below, the court found that defendant was not liable under Fla. Stat. ch. 672.314 to plaintiff for injuries caused by improper instructions or inadequate warnings as to poisonous ingredients used in a recipe. The court also found that absent allegations that defendant knew that there was reason to warn the public as to contents of a book, that the implied warranty in respect to sale of books by a merchant who regularly sells them was limited to a warranty of the physical properties of such books and not the material communicated therein.

Outcome

In response to two certified questions from the court below, the court found that a retail book dealer was not liable under Florida law, or the common law of implied warranties, to a purchaser of a cookbook for her injuries caused by improper instructions or lack of adequate warnings as to poisonous ingredients used in a recipe, absent allegations that the book seller knew that there were reasons to warn the public as to the contents.

Used Products

Tillman v. Vance Equipment Company

Supreme Court Of Oregon, 286 Ore. 747; 596 P.2d 1299 (1978)

OPINION BY: DENECKE

Plaintiff brought this action based upon the theory of strict liability in tort to recover for personal injuries caused by a 24-year-old crane sold by defendant, a used equipment dealer, to plaintiff's employer, Durametal. The court tried the case without a jury and found for the defendant. The plaintiff appeals and we affirm.

Durametal asked the defendant to locate a crane for purchase by Durametal. Defendant found one that looked suitable; Durametal inspected and approved it. The defendant purchased the crane and immediately resold it to Durametal. Defendant prepared documents making the sale "as is."

Durametal assigned plaintiff to operate the crane, including greasing it. Plaintiff believed the greasing of the gears could not be done properly without removing the gear cover and applying the grease while the gears were moving. While he was so greasing the gears, plaintiff's hand was drawn into them and he was injured.

Plaintiff alleged the defendant seller was liable because the crane was defectively designed in that it could not be properly greased without removing the protective gear covering and for failing to provide warnings of the danger. The trial court found for the defendant because the crane was a used piece of equipment and sold "as is."

The parties disagree about the effect of the "as is" disclaimer in the documents of sale. The issues raised include whether that disclaimer has any effect in an action of strict liability in tort, and whether, if so, it is effective to disclaim liability for a design defect as distinguished from a defect in the condition of the individual product. We do not answer these questions because we conclude that the trial court was correct in holding that a seller of used goods is not strictly liable in tort for a defect in a used crane when that defect was created by the manufacturer.

In order to determine whether the defendant seller may be held liable we are required to re-examine why we arrived at the decision that a seller "who is free from fault in the usual sense" should be held strictly liable for a defective product. Wights v. Staff Jennings, 241 Or 301, 306, 405 P2d 624 (1965).

"* * * Usually liability has been predicated on a breach of an implied warranty without explaining why the warranty was judicially implied. When the action was brought by the buyer against his immediate seller, it seemed enough that the plaintiff and defendant were parties to a contract, the warranty being born in some mysterious way out of the contractual relationship even in the absence of any promise express or implied in fact made by the seller. * * *." Wights v. Staff Jennings, supra, at 306.

Because of the impediments accompanying a contractual remedy, including the requirement of privity, we evolved the tort of strict liability. Redfield v. Mead, Johnson & Co., 266 Or 273, 285, 512 P2d 776 (1973) (specially concurring). Strict liability could be imposed upon a party with whom the plaintiff was not in privity. For this reason the manufacturer who created the defect could be sued directly. The injured party could usually obtain personal jurisdiction over the manufacturer by the use of the long-arm statutes. Because of the circumstances, there was no longer any urgent necessity to continue a cause of action against the seller who had not created the defect.

Nevertheless, courts did impose strict liability on the non-manufacturer sellers of new goods as summarized in a recent study:

> *"Over time most courts extended the rationale of these cases to both retailers and distributors. * * * Courts extended strict liability to retailers and distributors, in part, on the assumption that these groups would place pressure on the manufacturer to produce safe products. Courts also believed that retailers and distributors might be more accessible to suit than manufacturers." U.S. Dept of Commerce, Interagency Task Force on Product Liability: Final Report II-4, 5 (1976).*

As Mr. Justice Traynor said in Vandermark v. Ford Motor Company, 61 Cal 2d 256, 37 Cal Rptr 896, 391 P2d 168, 171 (1964):

> *"Retailers like manufacturers are engaged in the business of distributing goods to the public. They are an integral part of the overall producing and marketing enterprise that should bear the cost of injuries resulting from defective products. (See Greenman v. Yuba Power Products, Inc., 59 Cal 2d 57, 63, 27 Cal. Rptr. 697, 377 P2d 897). In some cases the retailer may be the only member of that enterprise reasonably available to the injured plaintiff. In other cases the retailer himself may play a substantial part in insuring the product is safe or may be in a position to exert pressure on the manufacturer to that end; the retailer's strict liability thus serves as an added incentive to safety. * * *."*

Mr. Justice Schaefer stated in Dunham v. Vaughan & Bushnell Mfg. Co., 42 Ill2d 339, 247 NE2d 401, 404 (1969): "The strict liability of a retailer arises from his integral role in the overall producing and marketing enterprise and affords an additional incentive to safety."

Moreover, if a jurisdiction has adopted the principle of strict liability on the basis of enterprise liability, the liability of the seller of either a new or used product would logically follow.

This court has never been willing to rely on enterprise liability alone as a justification for strict liability for defective products. See Markle v. Mulholland's, Inc., supra (265 Or at 265).

Instead, we have identified three justifications for the doctrine:

"* * * [C]ompensation (ability to spread the risk), satisfaction of the reasonable expectations of the purchaser or user (implied representational aspect), and over-all risk reduction (the impetus to manufacture a better product) * * *." Fulbright v. Klamath Gas Co., 271 Or 449, 460, 533 P2d 316 (1975).

While dealers in used goods are, as a class, capable like other businesses of providing for the compensation of injured parties and the allocation of the cost of injuries caused by the products they sell, we are not convinced that the other two considerations identified in Fulbright weigh sufficiently in this class of cases to justify imposing strict liability on sellers of used goods generally.

Our opinions have discussed, on other occasions, what we called in Fulbright the "implied representational aspect" of the justification for strict products liability. In Heaton v. Ford Motor Co., 248 Or 467, 435 P2d 806 (1967), both the majority and the dissent indicated that at least in some cases it was for the jury to decide what degree of safety the average consumer of a product expects. However, in Markle v. Mulholland's, Inc., supra (265 Or 259), a majority of the court agreed that the question was not solely a factual one.

We consider, then, whether the trier of fact may infer any representation as to safety from the sale of a used product.

We conclude that holding every dealer in used goods responsible regardless of fault for injuries caused by defects in his goods would not only affect the prices of used goods; it would work a significant change in the very nature of used goods markets. Those markets, generally speaking, operate on the apparent understanding that the seller, even though he is in the business of selling such goods, makes no particular representation about their quality simply by offering them for sale. If a buyer wants some assurance of quality, he typically either bargains for it in the specific transaction or seeks out a dealer who routinely offers it (by, for example, providing a guarantee, limiting his stock of goods to those of a particular quality, advertising that his used goods are specially selected, or in some other fashion). The flexibility of this kind of market appears to serve legitimate interests of buyers as well as sellers.

We are of the opinion that the sale of a used product, without more, may not be found to generate the kind of expectations of safety that the courts have held are justifiably created by the introduction of a new product into the stream of commerce.

As to the risk-reduction aspect of strict products liability, the position of the used-goods dealer is normally entirely outside the original chain of distribution of the product. As a consequence, we conclude, any risk reduction which would be accomplished by imposing strict liability on the dealer in used goods would not be significant enough to justify our taking that step. The dealer in used goods generally has no direct relationship with either manufacturers or distributors. Thus, there is no ready channel of communication by which the dealer and the manufacturer can exchange information about possible dangerous defects in particular product lines or about actual and potential liability claims.

In theory, a dealer in used goods who is held liable for injuries caused by a design defect or manufacturing flaw could obtain indemnity from the manufacturer. This possibility supports the argument that permitting strict liability claims against dealers in used goods will add to the financial incentive for manufacturers to design and build safe products. We believe, however, that the influence of this possibility as a practical factor in risk prevention is considerably diluted where used goods are involved due to such problems as statutes of limitation and the increasing difficulty as time passes of locating a still existing and solvent manufacturer.

Both of these considerations, of course, are also obstacles to injured parties attempting to recover directly from the manufacturer. However, although the provision of an adequate remedy for persons injured by defective products has been the major impetus to the development of strict product liability, it cannot provide the sole justification for imposing liability without fault on a particular class of defendants.

For the reasons we have discussed, we have concluded that the relevant policy considerations do not justify imposing strict liability for defective products on dealers in used goods, at least in the absence of some representation of quality beyond the sale itself or of a special position vis-à-vis the original manufacturer or others in the chain of original distribution. Accord: Rix v. Reeves, 23 Ariz. App 243, 532 P2d 185 (1975).

We have suggested, although we have never had occasion to rule on the question, that those who are in the business of leasing products to others may be strictly liable for injuries caused by defective products on the same basis as sellers of new products. Fulbright v. Klamath Gas Co., supra (271 Or at 455-458, 459). It has been urged that recognizing such a liability on the part of lessors while refusing to hold sellers of used goods liable would be logically inconsistent, because most leased goods are used when they reach the lessee. Hovenden v. Tenbush, supra (529 SW2d at 310). We see no such inconsistency when the focus of analysis is not on the status of the product but on that of the potential defendant. The lessor chooses the products which he offers in a significantly different way than does the typical dealer in used goods; the fact that he offers them repeatedly to different users as products he has selected may constitute a representation as to their quality; and it may well be that he has purchased them, either new or used, from a dealer who is directly related to the original distribution chain. Our rationale in the present case leaves the question of a lessor's strict liability an open one in this jurisdiction.

Affirmed.

In *Tillman*, the court held that a seller of a used crane would not be strictly liable in tort for a defect in the crane when the defect was created by the manufacturer. Retailers are an integral part of the overall production and marketing enterprise (this is called the so-called implied representational aspect of a retailer), and it is true that retailers should and do bear responsibilities and costs for defective products under certain circumstances. Under normal circumstances, a retailer may play a substantial part in insuring that a product is safe or in exerting pressure on a manufacturer to that end. However, a seller of used goods is not in such a unique position and would not bear this general responsibility. A seller of used goods, however, might be liable for negligence, for example, if a seller of used goods had actually caused a defect through or by improper preparation, maintenance, or if they knew about the existence of a defect, and/or failed to warn their buyer.

The issue of indemnity is also important in discussing the role of the retailer. Under normal circumstances where a retailer has been held liable in a product liability case without any proof of negligence on their part, the retailer is able to seek indemnity from the manufacturer. With used goods, there may be significant problems with a statute of limitations, or even with locating a solvent manufacturer, who is responsible for a defect—if one even exists!

As we may remember, UCC Section 2-314 warranty actions are applicable to the sale of used goods, but only to the extent reasonable. Don't forget, however, that warranties can be disclaimed and in most cases, used goods will be sold as is or with all faults - essentially negating all warranties. This is the usual case with the sale of a used car except in cases where fraud may have been present.

Real Estate Transactions

Property cases are especially interesting!

Kriegler v. Eichler Homes, Inc.

Court of Appeal of California, First Appellate District, Division Two
269 Cal. App. 2d 224; 74 Cal. Rptr. 749 (1969)

OPINION BY: TAYLOR, JUDGE

Respondent Kriegler filed this action for physical damage sustained as the result of the failure of a radiant heating system in a home constructed by appellants, Eichler Homes, Inc. and Joseph L. Eichler (hereafter Eichler), who cross-complained against the supplier, respondent, General Motors Corporation (hereafter General Motors) and the heating contractors, respondents, Anderson and Rother, individually and doing business as Arro Company (hereafter collectively referred to as Arro). Eichler appeals from the judgment in favor of Kriegler on the complaint and in favor of General Motors and Arro on the cross-complaint.

The questions presented are: 1) whether Eichler was liable to Kriegler on the theory of strict liability;...

The basic facts are not in dispute. In April 1957 Kriegler purchased a home in Palo Alto that had been constructed by Eichler in the last quarter of 1951 and sold to Kriegler's predecessors, the Resings, in January 1952. Eichler employed Arro as the heating contractor. Because of a copper shortage caused by the Korean war, Arro obtained terne coated steel tubing from General Motors. In the fall of 1951, Arro installed this steel tubing in the Kriegler home and guaranteed the radiant heating system in writing. Arro installed steel tubing radiant heating systems in at least 4,000 homes for Eichler.

In November 1959, as a result of the corrosion of the steel tubing, the radiant heating system of the Kriegler home failed. The emergency and final repairs required removal and storage of furniture, as well as the temporary acquisition by Kriegler and his family of other shelter.

Eichler concedes that the doctrine of strict liability in tort applies to physical harm to property (Gherna v. Ford Motor Co., 246 Cal.App.2d 639, 649 [55 Cal.Rptr. 94]) but argues that the doctrine cannot be applied to homes or builders. We do not agree. As set forth in Greenman v. Yuba Power Products, Inc., 59 Cal.2d 57 [27 Cal.Rptr. 697, 377 P.2d 897, 13 A.L.R.3d 1049], and Vandermark v. Ford Motor Co., 61 Cal.2d 256 [37 Cal.Rptr. 896, 391 P.2d 168], the strict liability doctrine applies when the plaintiff proves that he was injured while using the instrumentality in a way it was intended to be used as a result of a defect in design and manufacture of which plaintiff was not aware and which made the instrumentality unsafe for its intended use. So far, it has been applied in this state only to manufacturers, retailers and suppliers of personal property and rejected as to sales of real estate (Conolley v. Bull, 258 Cal.App.2d 183, 195 [65 Cal.Rptr. 689]). We recently pointed out in Barth v. B. F. Goodrich Tire Co., 265 Cal.App.2d 228, at pp. 252-253 [71 Cal.Rptr. 306], that the reasoning behind the doctrine applies to any case of injury resulting from the risk-creating conduct of a seller in any stage of the production and distribution of goods.

We think, in terms of today's society, there are no meaningful distinctions between Eichler's mass production and sale of homes and the mass production and sale of automobiles and that the pertinent overriding policy considerations are the same. Law, as an instrument of justice, has infinite capacity for growth to meet changing needs and mores. Nowhere is this better illustrated than in the recent developments in the field of products liability. The law should be based on current concepts of what is right and just and the judiciary should be alert to the never-ending need for keeping legal principles abreast of the times. Ancient distinctions that make no sense in today's society and that tend to discredit the law should be readily rejected as they were step by step in Greenman and Vandermark.

We find support in our view in the comments of our most eminent authority in the law of torts (see Prosser, Strict Liability to the Consumer in California, 18 Hastings L.J., 9, 20, and the exceptionally able and well-thought out opinion of the Supreme Court of New Jersey, in a case almost on all fours with the instant one (Schipper v. Levitt & Sons, Inc. (1965) 44 N.J. 70 [207 A.2d 314]). In Schipper, the purchaser of a mass-produced home sued the builder-vendor for injuries sustained by the child of a lessee. The child was injured by excessively hot water drawn from a faucet in a hot water system that had been installed without a mixing valve, a defect as latent as the incorrect positioning of the pipes in the instant case. In reversing a judgment of nonsuit, the Supreme Court held that the builder-vendor was liable to the purchaser on the basis of strict liability. In language equally applicable here, the court said: "When a vendee buys a development house from an advertised model, as in a Levitt or in a comparable project, he clearly relies on the skill of the developer and on its implied representation that the house will be erected in reasonably workmanlike manner and will be reasonably fit for habitation. He has no architect or other professional adviser of his own, he has no real competency to inspect on his own, his actual examination is, in the nature of things, largely superficial, and his opportunity for obtaining meaningful protective changes in the conveyancing documents prepared by the builder vendor is negligible. If there is improper construction such as a defective heating system or a defective ceiling, stairway and the like, the well-being of the vendee and others is seriously endangered and serious injury is foreseeable. The public interest dictates that if such injury does result from the defective construction, its cost should be borne by the responsible developer who created the danger and who is in the better economic position to bear the loss rather than by the injured party who justifiably relied on the developer's skill and implied representation."

"Buyers of mass produced development homes are not on an equal footing with the builder vendors and are no more able to protect themselves in the deed than are automobile purchasers in a position to protect themselves in the bill of sale." The court then pointed out that the imposition of strict liability principles on builders and developers would not make them insurers of the safety of all who thereafter came on the premises. In determining whether the house was defective, the test would be one of reasonableness rather than perfection.

As it cannot be disputed that Kriegler here relied on the skill of Eichler in producing a home with a heating system that was reasonably fit for its intended purpose, the trial court properly concluded that Eichler was liable to Kriegler on the basis of strict liability, and the judgment in favor of Kriegler must be affirmed on that ground alone.

Affirmed.

Kriegler was decided as a case of first impression on public policy grounds where a court is asked to interpret the purpose and effect of strict liability to determine if strict liability should be extended into an area, previously not considered. In *Kriegler*, the court held that there was essentially no difference between the mass production and sale of these homes, often called manufactured, modular, track, or development homes, and the mass production of autos. Thus, it was proper to hold the defendant liable on the basis of strict liability.

As we know, warranties under the UCC do not apply to real estate transactions. Warranties under Article 2 only apply to the sale/lease of movable and tangible goods. It is possible that other courts might apply the warranty of habitability (discussed below) to cases involving manufactured homes, and not products liability law at all.

As can be seen, the law in this area is both new and spotty; some courts will apply products liability to manufactured homes and some refuse to apply products liability concepts at all to transactions in real property, on the theory that doing so would raise questions about the types of homes that should or should not be covered. The rationale for imposing strict liability seems to have settled the law in so far as mass produced or manufactured housing - at least in those states that have adopted *Kriegler*.

Landlord-Tenant Cases

In landlord-tenant cases, a landlord is generally liabile for a dangerous condition found on a leased premises where there is a latent defect, or where there is a concealment of a known danger by the landlord, or where there is a contractual duty to repair undertaken by the landlord and the landlord failed to make the required repairs.

In *Becker v. IRM Corporation*, the judge noted that the common law had placed the risk concerning injuries sustained on leased premises on the tenant - essentially applying the doctrine of caveat emptor in these circumstances. Today, however, there is a clear trend to expand the responsibility of the landlord to provide the tenant with premises in a condition suitable for the use contemplated by the parties under the warranty of habitability. The *Becker* court said that a strict liability standard would be applied to a landlord who is engaged in the business of leasing dwellings when the defect that caused the injury to the tenant existed at the time the premises were leased to the tenant. The landlord is in a better position to bear the costs of injury due to defects in the premises rather than the tenant. This view is not universally held and the imposition of liability varies from state to state. Most states would apply a negligence standard rather than one in strict liability and would consider the issue under traditional property law, rather than products liability.

Even in states that follow *Becker*, decisions relate only to the initial lessor/landlord and hold that a subsequent purchaser of property who has not installed, altered or created the condition and who does not have actual or constructive knowledge of any defect should not be held to a strict liability standard. Liability for negligence under a reasonable landlord standard would apply.

It is safe to say that most jurisdictions apply traditional landlord-tenant law to defects in leased premises and not products liability at all.

Services

Courts have been reluctant to extend the definition of a product beyond the article manufactured, supplied, or sold and not to the process (service) under which it is supplied.

There are two types of service transactions: pure services and hybrid transactions that involve both products and services. Courts will generally not apply products liability at all to pure personal services, relying instead a negligence standard. A pure service transaction where products liability would not be applied may best be described as the negligent installation of a non-defective product.

In a mixed or hybrid transaction, it is clear that the product itself must be defective. For example, a New Jersey court held a beauty shop operator strictly liable when a defective permanent wave lotion was applied to a patron's hair.

Other courts disagree and have held that if a service component is involved at all, strict liability is not appropriate. For example, the plaintiff was injured when a defective needle, being used by a dentist, broke off in the patient's gum. The court assessed liability under a negligence standard.

In the case of a professional who renders services, where courts require proof of negligence, the standard of reasonableness will be that of a professional under similar circumstances. In practical terms, this standard of due or reasonable care will be higher than that of the ordinary, reasonable man because of the training required of a physician, lawyer, or some other professional.

QUESTIONS

1. Ryder Truck Rental Inc., the defendant, owns and rents commercial trucks. Defendant leased truck to a third party. During its use, the brake system failed and the vehicle collided with plaintiff, Martin.

   a. Does the doctrine of strict liability apply in this case?

   b. Is Ryder Truck Rental Inc. liable? Under what theory?

2. Kosters, the plaintiff, was at the grocery store. She was walking with a carton of 7UP bottles; when one fell out and exploded. A shard of glass struck her eye and she was blinded. Plaintiff brought suit against 7UP, the defendant.

   a. Does the doctrine of strict liability apply to the franchiser in this case?

   b. Is 7UP liable?

3. Cardozo, the plaintiff, purchased a cook book from defendant retail book dealer, True. While preparing a recipe, plaintiff, ate one of the ingredients. Shortly after, the plaintiff became severely ill and was hospitalized. The plaintiff claimed that the cookbook lacked a warning about the ingredient being poisonous if not cooked.

   a. Did the defendant impliedly warrant the book as reasonably fit for use?

   b. Is negligence applicable?

   c. Does strict liability apply to the publication in this case?

   d. Is True liable?

4. Vance Equipment Company, the defendant, is a used equipment dealer that sold a 24 year old crane to the plaintiff's, Tillman's, employer, Durametal. Durametal requested a crane that looked suitable and the defendant purchased one to resell to Durametal. Consequently, the defendant prepared documents, making the sale as is. Durmetal assigned the plaintiff to operate the crane, which involved greasing. To properly do so, the plaintiff had to remove its protective gear covering. While applying grease, the plaintiff's hand was drawn into the gears and he was injured. As a result, the plaintiff brought suit against the used equipment dealer.

   a. Was the product defectively designed?

   b. Does the doctrine of strict liability apply in this case?

c. Was there an implied warranty?

d. Is Vance Equipment Company liable? Is Durametal liable?

5. Kriegler, the plaintiff, purchased a home from the defendant, Eichler Homes Inc. Eichler employed Arro as a heating contractor. Due to a copper shortage, Arro purchased steel coated tubing from GM for the heating system in the Kriegler home, which he was guaranteed in writing. However, corrosion of the tubing caused the radiant heating system to fail. Kriegler filed for action against Eichler Homes Inc.

    a. Was the product defectively designed?

    b. Does the doctrine of strict liability apply to physical harm to property in real estate transactions?

    c. Is Eichler liable? Is GM liable? Is Arro liable?

    d. How did *Becker v. IRM* shape strict liability, specifically in relation to land-lord tenant cases? Has it been followed by a majority of jurisdictions?

Chapter Twelve

Parties to the Transaction

The tendency to expand the scope of both plaintiffs and defendants is a notable characteristic of the modern law of products liability.

Potential Plaintiffs

Buyers, users, consumers, and/or any other foreseeable parties, including bystanders, are all potential plaintiffs in a products liability case based on individual state law.

Potential Defendants

Generally, all parties in the vertical chain of distribution of a product are potential defendants. California provides the most extensive list of potential defendants which includes, but is not limited to, parties involved in designing, manufacturing, purchasing, producing, constructing, assembling, preparing, testing, inspecting, maintaining, repairing, installing, endorsing, selling, bailing, licensing, or otherwise marketing a product.

The manufacturer or final assembler of a product of a defective product is the most likely party to be held liable, since strict liability permits an injured party to sue a manufacturer directly, in the absence of the former requirement of privity. This is reflected in the following statement: "A manufacturer is strictly liable in tort when an article he places on the market, knowing it is to be used without inspection for defects, proves to have a defect that causes injury to a human being." (*Greenman*). In some cases, a retailer who sells products under his own name (retailer-brand name products) may also be liable to an injured user, but would be able to seek indemnity from the actual manufacturer. For example, giant retailers like Sears or Target or Walmart routinely sell products they themselves do not manufacture under their own brand name. This is sometimes referred to as brand-masking marketing.

What, however, would happen if the actual manufacturer is foreign-based, or not subject to legal process, or has filed for bankruptcy protection? If the plaintiff is unable to assert jurisdiction over a foreign defendant, the plaintiff would not be able to bring a lawsuit against the foreign defendant. If a company files for bankruptcy protection, any judgment creditors, or parties that have won a lawsuit, may not be paid because the judgment may have been discharged in the bankruptcy proceedings and the defendant may be judgment proof.

In most cases, the nature of the transaction involved will dictate who might be a potential defendant in a products liability suit.

Retailers, Wholesalers, And Distributors

Recall that under Comment f of Section 402A (strict liability), liability may be imposed on any party "engaged in the business of selling a product for use or consumption." i.e., manufacturer, wholesaler, retailer, or distributor, or even the operator of a restaurant.

In a negligence case, it may be difficult to maintain liability against a non-manufacturer seller, since such a party is normally a mere conduit with no affirmative duty to inspect a product or test a product for defects. This may be seen as the essence of the privity rule that insulated manufacturers from liability (caveat emptor) and held the non-negligent retailer harmless from liability. However, if a retailer does undertake to inspect, test, or assemble a product, it may be liable for its own conduct for failing to do so with reasonable care.

Case Study: Vandermark v. Ford Motor Company

Procedural Posture

Plaintiffs, a buyer and his sister, brought an action alleging breach of warranty and negligence against defendants, an automobile manufacturer and an automobile dealer, for personal injuries they sustained in an accident allegedly caused by defects in a new car. Plaintiffs appealed from judgments of the Superior Court of Los Angeles County (California).

Overview

Six weeks after purchasing his new car from the dealer, the buyer lost control of the car and collided with a light post. Plaintiffs claimed that there was a sudden failure of the car's braking system. The manufacturer had delegated the final steps of its process to the dealer and relied on the dealer to make the final inspections and adjustments necessary for the car to be ready for use. The trial court granted the manufacturer's motion for nonsuit, directed a verdict in favor of the dealer on the warranty action, and entered judgment on a jury verdict for the dealer on the negligence action. On appeal, the court concluded that it was error to grant nonsuit on issues of strict liability and negligence against the manufacturer and to direct a verdict for the dealer. The court held that the manufacturer could be strictly liable in tort and could not delegate its duty to deliver cars free from defects. The court extended the doctrine of strict liability to the dealer because it was in the business of selling cars, one of which proved to be defective. Although plaintiffs had proceeded under a warranty theory, they introduced substantial evidence to establish strict liability in tort.

Outcome

The court reversed the nonsuit granted in favor of the manufacturer. The court also reversed the judgment for the dealer on the warranty causes of action but affirmed the judgment in favor of the dealer on the negligence causes of action.

Vandermark, involving a suit against both Ford Motor, the manufacturer, and Maywood Bell Ford, the retailer, held that the retailer, "engaged in the business of distributing goods to the public," may be in a very good position to "exert pressure on the manufacturer" to assure safety and the imposition of liability in such circumstances serves as an "added incentive" to safety.

There are, however, some interesting exceptions or minority views, grounded in state law, where a retailer has been held not to be negligent:

- There is a widely held exception where a product is sold by a retailer in a sealed container;
- Where the basis of liability is for a latent defect that was not discoverable by reasonable inspection by the retailer;
- Some states have enacted specific statutes that exempt retailers from strict liability (Colorado, Kentucky, or Tennessee)—but not for their own negligence.

Because of the unique manner in which an express warranty or the warranty of fitness is created, an express warranty or implied warranty of fitness would only be applicable to those parties whose words or conduct created them. In contrast, the warranty of merchantability, in which there is an implied promise that goods are fair, average quality or are fit for their ordinary purposes is applicable to all sellers in the chain of distribution, but only if such parties are merchants. As you may recall, a merchant is defined as one who deals in goods of that kind on a regular basis or someone who holds themselves out as having special knowledge about such goods - generally referred to as an expert. Thus, the warranty of merchantability does not apply to the casual or occasional seller.

Remember that a retailer or wholesaler who is held liable under a theory of strict liability and who himself has not been negligent may be termed as an innocent seller. In that sense, the innocent seller would be entitled to seek indemnity from the manufacturer or some other party (if that party can be found and is available!).

Thiele v. Chick

Court Of Appeals Of Texas, First District, Houston, 631 S.W.2d 526 (1982)

OPINION BY: BASS, JUDGE

The following evidence was received:

1) The deposition of Officer C. L. Taylor, a traffic reconstruction expert who investigated the scene of the accident, was admitted. There was no eyewitness to the accident; the officer spoke with a man who had been driving along side Mr. Chick's truck just prior to the accident and who said that both trucks were doing about 30 mph. This man had pulled into a nearby service station as Chick's truck proceeded around the curve and overturned; when he pulled into the station he heard a loud pop and a rattling sound.

2) The deposition of Dr. Alvin D. Thomas, Jr., Technical Director of the Failure Analysis Laboratory for the Radian Corporation, a metallurgical engineer, who was asked to perform tests upon a load boomer by Dr. Thomas S. Mackey. He filed a report with Dr. Mackey.

3) The deposition of Dr. Thomas S. Mackey, the President of Key Metals and Minerals Engineering Corporation, a consulting engineering company, who is a metallurgical engineer. Mackey identified a load boomer he received from the plaintiff's attorney; one unit was intact, and the other had a separated hook.

After reading the Radian Corporation report, Dr. Mackey concluded that the load binder had both design and manufacturing defects in the socket and in the ball. The ball was "out of round" and pulled out of the socket. The tolerances that were measured by Radian Corporation were such that the original design made it difficult to produce a uniform, concerted load binder that would not be out of round in the socket and would not be out of round in the ball. In his opinion, the defect in the ball and socket existed before the accident. He testified that this boomer was bound to fail and that the faulty manufacture was a producing cause of the accident.

4) The testimony of Mr. E. E. Bollinger, Chief Dispatcher and Terminal Manager for

Woodard Trucking. He testified that Mr. Chick's truck should have weighed between 26,000 and 27,000 pounds and that his load was between 40,000 and 42,000 pounds. The policy of Woodard was to have at least four chains on this type of load, and he felt that the other chains were lost at the scene of the accident.

5) The testimony of Dr. Rex McLellan, Professor of Material Science at Rice University, with a degree in metallurgy. He testified that he performed metal structure tests of the boomer that failed and of a new boomer supplied by Thiele. McLellan concluded that the metal was not fatigued and that it had been torn by mechanical overloading. The boomer had a working load limit of about 8,000 pounds and a proof load limit of about 16,400 pounds. He found no great malformation in the ball.

6) The testimony of Mr. Joe Bob Duncan, a fellow trucker who observed Mr. Chick's load on the day of the accident, testified that he saw four chains on the truck.

7) The testimony of Mr. George Greene, Jr., a consulting mechanical engineer. He testified that he ran microscopic tests on the boomer and relied upon a previous metallurgical report for some of his findings; that he found no metallurgical problems with the steel; that he felt it was important for the manufacturer to notify consumers as to the load capacity of the boomer; that this was a defective design for a boomer; and that a boomer should last longer than this one, which was manufactured sometime between 1968 and 1972, did.

A letter written by Mr. Greene to Mr. Greg Laughlin, attorney, was admitted. The letter stated that:

> *"failure of the ball socket ... is imminent with usage. The design is such that no warning is apparent of an impending failure. The subject load binder is defectively designed and unreasonably dangerous to the user while being utilized in its intended manner."*

8) The deposition of Douglas Muster, Professor of Engineering at the University of Houston, was suppressed as to the appellant, Thiele, and applied only to Kulkoni. Muster testified that the boomer failed as a result of its faulty design and production.

9) The testimony of Ernest Craig, general manager for Triangle Transportation Company, was admitted. He was a truck driver in 1973 and for a total of eight years. He testified that an experienced truck driver can earn between twenty and thirty-five thousand dollars income per year.

10) The testimony of Mrs. Ethel Chick, widow of the deceased, confirmed that the deceased's salary was $ 200 per week and that he was in excellent health. "He was family-oriented. He liked ... to get together to go places, do things, go visit family, take the kids on trips. He hoped to buy a home for the family and to send the children to college." The son has been affected psychologically by his father's death. His school grades have deteriorated, and his mind wanders.

11) Freddie Chick, Jr., the deceased's son, age 11, testified that he remembers all the nice things he used to do with his dad.

* * * The jury found that the boomer was not defectively designed but that it was defectively manufactured by Thiele. It found that the defective manufacture was "a producing cause of the wreck" in which Fred Chick was killed. It did not find that the boomer was defective because of failure of the manufacturer to warn the user of the load capacity of the boomer. It found that two load binders were used to secure Mr. Chick's load, but that the use of two load binders was not a producing cause of his accident. The jury awarded $ 200,000 to Fred K. Chick, Jr. and $ 225,000 to Anna Ruth Chick.

Appellant, Thiele, filed a motion for judgment "non obstante veredicto" and, alternatively, a motion to disregard special issues and for additional findings. Thiele's bases for these motions were that the evidence was insufficient to sustain the verdict and that the jury's findings were incomplete. The appellee filed a motion for judgment on the verdict.

* * * The appellant, Thiele, argues that the total shifting of liability from the distributor to the manufacturer of a product is no longer the law.

The right of contribution among joint tortfeasors who have been held strictly liable to an injured consumer is recognized in Texas:

Any person against whom, with one or more others, a judgment is rendered in any suit on an action arising out of, or based on tort, except in causes wherein the right of contribution or of indemnity, or of recovery, over, by and between the defendants is given by statute or exists under the common law, shall, upon payment of said judgment, have a right of action against his co-defendant or co-defendants and may recover from each a sum equal to the proportion of all of the defendants named in said judgment rendered to the whole amount of said judgment ... Tex.Rev.Civ.Stat.Ann. art. 2212 (Vernon 1971).

The Texas Supreme Court devised a test to determine when one tortfeasor is entitled to indemnity from another under the provisions of art. 2212:

"In order to determine whether the loss should be shifted from one tortfeasor to another the proper approach is to consider the one seeking indemnity as though he were a plaintiff suing the other in tort, and then determine whether such a one as plaintiff, though guilty of a wrong against a third person, is nevertheless entitled to recover against his co-tortfeasor." Austin Road Co. v. Pope, 147 Tex. 430, 216 S.W.2d 563, 565 (1949). When the courts have found, even in strict liability cases, that one tortfeasor has violated a duty to another tortfeasor they have indemnified the injured tortfeasor...."

In Champion Mobile Homes v. Rasmussen, 553 S.W.2d 237 (Tex.Civ.App.-Tyler 1977, writ ref'd n. r. e.), the court held that the distributor of a dangerously defective mobile home had a right to indemnification from the manufacturer of the homes. The distributor had been held strictly liable for the plaintiff's injuries in the defective home. The problem was a latent defect in the electrical wiring system of which the distributor had been unaware. The distributor had done nothing wrong but to distribute the product. The court held that "the vendor owes no duty to the manufacturer to inspect for latent defects," and it awarded indemnification to the distributor.

Under the present law, Kulkoni, Inc. has a right to indemnity from August Thiele. The jury found that the producing cause of Mr. Chick's death was that the boomer had been defectively manufactured. This was a latent defect. There was no evidence that Kulkoni altered this product before distributing it. Although Kulkoni has been held strictly liable under § 402A as the "seller," it has not been proven that Kulkoni violated any duty toward August Thiele so as to preclude indemnification.

(T)he public has the right to and does expect, in the case of products which it needs and for which it is forced to rely upon the seller, that reputable sellers will stand behind their goods.

In B&B Auto Supply v. Central Freight Lines, Inc., 603 S.W.2d 814, 816-17 (Tex. 1980), the Supreme Court held that in negligence cases in which indemnity is governed by Tex.Rev.Civ.Stat.Ann. art. 2212a, there is no longer any reason to require one tortfeasor to indemnify another tortfeasor when both have been found negligent. But the court specifically stated that its holding:

"is not intended to bar indemnity in cases in which there is a contractual basis for indemnity or cases in which one party's liability is purely vicarious. We express no opinion whether this holding would extend to a strict liability case or a case involving a combination of negligent and strictly liable tortfeasors."

* * * The B&B Auto Supply opinion and the County of Nueces opinion are controlling in the present case. There were other considerations in the Lubbock Manufacturing opinion, including the fact that the parties had signed Mary Carter agreements, that distinguish it from the present case. Furthermore, there was more evidence in Lubbock to prove that International Harvester was "directly" liable to the plaintiffs than there was evidence in the present case to prove that Kulkoni was directly liable to the appellees. The Supreme Court has not specifically abolished the old indemnification rule in strict liability cases.

Appellant's points of error are denied, and the judgment of the trial court is affirmed in all respects.

In an indemnity case, courts will first look to the existence of a duty of reasonable care under a negligence standard. If a party who has been found liable under strict liability has not violated any duty, that is, the party is not negligent, that party can normally seek indemnity. Recall that indemnity is not the same as contribution, which is the actual assignment of a pro-rata share based upon a direct finding of fault. Contribution is accomplished by a process called impleading or through the filing of an independent action, where permissible, and where not barred by res judicata.

Used Product Sellers, Occasional Sellers, Component Part Manufacturers

As a matter of public policy, most courts will simply not hold a seller of used goods liable where the defect arose while the product was in the possession of or under the control of a previous owner, or the defect is due to a flaw in the manufacture or design of the product. However, in the event that a court might hold a used product seller strictly liable because of a defect in the product itself, the used product seller can also seek indemnity from the manufacturer. Remember, however, the existence of the statute of limitations or the unavailability of the original manufacturer make indemnity impossible or impractical!

The warranty of merchantability may be applicable to the sale of used goods, but only to the extent reasonable under the circumstances. Does this sound like a variation of the consumer expectations test? Who would decide the nature or extent of any warranty?

In the case of used goods, one who undertakes to rebuild a used product can be held liable if that work results in a defectively built used product. The theory of strict liability might be available in such cases because in effect, the rebuilt product may be considered as an entirely new product or perhaps was advertised as "good as new." Of course, if repairs are done improperly, the party can also be held liable for any negligence.

It is possible that a component manufacturer may be held liable for defects in a component part that makes its way into a final assembled product. However, it is more likely that the final assembler will be held liable for the defect and it would be up to that party to implead the component part manufacturer for contribution or perhaps full indemnity.

Successor Corporations

Consider the following question: Can a successor corporation (SC) that purchases the business or assets of another corporation be held strictly liable for injuries caused after the purchase as a result of a defective product sold by the prior corporation (PC) before the purchase?

Under the common law, liability could be imposed if:

- The successor corporation expressly or impliedly assumed the obligations and liabilities of the original corporation;
- There was a de facto merger of the two entities;

- There was a mere continuation of the original enterprise, despite a technical change in the business form;
- There was a fraudulent effort or sham to avoid the liabilities of the predecessor.

These principles are found in the case of *Ray v. Alad Corporation.*

Today, there are two main theories providing for liability in the area of products liability in cases of successor corporations:

The first theory is based on the "continuity of the enterprise" - also called the mere continuation rule of *Turner v. Bituminous Casting Co.*). There are four aspects of this rule:

- There is a continuity of management, personnel, physical location, assets and general business of the predecessor;
- There has been a dissolution of the predecessor and only one entity remains;
- There has been an assumption by the successor of the liabilities of the predecessor necessary for continuation of normal business operations;
- "Holding out" itself to the public by the successor as the effective continuation of the predecessor.

The second is the "product line" exception, where the successor corporation acquires all or substantially all of the manufacturing assets of the predecessor, or undertakes essentially the same manufacturing operations. It is fair to hold the successor corporation liable under these circumstances.

The product line exception, recognized in six states (California, Mississippi, New Jersey, New Mexico, Pennsylvania, and Washington), and the mere continuation rule of *Turner v. Bituminous Casting*, are based on a policy decision stemming from the virtual destruction of remedies against the predecessor corporation, and the ability of the successor corporation itself to spread the risks through such traditional methods as pricing or the purchase of insurance. There is also the fact that in many business transactions, a successor corporation could withhold some of the purchase price (escrow) or require an indemnity clause from the predecessor. Of course, a plaintiff could still sue the predecessor if the predecessor were available! This may be difficult if the prior corporation had been liquidated through a Chapter 7 bankruptcy proceeding, or simply has ceased to exist in any practical sense.

Recognize that these theories represent minority views. The majority view, which refuses to find liability for a corporation that purchases another corporation's assets under these theories—absent one of the four exceptions noted above—may be found in *Semenetz v. Sherling & Walden* (2006).

Lessors, Bailors, Licensors, Franchisers

In cases where a sale of a product is not involved, the preferred theory of liability is that of negligence. For example, in the case of a bailment for the benefit of the bailee - where the bailor is transferring possession, but not ownership of the goods for a fee - the bailor who did not manufacture the goods may not be held strictly liable for a manufacturing or a design defect in the goods but may be judged under a negligence standard. However, in some bailment arrangements, where the defect occurs at the beginning of the lease term and the bailor is the manufacturer, courts will impose strict liability but only if the defendant is in the business of leasing products of that type.

As we learned in the "7-Up case," in order to hold a franchiser liable, the franchiser must have been intimately involved in the design of the product or must have approved or retained the right to approve any product design. This is often the case in franchising, because the franchiser is required to maintain quality control over the franchise operation and over products distributed through the franchise operation.

Employers

In cases where an employee has been injured in the use of a product on the job, and where the injury arose out of and in the course of employment, many states have determined that their workers' compensation programs are the exclusive remedies—and not a products liability suit at all. In workers' compensation cases, damages are scheduled, and they are typically much less than those that are recoverable in products liability cases. In many cases, these damages are compensable through state insurance programs in which employers (and often employees) must participate. A number of states do permit an independent tort action (outside workers compensation) where the employer engages in intentional misconduct, such as the failure to warn of a danger known to the employer about which the employee did not know. (*Johns-Manville*, sometimes termed the Asbestos Case.)

There is also a limited exception or minority doctrine termed the dual capacity doctrine, where the employer is treated the same as a product supplier for the purpose of dangerous machinery or other products furnished by the employer for employee use in the workplace; for example, where the employer furnished the same product for the workplace as it sold to the public (a water cooler or coffee pot, manufactured by a defendant, also available to employees on the job). This permits an employee to sue an employer in an independent tort action as opposed to seeking redress under workers compensation laws in his capacity other than the employer. The dual capacity exception has not gained wide support and is a rather murky area of the law.

Providers of Services

Since strict liability will not generally lie in cases of the provision of pure services, a negligence standard will be applied to determine liability.

There are some interesting sub-topics:

Representational Conduct

Product certifiers and testers can be held liable for negligent conduct in the certification or testing process. One consideration for not applying a standard of strict liability would be the immense exposure of such parties because of their routine involvement with hundreds and perhaps thousands of different products. Similarly, a trade association that establishes safety guidelines or safety standards for their members may be held liable if it is negligent in creating these industry guidelines or standards.

Recall that in franchising cases, a licensor (franchiser) was held strictly liable for defective products marketed by its licensees and franchisees that followed the specs provided by the franchisor/licensor and that contained the Trade Mark or Logo of the franchisor/licensor.

Cases involving professional services (attorneys, accountants, financial planners) are most always decided under a theory of negligence, but under an enhanced "reasonable professional standard."

Builder-Vendors

In a few states (New Jersey, California, Florida) courts imposed strict liability on builder/ vendors for defective mass-produced or manufactured ("cookie cutter" or Levitt) homes. However, normally, the standard would be that of negligence.

Lessors may be required to repair conditions in leased premises where courts recognize the implied warranty of habitability or where state statutes require certain repairs. State "repair and deduct" statutes may also be applicable in certain circumstances.

In addition, occupiers (lessees) may owe an independent duty, judged by a negligence standard, to parties termed business invitees. There are a few cases in which the lessee has been held strictly liable to an invitee for activities termed abnormally or inherently dangerous such as blasting, or where chemicals are stored on the premises, or for other very dangerous activities. These, however, are not product cases.

There is another area of tort law - social host liability - where a social host - normally a home owner or someone who is hosting guests on their premises - may be held liable to a third party or even to the guest him/herself for injuries caused or sustained when a guest who had just a bit too much to drink sustains an injury - but that is the topic for another law course!

Questions

1. Plaintiff, Vandermark, bought a new car from a dealer. While driving, he collided with a light post due to a failure in the car's brake system. Furthermore, the manufacturer had delegated final inspections and adjustments to the car dealer. Plaintiff brought suit.

    a. Is the doctrine of negligence applicable?

    b. Was there a breach of warranty?

    c. Is the dealer liable? Is the manufacturer liable?

2. Mr. Chick, a truck driver, was transporting a load when his truck turned over. He died in the ensuing accident. Several witnesses claimed that the cause of the accident was directly linked to a faulty load boomer, supplied by Thiele.

    a. If the load boomer was, in fact, defectively designed, should the liability rest solely on the distributor? Or should the manufacturer be held liable as well?

    b. Does the doctrine of indemnity apply?

    c. Is Thiele liable?

3. How did *Champion Mobile Homes v. Rasmussen* shape the development of indemnification?

4. Plaintiff, Ray, fell from a defective ladder and sustained injuries. Consequently, he brought action against Alad Corporation (II). However, Alad Corporation (II) did not manufacture or sell the ladder. In fact, Alad Corporation (II) was simply the successor of the now dissolved Alad Corporation (I). Moreover, Alad Corporation (II) chose to manufacture the same line of ladders, under the old name, using the same equipment, designs, personnel, and soliciting Alad Corporation (I)'s customers.

    a. Is the successor corporation liable?

5. Find a modern successor corporation that faced liability for a defective product sold by the prior corporation due to the following:

    a. Continuity of the Enterprise

    b. The Product Line Exception

6. How did the actions of the Johns-Manville Corporation contribute to the development of liability toward employers?

Chapter Thirteen

THEORIES OF DAMAGES

What damages might an injured plaintiff expect to recover in a products liability case?

Economic loss or economic damages are termed as compensatory damages. They include a loss in value, loss of use, cost of replacement or repair of the product itself, or loss of profits under certain circumstances for the unavailability of the product. These damages are ascertainable because the losses can be traced through documentary proof and expert testimony. Compensatory damages result as an immediate, direct, and proximate result from the tortious conduct.

In general, damages must be foreseeable and must not be remote; that is, they must flow naturally and directly from the breach and must be of the type and character that will ordinarily result from a defective product. A plaintiff is entitled to recover all foreseeable damages in a cause of action in tort - either negligence or strict liability.

Consequential damages for lost profits in a contract (warranty) action are damages which do not flow directly and immediately from the act of the plaintiff, but resulting from the act. In the case where a plaintiff is seeking damages for lost profits, courts require that the damages be "within the clear contemplation of the parties at the time the contract was created." The English case of *Hadley v. Baxendale* (the crank shaft case) exemplifies this important point.

In the case of personal injury as a result of defective consumer goods (goods purchased for personal, family or household use), UCC Section 2-719 explicitly states that an attempt to limit or exclude such damages would be unconscionable - thus not enforced by a court. In the case of producer goods, however, where the loss is commercial, a limitation or exclusion of consequential damages is not unconscionable and may be compensable through business insurance, or in the case of an injury to an employee or worker, through the workers' compensation system.

The term pecuniary loss refers to actual, provable damages for personal injury or harm or damage to property.

Punitive or exemplary damages are damages awarded to a plaintiff over and above provable damages, where a wrong done to the plaintiff was aggravated by circumstances of violence, oppression, or malice; as a result of fraud (proving scienter); through wanton or wicked conduct on the part of the defendant; to punish a defendant for evil behavior; or to make an example of the defendant.

In general, punitive damages are not available in contract actions, except in cases of fraud, but may be available in certain tort actions, where the conduct of the defendant was deemed to be outrageous, reprehensible and intentional, or showing flagrant indifference to public safety.

Acosta v. Honda Motor Company, Ltd.

United States Court of Appeals for the Third Circuit, 717 F.2d 828 (1983)

While riding his used motorcycle, plaintiff was injured when the rear wheel collapsed from a 35 mile per hour impact with a ditch four inches deep. Plaintiff filed a strict products liability action against defendants, the motorcycle manufacturer, rear wheel manufacturer and assembler, and distributor. After the jury found defendants liable for compensatory and punitive damages, the district court only granted defendant distributor's motion for judgment notwithstanding the verdict (JNOV) with respect to punitive damages. Both sides appealed. Despite noting that Virgin Islands law permitted the award of punitive damages against defendants who were found strictly liable for having marketed defective products, the court reversed the denial of defendants' JNOV motion as to punitive damages by holding that the evidence was not clear and convincing that defendants acted with outrageous or reckless disregard for the safety of users. In short, defendants neither knew nor had reason to know that the rear wheel of plaintiff's motorcycle was defective in design or manufacture. As such, the court vacated and remanded the award of attorney fees.

OPINION BY: BECKER, CIRCUIT JUDGE

*** III.

Defendants' principal contention on appeal is that the evidence was insufficient as a matter of law to sustain the award of punitive damages and that the district court erred in submitting the issue to the jury in the first place. Before turning to that question, however, we first must address their argument that punitive damages are unavailable in this case because, no matter what the evidence, punitive damages are fundamentally inconsistent with a regime of strict products liability in general, and with section 402A in particular.

A. The Availability of Punitive Damages in the Strict Liability Context

Although this question is one of first impression in the Virgin Islands, we do not lack guidance. Many courts, both state and federal, have already considered the issue, and the overwhelming majority have concluded that there is no theoretical problem in a jury finding that a defendant is liable because of the defectiveness of a product and then judging the conduct of the defendant in order to determine whether punitive damages should be awarded on the basis of 'outrageous conduct' in light of the injuries sustained by the plaintiff. Hoffman v. Sterling Drug, Inc., 485 F.2d 132, 144-47 (3d Cir. 1973); Thomas v. American Cystoscope Makers, Inc., 414 F. Supp. 255, 263-267 (E.D. Pa. 1976). Punitive damage awards provide a useful function in punishing the wrongdoer and deterring product suppliers from making economic decisions not to remedy the defects of the product.

Neal v. Carey Canadian Mines, Ltd., 548 F. Supp. 357 (E.D. Pa. 1982) (Bechtle, J.) (construing Pennsylvania law).

* * * As long as a plaintiff can carry his burden of proof under section 402A, there is no inconsistency in his also being permitted to offer proof regarding the nature of the manufacturer's conduct.

The Restatement (Second) of Torts does include a generally applicable provision regarding punitive damages. Section 908(2) declares:

Punitive damages may be awarded for conduct that is outrageous, because of the defendant's evil motive or his reckless indifference to the rights of others. In assessing punitive damages, the trier of fact can properly consider the character of the defendant's act, the nature and extent of the harm to the plaintiff that the defendant caused or intended to cause and the wealth of the defendant.

Nowhere in that section or the comments did the drafters suggest that these principles should not apply to strict products liability, and we concur with the considered opinion of the Court of Appeals for the Fifth Circuit that "punishment and deterrence, the basis for punitive damages . . ., are no less appropriate with respect to a product manufacturer who knowingly ignores safety deficiencies in its product that may endanger human life" than in other cases in which "the defendant's conduct shows wantonness or recklessness or reckless indifference to the rights of others." Dorsey v. Honda Motor Co., 655 F.2d 650, 658 (5th Cir. 1981) (construing Florida law), opinion modified on rehearing, 670 F.2d 21 (5th Cir.), cert. denied, 459 U.S. 880, 103 S. Ct. 177, 74 L. Ed. 2d 145 (1982).

Some courts and commentators, however, have suggested that the policies underlying punitive damages are so incompatible with those animating strict products liability that punitive damage awards should not be permitted against defendants found liable under 402A. These arguments essentially break down into three groups: contentions that punitive damages will upset the delicate balance struck in the creation of a strict products liability regime, assertions that the goals of punitive damages are unachievable in the strict products liability context, and arguments that the imposition of punitive damages in 402A cases will have extremely undesirable economic and social consequences. We disagree that these considerations warrant our precluding the award of punitive damages, and we discuss each in turn.

B. Standard of Proof

Although we reject each of the various arguments against awarding punitive damages in the strict liability context, we agree with Judge Friendly's observation in Roginsky, supra, that "the consequences of imposing punitive damages in a case like the present are so serious" that "particularly careful scrutiny" is warranted. 378 F.2d at 852 (denying petition for rehearing); cf. Comment, Criminal Safeguards and the Punitive Damages Defendant, 34 U. Chi. L. Rev. 408, 417 (1967) ("If one accepts the proposition that the consequences of punitive damages can be 'momentous and serious,' then justice requires increasing the burden of persuasion of the plaintiff in a punitive damages action.") We therefore hold under Virgin Islands law that a plaintiff seeking punitive damages, at least in an action in which liability is predicated on section 402A, must prove the requisite "outrageous" conduct by clear and convincing proof. Accord Wangen v. Ford Motor Co., supra; Model Uniform Product Liability Act § 120(A), 44 Fed. Reg. 62748 (1979).

C. The Standard Applied

Applying the "clear and convincing" standard to the facts of this case, we conclude that the district court should have entered judgments n.o.v. on the punitive damages issue for all three defendants, and not just for American Honda. We recognize, of course, that we are bound to "view all the evidence and the inferences reasonably drawn therefrom" in plaintiff's favor, see Chuy v. Philadelphia Eagles Football Club, 595 F.2d 1265, 1273 (3d Cir. 1979) (in banc), and that "our limited function at this point is to ascertain from a review of the record whether there is sufficient evidence to sustain the verdict of the jury on this issue," id. It nevertheless appears to us that the record "is critically deficient of that minimum quantum of evidence from which a jury might reasonably afford relief." Denneny v. Siegel, 407 F.2d 433, 439 (3d Cir. 1969).

> Plaintiff's evidence allegedly supporting his claim for punitive damages essentially consisted of the following:
>
> The rear wheel of his motorcycle collapsed from a thirty-five mile per hour impact with a ditch four inches deep;
>
> The particular wheel of plaintiff's motorcycle suffered from an inherent lack of strength as evidenced by the fact that it weighed sixteen percent less than several other randomly sampled rear wheels of motorcycles of the same model;
>
> The owner's manual represented the CB750 as a high-speed touring motorcycle

> but provided no warning that the rear wheel might collapse upon the type of impact that occurred in this case;
>
> Although the owner's manual instructed users to set and maintain the tension of the motorcycle's shock absorbers and wheel spokes, the manual did not warn that the failure to do so might result in the collapse of the wheel;
>
> Defendants merely spot-checked rear wheels during the assembly process and did not crush test or weigh each wheel;
>
> Plaintiff's expert witness testified that the above evidence constituted defective manufacture and a failure adequately to inspect or to warn; and
>
> Plaintiff's expert concluded that defendant's conduct manifested a "colossal disregard for the safety of the users of the motor vehicle," App. II at 125-26.

Plaintiff contends that the jury was entitled to infer from this evidence that defendants recklessly disregarded his rights and safety as a user of the motorcycle. We cannot agree. As we have suggested above, section 908 of the Restatement declares that reckless or outrageous conduct on the part of the defendant is the touchstone of punitive damages. See Berroyer v. Hertz, 672 F.2d 334 (3d Cir. 1982); Chuy v. Philadelphia Eagles, supra, 595 F.2d at 1277. Although section 908 does not elaborate on the kind of conduct for which punitive damages are appropriate, comment b refers to section 500, which in turn provides:

The actor's conduct is in reckless disregard of the safety of another if he does an act or intentionally fails to do an act which it is his duty to the other to do, knowing or having reason to know of facts which would lead a reasonable man to realize, not only that his conduct creates an unreasonable risk of physical harm to another but also that such risk is substantially greater than that which is necessary to make his conduct negligent.

The commentary accompanying section 500 explains further:

Recklessness may consist of either of two different types of conduct. In one the actor knows, or has reason to know . . . of facts which create a high degree of risk of physical harm to another, and deliberately proceeds to act, or to fail to act, in conscious disregard of, or indifference to, that risk. In the other the actor has such knowledge, or reason to know, of the facts, but does not realize or appreciate the high degree of risk involved, although a reasonable man in his position would do so. An objective standard is applied to him and he is held to the realization of the aggravated risk which a reasonable man in his place would have, although he does not himself have it.

* * *

For either type of conduct, to be reckless it must be unreasonable; but to be reckless, it must be something more than negligent. It must not only be unreasonable, but it must involve a risk of harm to others substantially in excess of that necessary to make the conduct negligent. It must involve an easily perceptible danger of death or substantial physical harm, and the probability that it will so result must be substantially greater than is required for ordinary negligence.

We have examined the evidence; viewed in the light most favorable to plaintiff, it does not show that the conduct of any defendant was outrageous or reckless. Indeed we discern no basis upon which the jury could have concluded that defendants knew or had reason to know that the rear wheel of Acosta's motorcycle was defective in design or manufacture and that they decided not to remedy the defect in conscious disregard of or indifference to the risk thereby created. Although the wheel had been used in over 275,000 motorcycles, and the model first offered in 1970 (six years before plaintiff's accident), there was no evidence of previous consumer complaints or lawsuits that might have called to defendants' attention that there might be a problem. Moreover, plaintiff offered no proof that defendants developed or failed to modify the engineering designs for the rear wheel of the CB750 with any knowledge or reason to know of its alleged lack of safety. Such matters would have been admissible on the punitive damages issues.

In short, a jury could not have reasonably concluded that the evidence by the clear and convincing standard showed defendants to have acted with reckless disregard for the safety of users of the CB750. Accordingly, we hold that the district court should have granted defendants' motions for directed verdicts on the punitive damage claim and that it was error to deny the subsequent motions for judgment n.o.v. on behalf of Honda and Daido Kogyo.

VI. Conclusion

For the foregoing reasons, we will reverse the judgment of the district court denying Honda's and Daido Kogyo's motions for judgment n.o.v. on the award of punitive damages and the district court will be directed to enter judgment for Honda and Daido Kogyo on that claim. We will vacate the award of attorney's fees and remand the case to the district court for reconsideration of that award in light of our disposition of the punitive damages issue. In all other respects, the judgment of the district court will be affirmed.

There are many examples of punitive damage awards in the law. In antitrust cases, courts will award a variation of punitive damages, termed treble damages (triple the amount of compensatory damages), against a defendant that has been found to be in violation of one of the per se rules of antitrust, such as price fixing, horizontal division of markets, or engaging in a group boycott.

In strict liability cases, the issue of awarding punitive damages usually occurs after the case-in-chief is presented where the plaintiff can offer proof regarding the nature of the defendant's conduct (sometimes called Step 2). This may present a special problem for a jury who has been instructed that it should not consider the conduct of the defendant in a strict liability case, and which is then asked to award punitive damages for intentional conduct. A separate jury might be empanelled to determine if punitive damages are appropriate.

It should also be recognized that while the normal quantum of proof in civil cases is proof by a preponderance of evidence (is it more or less likely that the event took place), courts will require clear and convincing proof of the conduct required to award punitive damages. The jury can award huge sums in products liability cases like *Pinto,* where the conduct of the defendant was particularly egregious.

In recent years, there has been an attempt to limit or cap punitive damages to a set amount or to some multiple of the actual damages proved. The United States Supreme Court entered the debate by deciding that punitive damages had to bear some reasonable relationship to the actual, provable damages or the award of unreasonable punitive damages would violate the equal protection clause of the Constitution. It seems that an award of punitive damages in a ration more than 9 or 10 to 1 might be problematic in light of the analysis employed in *Gore v. BMW*!

Comment b of Section 500 of the Restatement of Torts (Second) sets forth the type of conduct required for the imposition of punitive damage awards.

> *"Recklessness may consist of either of two different types of conduct. If one actor knows, or has to reason to know of the facts which create a high degree of risk of physical harm to another, and deliberately proceeds to act, or fails to act, in conscious disregard of, or indifference to, that risk. In the other, the actor has such knowledge, or reason to know, of the facts, but does not realize or appreciate the high degree of risk involved, although a reasonable man in his position would do so. An objective standard is applied to him and he is held to the realization of the aggravated risk, which a reasonable man in his place would have, although he does not himself have it."*
>
> *"It must involve an easily perceptible danger of death or substantial physical harm, and the probability that it will so result must be substantially greater than is required for ordinary negligence."*
>
> *"... But to be reckless, it must be more than negligent."*

Fischer v. Johns-Manville Corporation

Supreme Court of New Jersey, 103 N.J. 643; 512 A.2d 466 (1986)

OPINION BY: CLIFFORD, JUDGE

* * *

Defendant argues that allowing proofs of a defendant's misconduct in a strict liability case invites the risk of confusing juries. Presumably the fear is that jurors will be unable in their evaluation of the strict liability claim to disregard whatever evidence there may be of defendant's misconduct, and hence will be unable to return a fair verdict. The fear is unfounded. Our faith in the jury system is greater than the argument suggests. Juries are often called on to consider alternative theories and to conduct deliberations in stages, as when given interrogatories or a special verdict sheet. See Rule 4:39-2, Rule 4:39-1. We are confident that a careful charge, clearly explaining the elements necessary for each finding, can assist juries in reaching fair verdicts on both the liability phase and, should they reach the question, punitive damages in a failure-to-warn, strict products liability case.

* * * the massive amount of litigation generated by exposure to asbestos. Although we are mindful of the fact that the case before us involves one worker, whose exposure to asbestos caused legally compensable injury to him and his wife -- it is not a class action, not a "mass" case -- nevertheless we would be remiss were we to ignore the society-wide nature of the asbestos problem. Recognizing the mass-tort nature of asbestos litigation, we address the concerns that that characteristic of the litigation brings to a decision to allow punitive damages.

Studies show that between eleven million and thirteen million workers have been exposed to asbestos. Special Project, "An Analysis of the Legal, Social, and Political Issues Raised by Asbestos Litigation," 36 Vand.L.Rev. 573, 580 (1983). More than 30,000 lawsuits have been filed already for damages caused by that exposure, with no indication that there are no more victims who will seek redress. Of the multitude of lawsuits that are faced by asbestos defendants as a group, Johns-Manville alone has been named in more than 11,000 cases. New claims are stayed because Johns-Manville is attempting reorganization under federal bankruptcy law. In re Johns-Manville Corp., 26 B.R. 420 (Bankr.S.D.N.Y.1983).

Defendant argues that the amount of compensatory damages assessed and to be assessed is so great that it will effectively serve the functions of punitive damages -- that is, defendants are more than sufficiently punished and deterred. We are not at all satisfied, however, that compensatory damages effectively serve the same functions as punitive damages, even when they amount to staggering sums. Compensatory damages are often foreseeable as to amount, within certain limits difficult to reduce to a formula but nonetheless familiar to the liability insurance industry. Anticipation of these damages will allow potential defendants, aware of dangers of a product, to factor those anticipated damages into a cost-benefit analysis and to decide whether to market a particular product. The risk and amount of such damages can, and in some cases will, be reflected in the cost of a product, in which event the product will be marketed in its dangerous condition.

Without punitive damages a manufacturer who is aware of a dangerous feature of its product but nevertheless knowingly chooses to market it in that condition, willfully concealing from the public information regarding the dangers of the product, would be far better off than an innocent manufacturer who markets a product later discovered to be dangerous -- this, because both will be subjected to the same compensatory damages, but the innocent manufacturer, unable to anticipate those damages, will not have incorporated the cost of those damages into the cost of the product. All else being equal, the law should not place the innocent manufacturer in a worse position than that of a knowing wrongdoer.

Punitive damages tend to meet this need.

Defendant argues further that the cumulative effect of punitive damages in mass-tort litigation is "potentially catastrophic." The Johns-Manville bankruptcy is offered as proof of this effect. We fail to see the distinction, in the case of Johns-Manville, between the effect of compensatory damages and that of punitive damages. The amount of punitive damages and the determination that they would cause insolvency that could be avoided in their absence are so speculative as to foreclose any sound basis for judicial decision. See also Jackson v. Johns-Manville, supra, 781 F.2d at 403 n. 11 ("defendants * * * do not indicate why their ability to pay future damage awards will be more affected by punitive damage awards than by the multiplicity of compensatory damage awards.").

Heretofore the typical setting for punitive damage claims has been the two-party lawsuit in which, more often than not, a punitive damages award was supported by a showing of some element of malice or intentional wrongdoing, directed by a defendant to the specific plaintiff. Even if the actual object of the malicious conduct was unknown to defendant, the conduct nevertheless was directed at a single person or a very limited group of potential plaintiffs.

Punishable conduct in a products liability action, on the other hand, will often affect countless potential plaintiffs whose identities are unknown to defendant at the time of the culpable conduct. We agree with the Illinois court that the mere fact that a defendant, "through outrageous misconduct, * * * manage[s] to seriously injure a large number of persons" should not relieve it of liability for punitive damages. Froud v. Celotex Corp., 107 Ill.App.3d 654, 658, 63 Ill.Dec. 261, 264, 437 N.E.2d 910, 913 (1982), rev'd on other grounds, 98 Ill.2d 324, 74 Ill.Dec. 629, 456 N.E.2d 131 (1983).

Of greater concern to us is the possibility that asbestos defendants' assets may become so depleted by early awards that the defendants will no longer be in existence and able to pay compensatory damages to later plaintiffs. Again, it is difficult if not impossible to ascertain the additional impact of punitive damages as compared to the impact of mass compensatory damages alone.

Many of the policy arguments against punitive damages in mass tort litigation cases can be traced to Roginsky v. Richardson-Merrell, Inc., 378 F.2d 832 (2d Cir.1967). The Roginsky court denied punitive damages to a plaintiff who suffered cataracts caused by MER/29, an anti-cholesterol drug. Although the denial of punitive damages rested on a determination that the evidence was insufficient to send the matter to the jury, the court expressed several concerns over allowing punitive damages for injuries to multiple plaintiffs. The fear that punitive damages would lead to "overkill" turned out to be unfounded in the MER/29 litigation. Approximately 1500 claims were made, of which only eleven were tried to a jury verdict. Punitive damages were awarded in only three of those cases, one of which was reversed on appeal. (Roginsky, supra, 378 F.2d 832.)

Owen I, supra, 74 Mich.L.Rev. at 1324, 1330 n. 339. While we do not discount entirely the possibility of punitive damage "overkill" in asbestos litigation, we do recognize that the vast majority of cases settle without trial.

Accepting the possibility of punitive damage "overkill," we turn to means of addressing that problem. Because the problem is nationwide, several possible remedial steps can be effective only on a nationwide basis, and hence are beyond our reach. One such solution is the setting of a cap on total punitive damages against each defendant. E.g., Owen II, 49 U.Chi.L.Rev. at 48-49 & n. 227. Such a cap would be ineffective unless applied uniformly. To adopt such a cap in New Jersey would be to deprive our citizens of punitive damages without the concomitant benefit of assuring the availability of compensatory damages for later plaintiffs. This we decline to do.

* * * At the state court level we are powerless to implement solutions to the nationwide problems created by asbestos exposure and litigation arising from that exposure. That does not mean, however, that we cannot institute some controls over runaway punitive damages. When a defendant manufacturer engages in conduct warranting the imposition of punitive damages, the harm caused may run to countless plaintiffs. Each individual plaintiff can fairly charge that the manufacturer's conduct was egregious as to him and that punitive damages should be assessed in his lawsuit. "Each tort committed by the defendant is individual and peculiar to that particular plaintiff who has brought suit." Neal v. Carey Canadian Mines, 548 F.Supp. 357, 377 (E.D.Pa.1982), aff'd sub nom. Van Buskirk v. Carey Canadian Mines, Ltd., 760 F.2d 481 (3d Cir.1985). Nonetheless, there should be some limits placed on the total punishment exacted from a culpable defendant. We conclude that a reasonable imposition of those limits would permit a defendant to introduce evidence of other punitive damage awards already assessed against and paid by it, as well as evidence of its own financial status and the effect a punitive award would have. We note with approval that this approach has already been looked on with favor by our trial courts. See Brotherton v. Celotex Corp., 202 N.J. Super. 148, 163 (Law Div.1985).

We realize that defendants may be reluctant to alert juries to the fact that other courts or juries have assessed punitive damages for conduct similar to that being considered by the jury in a given case. Although the evidence may convince a jury that a defendant has been sufficiently punished, the same evidence could nudge a jury closer to a determination that punishment is warranted. That is a risk of jury trial. The willingness to accept that risk is a matter of strategy for defendant and its counsel, no different from other strategy choices facing trial lawyers every day.

When evidence of other punitive awards is introduced, trial courts should instruct juries to consider whether the defendant has been sufficiently punished, keeping in mind that punitive damages are meant to punish and deter defendants for the benefit of society, not to compensate individual plaintiffs.

A further protection may be afforded defendants by the judicious exercise of remittitur. Should a trial court determine that an award is "manifestly outrageous" or "grossly excessive," Cabakov v. Thatcher, supra, 37 N.J. Super. at 260, it may reduce that award or order a new trial on punitive damages. In evaluating the excessiveness of challenged punitive damage awards, trial courts are expressly authorized to consider prior punitive damage awards.

* * * We hold that punitive damages are available in failure-to-warn, strict products liability actions when a manufacturer is (1) aware of or culpably indifferent to an unnecessary risk of injury, and (2) refuses to take steps to reduce that danger to an acceptable level. This standard can be met by a showing of "a deliberate act or omission with knowledge of a high degree of probability of harm and reckless indifference to consequences." Berg v. Reaction Motors, supra, 37 N.J. at 414.

* * * The purpose and nature of punitive damages must be carefully explained to the jury. In determining whether a defendant's conduct was sufficiently egregious to justify punitive damages, fact-finders should consider the seriousness of the hazard to the public; the degree of the defendant's awareness of the hazard and of its excessiveness; the cost of correcting or reducing the risk; the duration of both the improper marketing behavior and its cover-up; the attitude and conduct of the enterprise upon discovery of the misconduct; and the defendant's reasons for failing to act. See Owen I, supra, 74 Mich.L.Rev.; Thiry v. Armstrong, supra, 661 P.2d at 519; Gryc v. Dayton-Hudson, 297 N.W.2d 727, 739 (Minn.), cert. denied, 449 U.S. 921, 101 S.Ct. 320, 66 L.Ed.2d 149 (1980).

If a fact-finder decides to award punitive damages, additional considerations can guide a determination of the appropriate amount. Punitive damages should bear some reasonable relationship to actual injury, but we have consistently declined to require a set numerical ratio between punitive and compensatory damages. Nappe, supra, 97 N.J. at 50; Leimgruber, supra, 73 N.J. at 457-58. The reasonableness of the relationship of punitive damages to actual injury must be considered in light of other factors in each case. For example, some particularly egregious conduct may generate only minimal compensatory damages. In such cases higher punitive damages would be justified than when substantial compensatory damages are awarded. The profitability of the marketing misconduct, where it can be determined, is relevant. Other factors to be considered include the amount of the plaintiff's litigation expenses, the financial condition of the enterprise and the probable effect thereon of a particular judgment, and the total punishment the enterprise will probably receive from other sources.

Finally, there looms the question of the quality of proof required to sustain a punitive damages award. Our dissenting colleagues urge adoption of a "clear and convincing" standard to replace New Jersey's traditional "preponderance of the evidence" rule. The dissent makes a persuasive argument to support such a change and has cited policy considerations that deserve careful consideration.

> However, the fact remains that the parties have not briefed or argued that issue, nor have the courts below addressed it. So significant a shift in our law should come, if at all, only after it has been fully litigated. Under the circumstance we are content to leave for another day the definitive resolution of so portentous a question.
>
> Judgment affirmed.

Liquidated Damages

Liquidated damages are predetermined damages found in a contract, where a specific sum of money has been expressly stipulated by the parties as the amount of damages to be recovered by either party in case of a breach by the other party. In order for a court to enforce a liquidated damage clause, a court would determine whether the stipulated amount was a reasonable estimate of the expected or anticipated damages in light of the difficulty of proof or of the commercial setting; and that the damages are not seen as a penalty (sometimes dealing with the amount of the damages in question).

Liquidated damage clauses are most often found in construction contracts or in a wide variety of both commercial and residential lease agreements.

Under the UCC (Section 2-718), damages for breach may be liquidated, subject to the same general standards as under the common law: They must be "… reasonable in the light of the anticipated or actual harm caused by the breach, the difficulties of proof of loss, and the inconvenience or non-feasibility of otherwise obtaining an adequate remedy. A term fixing unreasonably large liquidated damages is void as a penalty." In terms of warranty actions (Section 2-719), an agreement between the parties may provide that the measure of damages in warranty cases may "limit the buyer's remedies to return of the goods and repayment of the price or to repair and replacement of nonconforming goods or parts" and this remedy my be the "sole or exclusive remedy." Thus, if personal injury is claimed, the warranty provisions above may prove to be problematic, although not entirely insurmountable today where a plaintiff has been injured as a result of a defect in a consumer good—one used for "personal, family, or household use)!

Nominal Damages

Nominal damages are a trifling sum awarded to a plaintiff in an action where there is no substantial loss or injury, or where there has only been a "technical violation."

Damages For Pain And Suffering Or For Emotional Distress, Or "Add On" Damages

Damages for pain and suffering or emotional distress are often highly speculative and subjective and may likewise be subjected to some limitation or "cap" under various state statutes. This area of the law has been subjected to much public scrutiny and debate because of abuses - actual or perceived. It is a rule in most states that a plaintiff will only be permitted to collect damages for "pain and suffering" or emotional distress after a prior physical harm has been proven. In some states, however, damages for emotional distress have been found to be "actual or real damages" in their own right.

Because of the variety of potential causes of action, courts have set down the following general rules or guidelines:

- If a plaintiff has suffered only economic loss or a loss of profits, and there is no allegation of personal injury or injury to the property of another (where there has only been "injury to the product itself"), the plaintiff should bring a suit for breach of warranty against the manufacturer and not in tort: "the tort concern for safety is reduced when an injury is only to the product itself." An exception might be a suit for breach of warranty is foreclosed on other grounds (statute of limitations, notice requirements, etc.)
- If a plaintiff has suffered personal injury, the plaintiff should file a suit in tort, most likely under a theory of strict liability, and/or perhaps negligence. East River lays out an interesting and fundamental point: Where a product "injures only itself," the reasons for imposing a tort duty in either strict liability or negligence are weak, and the reasons for filing a contract (warranty) action are strong! The corollary is equally true where there has been personal injury.

Generally, commercial buyers cannot rely on strict liability or negligence for recovery of pure economic damages. They must rely on warranties when seeking economic damages.

Strict liability should be used if a defective product causes physical harm to a person or causes damage to the property of another.

The commercial buyer of a producer good may be limited to repair or replacement of the product or parts only and not to other economic losses if stipulated in the contract.

If the plaintiff can show physical harm to a person or property based upon strict liability, then the courts will also permit him or her to recover compensation for economic losses that flow from the physical harm.

What about the issue of emotional distress (damages for pain and suffering) when it is not accompanied by any proof of physical injury?

Gnirk v. The Ford Motor Company

United States District Court for the District of South Dakota, Central Division, 572 F. Supp. 1201 (1983)

OPINION BY: PORTER, JUDGE

MEMORANDUM OPINION

I

Plaintiff Wilma Gnirk seeks compensatory damages against The Ford Motor Company (Ford) for emotional distress inflicted upon her while witnessing the death of her child, a passenger in a Ford car. Ford moves for summary judgment, contending that plaintiff, as a "bystander" cannot recover for emotional distress because (1) it was not intentionally inflicted upon her by Ford; and (2) since she sustained no "accompanying physical injury, i.e., a physical impact and attendant, contemporaneous physical injury", even if Ford's legal liability for her child's death were assumed, she may not recover. Ford further contends that all damages incident to the child's death must be sought under the South Dakota wrongful death act, SDCL 21-5-7 which act does not allow recovery for emotional distress. For the reasons following, Ford's motion for summary judgment is denied.

II

Plaintiff alleges that on November 20, 1980 she and her thirteen month old son were traveling in a 1976 Ford L.T.D. car. She co-owned and was then driving the car. In order to open a fence gate she stopped the car, shifted the gear selector into park, and left the engine running. She got out on the driver's side, leaving her son in the front seat with a seat belt fastened around him. While she was opening the gate the car gear shifted from park to reverse and the car backed up, struck a post, and then went forward a distance into a stock dam. From the time the car first moved, plaintiff chased it and tried unsuccessfully several times to get into the moving car to stop it. When it finally stopped, the car was completely submerged in the stock dam. The child was in the car alone. Plaintiff, a non-swimmer, entered the water but could not locate the car. She then walked a mile and a half to the nearest farmhouse for help.

The event above described, plaintiff alleges, caused her great depression, insomnia, permanent psychological injury, and physical illness.

Plaintiff's claim is analyzed under 402A. This is not to say it is the only theory which will survive defendant's motion. Essentially the same principles apply to an action under 402A as to an action for breach of implied warranty. Pearson v. Franklin Laboratories, Inc., 254 N.W.2d 133, 138-39 (S.D. 1977).

III

Upon the facts here, it is appropriate to view plaintiff in the role of a user of Ford's product, rather than as a "bystander". Bystander cases are typically void of any product liability implications running from the defendant tortfeasor to the bystander-plaintiff. Having no connection with the tortfeasor, or his negligent tort, the only part played by the bystander is to serve as the unwilling eyewitness to the death or injury of the victim by the tortfeasor. Thus, the bystander has nowhere to look but to the common law rules of negligence, if she [he] is to find a legal duty upon the tortfeasor not to inflict emotional distress upon her by negligently killing or injuring the victim in her presence.

Plaintiff here has a legal connection with Ford which goes to the heart of the case, making it unnecessary for her, or for this court, to look beyond the Restatement (Second) of Torts § 402A (1965) [hereinafter cited as 402A]. By virtue of her status as the user of the Ford car involved, at the time involved, Ford under 402A owed to plaintiff an independent legal duty not to harm her. Engberg v. Ford Motor Co., 87 S.D. 196, 205 N.W.2d 104 (1973); Shaffer v. Honeywell, Inc., 249 N.W.2d 251 (S.D. 1976). Moreover, Ford's duty to plaintiff under Engberg stems not from the South Dakota wrongful death act but rather from 402A. Ford's legal duty to plaintiff under 402A endures even if the victim does not survive.

IV

In 1918 the South Dakota Supreme Court considered an issue pertinent to the damage issue here. In Sternhagen v. Kozel, 40 S.D. 396, 167 N.W. 398 it was plaintiff's claim that, owing to an alleged tort "she suffered a severe fright and through such fright received a severe mental and physical shock." The Court saw the question presented as whether or not "one, who, through a tort committed against him, suffers a fright -- which fright is not the result of an accompanying physical injury, but is itself the proximate cause of a physical injury -- can recover damages for such fright and the resulting physical injury." The Court answered as follows:

> *"Without determining whether one could recover for fright alone, such fright not accompanying physical injury either as its result or cause we are of the opinion that: When physical injury accompanies a fright as its effect, the injured party may recover for the fright, for the physical injury, and for any mental injury accompanying such fright and physical injury, exactly as one can recover where the fright is the result of a physical injury."*

Two South Dakota cases were cited by defendant. First National Bank of Jacksonville v. Bragdon, 84 S.D. 89, 167 N.W.2d 381 (1969) involved a counterclaim by debtors against a creditor for malicious conduct in debt collection. Chisum v. Behrens, 283 N.W.2d 235 (1979) was a suit by a widow against a mortician concerning the care of the body of the deceased husband. Both cases involved claimed intentional or malicious conduct, by the creditor in Bragdon, and by the mortician in Chisum. Chisum adhered to the rule stated in Bragdon that "where the act is willful or malicious, as distinguished from being merely negligent, recovery may be had for mental pain, though no physical injury results."

The issue in both Bragdon and Chisum involved infliction of mental pain by intentional or malicious misconduct. The issue in the instant case involves tortiously but unintentionally inflicted injury. Sternhagen is more in point, but the opinion did not discuss the facts of the case. The Sternhagen court did not indicate what physical phenomena or manifestation is sufficient to constitute the "physical injury" referred to in the quotation from the case, supra [40 S.D. 392, 167 N.W. 399]. That issue has not yet been addressed by the state Supreme Court. In the absence of a controlling statute or decision of the highest court of the state, this court, exercising diversity jurisdiction, 28 U.S.C. § 1332, must apply the rule it believes the Supreme Court of South Dakota would adopt. McElhaney v. Eli Lilly & Co., 564 F. Supp. 265, 268 (D.S.D. 1983).

In recent years, [due to increased understanding of the relationship between physical and psychic injury] courts have realistically construed the term "physical injury". See, e.g., Haught v. Maceluch, 681 F.2d 291, 299 n.9 (5th Cir. 1982) (applying Texas law; depression, nervousness, weight gain, and nightmares are equivalent to physical injury); D'Ambra v. United States, 396 F. Supp. 1180, 1183-84 (D.R.I. 1973) ("psychoneurosis" or acute depression constitutes physical injury); Corso v. Merrill, 119 N.H. 647, 658, 406 A.2d 300, 307 (1979) (depression constitutes a physical injury); Mobaldi v. Board of Regents, 55 Cal. App. 3d 573, 578, 127 Cal. Rptr. 720, 723 (1976) (depression and weight loss constitute physical injury overruled on other grounds, Baxter v. Superior Court, 19 Cal. 3d 461, 466 n.4, 563 P.2d 871, 874 n.4, 138 Cal. Rptr. 315, 318 n.4 (1977); Hughes v. Moore, 214 Va. 27, 29, 35, 197 S.E. 2d 214, 216, 220 (1973) (anxiety reaction, phobia and hysteria constitute physical injury); Daley v. LaCroix, 384 Mich. 4, 15-16, 179 N.W.2d 390, 396 (1970) (weight loss and nervousness constitute physical injury); Toms v. McConnell, 45 Mich. App. 647, 657, 207 N.W.2d 140, 145 (1973) (depression constitutes physical injury).

- - - - - - - - - - - - - - Footnotes - - - - - - - - - - - - - - -

6 An increasing number of courts have dispensed with the requirement that plaintiff's emotional distress must have manifested itself in some form of physical injury in order to be recoverable. See Paugh v. Hanks, 6 Ohio St. 3d 72, 451 N.E. 2, 451 N.E.2d 759 (1983); Culbert v. Sampson's Supermarkets, Inc., 444 A.2d 433, (Me. 1982); Barnhill v. Davis, 300 N.W.2d 104, (Iowa 1981); Molien v. Kaiser Foundation Hospitals, 27 Cal. 3d 916, 616 P.2d 813, 167 Cal. Rptr. 831 (1980); Sinn v. Burd, 486 Pa. 146, 404 A.2d 672 (1979); Leong v. Takasaki, 55 Hawaii 398, 520 P.2d 758 (1974).

There is no fine line distinguishing physical from emotional injury. D'Ambra v. United States, 396 F. Supp. 1180, 1184 (D.R.I. 1973) (quoting from Sloane v. Southern Cal. Ry. Co., 111 Cal. 668, 680, 44 P. 320, 322 (1896); Molien, 27 Cal. 3d at 929, 616 P.2d at 820-21, 167 Cal. Rptr. at 838-39. The Restatement acknowledges this much:

[Emotional distress] accompanied by transitory, non-recurring physical phenomena, harmless in themselves, such as dizziness, vomiting, and the like, does not make the actor liable where such phenomena are in themselves inconsequential and do not amount to any substantial bodily harm. On the other hand, long continued nausea or headaches may amount to physical illness, which is bodily harm; and even long continued mental disturbance, as for example in the case of repeated hysterical attacks, or mental aberration, may be classified by the courts as illness, notwithstanding their mental character.

Restatement (Second) of Torts, § 436A comment c (1965).

Comment c, above quoted, is a reasonable rule or guide for trial of the issue of whether plaintiff sustained bodily injury proximately caused by alleged emotional disturbance inflicted by Ford. If plaintiff makes out a case for the jury on the issue, and if the jury find for her on the issue she is entitled to recover damages for emotional distress suffered during the event in which her son drowned, for physical injury proximately caused, and for any mental injury accompanying such emotional distress and physical injury, Sternhagen, supra, 167 N.W. 398.

This court believes that the South Dakota Supreme Court would so rule if confronted with the damage issue here presented. This court is mindful that in the past, the first and second Restatement of Torts is a source the South Dakota Supreme Court has frequently relied upon in formulating rules of tort law. See McElhaney v. Eli Lilly & Co., supra, 564 F. Supp. 265, 269. South Dakota cases cited at fn. 11.

At the request of both plaintiff and Ford (under FRCP 12(b) this court treats Ford's original motion to dismiss (FRCP 12(b)(6) as a motion for a summary judgment (FRCP 56), in favor of Ford, as to count three. The parties in briefing referred to a deposition of plaintiff taken December 29, 1981 and to her later deposition taken May 16, 1983. A motion for summary judgment may be granted "only when, viewing the facts and inferences that may be derived therefrom in the light most favorable to the non-moving party, the moving party establishes that there is no genuine issue of material fact and that it is entitled to judgment as a matter of law." Impro Products, Inc. v. Herrick, 715 F.2d 1267, 1272 (8th Cir. 1983).

The court concludes that a genuine issue of fact exists concerning whether the event in which her son lost his life inflicted great depression, insomnia, and permanent psychological injury upon plaintiff, which injury proximately caused bodily injury to plaintiff. The court has not considered it, concluding that the Ford motion must be overruled in any event.

In *Gnirk,* the plaintiff had sued for injury for emotional distress as a user of the Ford product and not as bystander. The court finessed the issue by concluding that emotional distress and evidence of illness of a mental character is an illness in itself (a distinct physical harm) and is thus recoverable, adopting an expansive and broad view of physical harm to include evidence of emotional distress!

Under which circumstances might a bystander be able to sue for damages for emotional distress relating to a defective product? One approach to finding liability is called the zone of danger theory where recovery will be permitted where the plaintiff him/herself is within a zone of danger. In *Dillon v. Legg,* the court laid down a more detailed rule in which:

- The parties must be closely related;
- The plaintiff must be sufficiently near the scene of the accident; (within the zone of danger)
- The plaintiff must contemporaneously observe the accident or incident.

Aren't these elements merely an extension of the foreseeability requirement enunciated by Judge Cardozo in *Palsgraf*?

What might be the result if grandma learns through a news broadcast that her granddaughter had been killed when an RV in which she was sitting had rolled into a lake when the breaking system failed due to a design or manufacturing defect? Grandma collapses and breaks her leg and pelvis, suffering severe emotional distress in the process as well. What about the situation where grandma witnesses an accident via a video phone or through some other cutting-edge technology?

QUESTIONS

1. A shaft in Hadley's, the plaintiff's, mill broke down causing the mill to stop operations. As a result, Hadley hired Baxendale, the defendant, to transport the broken mill shaft to an engineer to create a duplicate. Hadley stressed to Baxendale that the shaft must be sent immediately. Baxendale agreed to send it the next day. However, Baxendale did not deliver the shaft as promised and Hadley brought suit for the loss of profits caused by the halt of operations at the mill. Baxendale claimed he lacked any knowledge that the mill would be inoperable without the shaft?

   a. Is Baxendale liable? See *Hadley v. Baxendale*, 156 Eng. Rep. 145 (1845).

   b. How did the decision shape the development of consequential damages?

2. Acosta, the plaintiff, was riding his motorcycle at 35mph when he hit a 4 inch deep hole, which caused the rear wheel to collapse and injure him. Acosta brought suit against Honda Motor Company LTD, the defendant. Moreover, the plaintiff's motorcycle lacked the same strength as several other wheels from the same model that were randomly sampled. Additionally, the owner's manual lacked any warning about the collapse of the rear wheel from such an impact. It should also be noted that the defendant merely spot-checked the rear wheels as opposed to a crush test or weighing each wheel.

   a. Did Honda act recklessly?

   b. Is Honda liable for punitive damages?

3. Johns-Manville Corporation, the defendant, is a supplier of asbestos material. Fischer, the plaintiff, is bringing suit for damages for lung diseases suffered as a result of his exposure to asbestos. Research *Fischer v. Johns-Manville Corporation.*

   a. Does strict liability apply?

   b. Was there a breach of warranty?

   c. Does negligence apply?

   d. Is the Johns-Manville Corporation liable for punitive damages?

4. Find a case where liquidated damages come into play. How does it differ from a case with punitive damages? Why?

5. How did the *Dillon v. Legg* case help shape the development of the zone of danger theory?

6. Gnirk, the plaintiff, and her 13 month old son were traveling in a 1976 Ford that she co-owned. In order to open a fence gate, she had to stop the car. So, she put the car in park and got out, leaving her son in the car. However, as she was doing so, the car shifted to reverse and rolled into a stock damn, where it became submerged in water. The plaintiff was a non-swimmer. Plaintiff asserts that the event has caused depression, insomnia, permanent psychological injury, and physical injury. Gnirk brought suit against the Ford Motor Company.

   a. Is The Ford Motor Company liable for the emotional distress of Gnirk?

Chapter Fourteen

Defenses to Product Liability Suits

Defendants may claim a variety of defenses to a suit involving products liability.

Contributory Negligence

Contributory negligence involves a plaintiff's failure to exercise reasonable care for his or her own safety. The basic test of contributory negligence is whether the plaintiff created foreseeable, unreasonable risks to his own safety by or through their own conduct. At common law, contributory negligence was a total or absolute bar to recovery by a plaintiff; today, the allegation of contributory negligence may be evaluated under a standard of comparative negligence, under which a court will apportion damages based upon the principle of comparative fault between a plaintiff and a defendant.

The theory of contributory negligence rests on the view that a plaintiff has a duty to use reasonable care in the conduct of his or her own affairs; that the plaintiff breached this duty of reasonable care; and that the plaintiff's failure proximately caused all or some of the plaintiff's own injuries.

Section 402A, comment n notes that contributory negligence is not a defense in strict liability cases if there is a mere failure to discover a defect or to take steps to guard against its existence. This statement has caused much discussion and debate in the products liability bar, as well as in the courts!

McCown v. International Harvester Co.

Supreme Court of Pennsylvania, 342 A.2d 381 (1975)

OPINION BY: JONES, JUDGE

Appellant, manufacturer of large over-the-road tractors, was held liable under Section 402A of Restatement (Second) of Torts (1965) for the injuries sustained by the appellee in a one-vehicle accident. The Superior Court affirmed and we granted allocatur limited to the issue of the availability of contributory negligence as a defense to a 402A action.

Appellee was injured while driving a tractor manufactured by appellant. The design of the steering mechanism of the tractor made the vehicle unusually difficult to maneuver.

Specifically, twelve to fifteen percent more mechanical effort than that normally expended had to be applied to the steering wheel to accomplish any given turn. Appellee, after driving the vehicle for several hours, stopped for an equipment check on the blacktopped shoulder of the Pennsylvania Turnpike. After completing the inspection the appellee proceeded to reenter the Turnpike.

Unrelated to any steering difficulty appellee struck a guardrail adjoining the shoulder with the right front tire of the tractor. This collision caused the steering wheel to spin rapidly in the direction opposite to the turn. The spokes of the spinning steering wheel struck appellee's right arm, fracturing his wrist and forearm. Evidence adduced at trial indicated that the force and speed of the steering wheel's counterrotation were directly related to the design of the steering mechanism.

For the purposes of this appeal appellant concedes the defect in the steering system's design, but argues that appellee's contributory negligence in colliding with the guardrail should at least be considered in determining appellee's recovery. We disagree and affirm.

In Webb v. Zern, 422 Pa. 424, 220 A.2d 853 (1966), this Court adopted Section 402A of the Restatement and in Ferraro v. Ford Motor Co., 423 Pa. 324, 223 A.2d 746 (1966), permitted the assertion of assumption of the risk as a defense to a 402A action, citing with approval comment n to Section 402A. Today, we complete our acceptance of the principles delineated in comment n by rejecting contributory negligence as an available defense in 402A cases.

Appellant's position that contributory negligence should affect 402A liability could have two possible applications. Either contributory negligence should serve to diminish any recovery in an amount adjudged equal to a plaintiff's lack of care, or as in most other tort actions, contributory negligence should be available as a complete defense to liability.

Acceptance of the appellant's first alternative would create a system of comparative assessment of damages for 402A actions. Neither the General Assembly by statute nor this

Court by case law has established such a scheme of comparative negligence in other areas of tort law. Without considering the relative merits of comparative negligence, we think it unwise to embrace the theory in the context of an appeal involving Section 402A.

Adoption of contributory negligence as a complete defense in 402A actions would defeat one theoretical basis for our acceptance of Section 402A. "Our courts have determined that a manufacturer by marketing and advertising his products impliedly represents that it is safe for its intended use." Salvador v. Atlantic Steel Boiler Co., 457 Pa. 24, 32, 319 A.2d 903, 907 (1974). Based on that implied representation is the consumer's assumption that a manufacturer's goods are safe. Recognition of consumer negligence as a defense to a 402A action would contradict this normal expectation of product safety. One does not inspect a product for defects or guard against the possibility of product defects when one assumes the item to be safe. The law should not require such inspection or caution when it has accepted as reasonable the consumer's anticipation of safety. We reject contributory negligence as a defense to actions grounded in Section 402A.

Judgment affirmed.

CONCUR BY: POMEROY

Contrary to what the opinion of the Court seems to suggest, the answer to the question presented by this appeal is not to be found altogether in the language of Comment to Section 402A. Comment n provides, on the one hand, that the negligent failure to discover a defect in a product or to guard against the possibility of its existence is not defense to a strict liability action, and, on the other hand, that assumption of risk is a defense. But the conduct of John McCown, the appellee, fits into neither of the above categories. His negligence, if any, was the manner of his operation of an International Harvester tractor. Although Comment n is silent with regard to the consequences of negligent use of a product, it points to a resolution of the issue by referring to Section 524 of the Restatement (Second) of Torts. That section provides that in general "the contributory negligence of the plaintiff is not a defense to the strict liability of one who carries on an abnormally dangerous activity." Neither the Comments to Section 524 nor Comment n to Section 402A offer a rationale for the application of this rule in products liability cases, but I am satisfied that the elimination of the defense of plaintiff's negligence is in accord not only with the weight of authority in other jurisdictions but also with the policy which underlies the concept of strict liability in tort.

The strict liability of Section 402A is founded in part upon the belief that as between the sellers of products and those who use them, the former are the better able to bear the losses caused by defects in the products involved. See Bialek v. Pittsburgh Brewing Company, 430 Pa. 176, 187 n. 2, 242 A.2d 231, 236 n. 2 (1968); Restatement (Second) of Torts § 402A, Comments c & f. This greater loss-bearing capacity is unrelated to negligence in the manufacture or marketing of products. Indeed, retail and wholesale sellers of chattels are themselves often in no position to discover or avoid defects in their inventories, even by the exercise of a high degree of care. Thus, defendants in Section 402A actions are subjected to liability without regard to fault. It is a proper corollary to this principle that the lesser loss-bearing capacity of product users exists independently of their negligence or lack of it. It follows that such negligence should not ordinarily or necessarily operate to preclude recovery in a strict liability case. On the other hand, where assumption of risk is involved, the "loss-bearing" policy underlying Section 402A is outweighed by a countervailing policy, one which refuses recovery to persons who consciously expose themselves to known dangers. This policy is deemed stronger than the one, reflected in the normal law of contributory negligence, which denies recovery to individuals whose conduct is merely lacking in due care under the circumstances.

This is not to say, however, that evidence of ordinary negligence on the part of a plaintiff is never relevant in a Section 402A action; such evidence may bear directly upon the determination of whether the plaintiff has proved all the elements necessary to make out a cause of action. Thus, negligence in the use of a product may tend to show that the plaintiff caused a defect and therefore that the product was not defective when sold. See Comment g to Section 402A. Again, if the negligent use of a product amounts to abnormal use, it may be inferred that the product was not defective at all, for a product is not defective if it is safe for normal handling and use. See Comment h to Section 402A. Similarly, negligence in the use of a product may have a bearing on the question whether a defect in a product was the legal cause of the plaintiff's injury. See Restatement (Second) of Torts §§ 5 and 9 and the Comments to these sections.

What has been said is not intended as an exhaustive listing of the purposes for which evidence of the plaintiff's negligence may be relevant in Section 402A cases. It is intended merely to indicate that, although such negligence is not per se a bar to recovery, it may nevertheless have that effect in a proper case where it negates an essential element of the cause of action. I do not read the opinion of the Court as suggesting anything to the contrary.

In *McCown*, the court stated that "The law should not require such inspection or caution when it has accepted as reasonable the consumer's anticipation of safety." However, comment n continues: "…the form of contributory negligence which consists in voluntarily and unreasonable proceeding to encounter a known danger, and commonly passes under the name assumption of risk, is a defense under this section as in other cases of strict liability."

Assumption of Risk

"Volenti Non Fit Injuria - To a willing person, injury is not done!"

Assumption of risk is available in both negligence and strict liability cases.

Heil Co. v. Grant

Court of Civil Appeals of Texas, 534 S.W.2d 916 (1976)

DUNAGAN, CHIEF JUSTICE.

This is a products liability case which involves the doctrines of assumption of risk and misuse. * * * Valmarie Grant and her children sued for the death of James Grant (hereinafter referred to as Decedent), their husband and father respectively. The defendant-appellant is the Heil Company, a major manufacturer of hydraulic hoists.

* * *

Decedent and Vernon [Grant] were working beneath the raised bed [of a dump truck] when it somehow descended. Vernon jumped away but Decedent did not. Heil Company's engineer found no malfunction in the hoist mechanism and concluded that the pullout cable had been tripped. Immediately before the accident, Vernon told Decedent that if he hit the pullout cable, the bed would come down.

* * *

Plaintiffs sued the Heil Company under a theory of strict liability for defective design of the hoist mechanism and for failure to warn of the hazard.

* * *

The Heil Company pleaded, offered evidence of and requested Special Issues on the defenses of assumption of risk and misuse. The trial court, applying the Dead Man's Statute, excluded that portion of Vernon Grant's testimony which related to those defenses and refused to submit Special Issues thereon since there was no other evidence to support such issues. Heil Company's primary contention before this court is that the exclusion of Vernon Grant's testimony was harmful error because that testimony was admissible and established or raised fact issues of those defenses.

* * *

Plaintiff's contend that Vernon Grant's warning to Decedent ("I stated * * * that if he hit the cable, the bed would come down") did not constitute evidence that Decedent "knew" of the risk. Plaintiffs argue that Decedent might not have heard, understood or remembered the warning and that Vernon Grant's testimony was merely evidence that Decedent could have known of the risk.

An injured person's knowledge of a dangerous condition or defect is measured subjectively; i.e., by that person's actual, conscious knowledge. Massman-Johnson v. Gvndolf, 464

S.W.2d 555, 557 (Tex. 1972). The fact that the injured person should have known of the danger will not support the assumption of risk defense. Halepeska v. Callihan Interests, Inc., [371 S.W.2d 368 (Tex. 1963)]. Sometimes, however, that person may know such facts as to be charged with knowledge of the danger. Halepeska v. Callihan Interests, Inc., supra. This standard would be applied when it was difficult or impossible to determine the state of the injured person's mind; as it was in the instant case of a fatal injury. The "actual knowledge or charged knowledge" test has been applied in determining the strict liability of a supplier of defective products. See Rourke v. Garza, 530 S.W.2d 794 (Tex. 1975).

* * *

Whether an injured person actually knew of the danger is peculiarly within the province of the jury. Hillman-Kelley v. Pittman, 469 S.W.2d 669, 692 (Tex.Civ.App.-El Paso 1972, n.w.h.). Here, there was some evidence from which the jury could have found that Decedent "knew" of the danger, to-wit: the fact that he had been told of the effect of hitting the pullout cable. Although the jury could also have found that Decedent did not know of the danger because he did not hear, understand or remember the warning, we are not able to say, as a matter of law, that he did not know of that danger.

Plaintiffs argue that even if Decedent had knowledge of some danger, there is no evidence that he knew of the specific defect involved. Knowledge of the general hazard involved in operating a punch-press machine will not support the assumption of risk defense. Rhoads v. Service Machine Co., 329 F.Supp. 367 (E.B.Ark. 1971). The general hazard in the instant case was working beneath the raised bed of the dump truck. Vernon Grant and Heil Company's engineer both concluded that the bed descended because the pullout cable was tripped. This evidence indicates that the specific danger was that striking the pullout cable would cause the bed to descend. The jury, upon consideration of Vernon Grants testimony, could have found that Decedent knew of this specific hazard. Plaintiffs also contend that the requisite knowledge must be of a "defect," and that "knowledge that a phenomenon will occur in a product * * * is not knowledge that the product is dangerously defective." [Henderson v. Ford Motor Co., 519 S.W.2d 67, 89 (Tex. 1974)] * * * It is clear, however, that the assumption of risk defense is premised upon knowledge of the dangerous condition of a product rather than recognition of its defectiveness.

* * *

Plaintiffs argue that even if Decedent knew of the danger of the pullout cable, there is no evidence that he knew of the other dangerous defects, to-wit: the defectively designed control valve; the failure to supply a support brace; and the failure to instruct as to proper bracing. These defects may well have been producing or proximate causes of the death in that (1) but for the defects, the death might not have occurred, and (2) the death was a foreseeable result of the defects. * * * In our opinion, however, all of the above producing causes were part of the same danger. The assumption of risk defense is based upon the injured person's awareness of the danger of injury rather than an awareness of the producing causes of the injury. Since there was some evidence that Decedent knew of the specific danger in hitting the pullout cable, Plaintiffs' argument is without merit.

The danger encountered must be both known and appreciated to raise the assumption of risk defense. * * * Again, the test is subjective. * * * We look for some evidence that Decedent actually appreciated the risk or was in possession of facts from which he would be legally charged with appreciation of the danger. Halepeska v. Callihan Interests, Inc., supra, 371 S.W.2d at 379. If by reason of age, or lack of information, experience, intelligence or judgment, Decedent did not understand the risk involved, he will not be taken to have assumed that risk. Restatement (Second) of Torts, Section 496D, comment c.

* * *

There is some evidence that Decedent might not have appreciated the danger of hitting the pullout cable. However, by reason of Decedent's information, age and experience, we conclude that there was some evidence of probative force that he did appreciate that danger. Thus, an issue for the jury exists. Plaintiffs' final point in support of their contention of no evidence of the necessary elements of the assumption of risk defense is that Decedent's encounter of the risk was not shown to have been voluntary. A voluntary encounter means by free and intelligent choice. * * * We have thoroughly considered each of these arguments and find them to be without merit. We conclude that there was some evidence that would support a jury finding that Decedent's encounter with the risk was by free and intelligent choice.

Plaintiffs, second contention under * * * Point I is that any error in excluding the testimony of Vernon Grant which related to assumption of risk was harmless because that defense is inapplicable when strict liability is based upon a failure to warn of a dangerous condition. Plaintiffs rely upon statements to the effect that when there is a breach of the duty to warn, there is no assumption of the risk. * * * These statements were made in situations in which no warning had been given to the injured person. The function of the warning is to give that person knowledge and an opportunity to appreciate the danger. * * * The supplier of a defective product is usually in the best position to supply this warning but there is no reason why the warning cannot come from another source. "One who voluntarily chooses to use a chattel with a complete realization, regardless of how it was acquired, of the risks to which he thus exposes himself voluntarily assumes such risks * * *" 1 Hursh & Bailey, American Law of Products Liability 2d, sec. 2: 107 (Emphasis added.)

* * *

Plaintiffs' final argument * * * is that any error in excluding evidence of assumption of risk was harmless because that defense is inapplicable when strict liability is based upon the defective design of a product being used in a manner reasonably foreseeable to the supplier. Plaintiffs argue that the supplier is in the best position to discover a design defect

> and should not be permitted to avoid liability on the ground that the injured person made a foolish judgment to encounter the danger. The thrust of this argument is that assumption of risk should not be applicable in any case when strict liability is based upon the defective design of a product. The defense of assumption of risk was held available in such a case in Rourke v. Garza, supra, 530 S.W.2d 794.
>
> PLAINTIFFS' CONTENTION IS OVERRULED.

Comment n continues further: "If the user or consumer discovers the defect and is aware of the danger, and nevertheless proceeds unreasonably to make use of the product and is injured by it, he is barred from recovery."

There are two types of assumption of risk: Express or contractual assumption of risk and implied assumption of risk. Express assumption of risk, also known as contractual assumption of risk, occurs where there is an agreement between the parties that one party will bear the risk of injury, even it is caused by the other party's negligence. Assumption of risk may also be seen where there are limitations placed on liability to specific dollar amounts. These contracts will be enforced so long as they are reasonable, are not unconscionable, and do not violate public policy.

Implied assumption of risk rests on the plaintiff's implied consent to relieve the defendant of the obligation of due care toward him/her and to take his/her chances of harm from a particular risk. There are three general aspects of implied assumption of risk:

- The nature and extent of risk is fully appreciated and known;
- The risk must be voluntarily encountered;
- The risk is "normal and natural" and not one that could not reasonably be expected.

In other areas of contract law, a disclaimer (or a so-called exculpatory clause) may not be enforced if it contravenes public policy and includes those offered by a public institution (any institution or business owned or operated by the government or by a branch of the government) or quasi-public institutions (a private institution or business that deals in a necessary and/or vital service and one that invites the public to its premises in large numbers). Institutions or businesses such as banks, amusement parks, casinos, etc., may fall under thus rule today. Refer to *Hy-Grade Oil v. New Jersey National Bank*, which involved an exculpatory clause offered by a bank in connection with the use of a night depository by a customer that was refused enforcement by New Jersey courts.

The area of warranty disclaimers (2-316) and limitations (2-719) were discussed in the materials on warranties.

In warranty cases, assumption of risk deals with the element of reliance and is associated with the rule that a buyer can not sue for breach of warranty for a defect if the defect would have been discovered through a reasonable inspection. A plaintiff cannot rely on statements made by a seller if a reasonable inspection would have revealed the falseness of any assertions or statements. Thus, a party who voluntarily chooses to use a chattel with knowledge of the risks to which he or she is exposed voluntarily assumes such risks.

In strict liability cases, implied assumption of risk involves a plaintiff who voluntarily encounters a risk that he subjectively knows and appreciates. In Heil, the court noted that knowledge of some general hazard involved in operating a product will not support the assumption of risk defense. There must be actual or charged knowledge of a specific hazard by using a subjective test relating to the extent of knowledge of a plaintiff.

Misuse, however, is a well-recognized and acceptable defense in a strict liability case.

MISUSE

PERFECTION PAINT & COLOR V. KONDURIS

Court of Appeals of Indiana, 147 Ind. App. 106; 258 N.E.2d 681 (1970)

OPINION BY: PFAFF, JUDGE

The plaintiff-appellee, Kosmos Alexander Konduris, instituted this action on behalf of his deceased father, Kosmos Kountouris, who died from burns inflicted in a fire in the plant of his employer, Alrimo Pizza, Inc. (Alrimo). The defendant-appellant, Perfection Paint & Color Company (Perfection), furnished Alrimo with a lacquer reducer for the purpose of removing a paint film on Alrimo's storage room floor. The lacquer reducer proved to be highly flammable and when applied to the storage room floor was ignited by an operative gas hot water heater in one corner of the storage room. This fire resulted in the death of Kosmos Kountouris.

Misuse of a defective product is a defense to strict liability in tort.... Judge Sharp of this court correctly stated that the defense of misuse is available when the product is used "for a purpose not reasonable to the manufacturer" or when the product is used "in a manner not reasonably foreseeable for a reasonably foreseeable purpose". Cornette v. Searjeant Metal Products, supra (concurring opinion). The contributory negligence of the plaintiff in failing to discover a defect in a product or in failing to guard against the existence of a defect is not misuse of the product and is, therefore, not a defense to strict liability in tort. § 402A, supra, Comment n at 356. A consumer who incurs or assumes the risk of injury by virtue of his continuing use of a product after having discovered a defect or who uses a product in contravention of a legally sufficient warning, misuses the product and, in the context of the defenses of incurred risk, is subject to the defense of misuse.

A legal description of those acts which constitute a "misuse" of a product has proven to be difficult to achieve. The problem appears to us to be one of failing to differentiate between misuse of a product which does not exhibit any defective condition until misused, or which does not appear to be defective and unreasonably dangerous, and misuse of a product when the defective and unreasonably dangerous condition is either discovered by the consumer or brought to his attention by a legally sufficient warning. While in either situation a product is being misused, the former constitutes the true category of misuse while the latter form of misuse is tantamount to the traditional concepts of incurred or assumed risk. The former, which Judge Sharp in Cornette, supra, previously categorized as use of a product for a purpose not reasonably foreseeable to the manufacturer "or use of the product in a manner not reasonably foreseeable for a reasonably foreseeable purpose", will apply in a situation in which a product is used for a purpose which is unforeseeable with that for which it was manufactured, or when used for a foreseeable purpose, is subjected to an unforeseeable or overly harsh use. We again refer to Greeno v. Clark Equipment Company, supra, at 429 of 237 F. Supp., wherein it is stated:

> *"Neither would contributory negligence constitute a defense, although a use different from or more strenuous than that contemplated to be safe by ordinary users/consumers, that is 'misuse' would either refute defective condition or causation."*

The latter form of misuse, that which is analogous to the defenses of incurred or assumed risk, occurs when a product, being used in the manner intended by the manufacturer and for the purpose intended by the manufacturer, proves to be defective and the defect is discovered, or when a defective and unreasonably dangerous product, acknowledged to be such by a manufacturer's warnings or instructions on proper use, is used in contravention of the instructions or warnings.

Appellant's lacquer reducer is admittedly a defective and unreasonably dangerous product. Because the lacquer reducer is "more dangerous than would be contemplated by the ordinary consumer/user with the ordinary knowledge of the community as to its characteristics and uses", Greeno v. Clark Equipment Company, supra, appellant owed a duty to consumers to warn of the product's unreasonably dangerous propensities, and did so warn of the product's defective condition on the container. Using the product, however, on a concrete floor in order to remove a paint film was not a use of the product inconsistent with the use for which the lacquer reducer was manufactured. It is undisputed that subsequent to the drying problems encountered in the application of appellant's epoxy paint on the concrete floors, appellant, after declaring that it would remedy the drying problem, provided paint remover, lacquer reducer, instructions, and on the scene supervision of the paint removing operation. Not only was the use of appellant's lacquer reducer a foreseeable use of the product, appellant furnished and expressly directed the use of its product in order to remove the paint film from the storage room floor. The use of the lacquer reducer for this purpose was unquestionably done for a reasonably foreseeable purpose inasmuch as the record establishes that the manufacturer provided the product for the express purpose of removing the paint film, gave directions as to its use, supervised the operation and, additionally, the manufacturer, by its representative, applied the product to the storage room floor immediately prior to the fire.

The question of misuse in this case is not, therefore, one of using a product for an unforeseeable purpose or overly harsh or unforeseeable use for a foreseeable purpose; rather, the question is whether or not the defective and unreasonably dangerous lacquer reducer was used in contravention of warnings and instructions on the correct use of said product.

The jury must make the determination of whether or not a defective product was misused. In this case there is evidence from which the jury could have determined that either the appellant's representative, Mr. Francis, or Alrimo misused the product. Misuse on the part of the seller is properly categorized as negligence, but even though the jury found that the appellant was not negligent, this finding does not automatically presuppose misuse on the part of the consumer. The defense of misuse will defeat strict liability in tort when a jury determines that the consumer misused the product. If the evidence is conflicting on this point, as it is in this instance, we are not at liberty to invade the province of the jury on this question, and its de termination that the lacquer reducer was not misused must stand.

For the foregoing reasons, the trial court was correct in refusing to direct a verdict in favor of the defendant-appellant and in overruling its motion for a new trial.

Judgment affirmed. Costs are to be taxed against the appellant.

Hoffman, P.J., Sharp and White, JJ., concur.

The defense of misuse may occur where a product is used for a purpose not reasonably foreseeable by the manufacturer, e.g., using a carving knife to trim a Christmas tree; using a lawn mower to trim a hedge; using a product in contravention of legally sufficient warnings (for example, "do not use in an enclosed, unventilated room"); using a product after having discovered a defect (sounds a lot like assumption of risk!); abnormal handling of a product; or abnormal consumption, for example, taking twenty tablets of x-lax at one time. However, it may be foreseeable that a product would be misused based upon the facts, market surveys, incident reports, etc., and such misuse may not qualify as misuse in a legal sense. The defendant may have to take specific precautions to guard against such foreseeable misuse, especially where the plaintiff was unable to comprehend the inherent danger in any misuse of the product, for example, misuse by a child.

As a part of the proof relating to misuse, the defendant may introduce evidence that the product was not in a defective condition when it left the seller's hands. Generally, if a product is not defective at the time of its delivery, the defense of misuse will lie and will be an absolute defense. "Such a safe condition at the time of delivery by the seller will include proper packaging, necessary sterilization, and other precautions required to permit the product to remain safe for a normal length of time when handled in a normal manner." (Comment g to Section 402A.)

Comment h to Section 402A provides some interesting examples of misuse:

> *"If the injury results from abnormal handling, as where a beverage is knocked against a radiator to remove the cap, or from abnormal preparation for use, as where too much salt is added to food, or from abnormal consumption, as where a child eats too much candy and is made ill, the seller is not liable. Where, however, he has reason to anticipate that danger may result form a particular use, as where a drug is sold which is safe only in limited doses, he may be required to give adequate warning of the danger, and a product sold without such warning is in a defective condition."*

Recently, a court determined that a drug manufacturer may be held liable for an injury to a child for use of a drug even though the drug was intended and labeled for use by an adult, if the manufacturer knew or should have known that the drug would be prescribed for use by the child. Evidence of sales to pediatricians provided strong evidence of liability on the part of a manufacturer that a product designed to be used for adults was being misused.

Comparative Negligence

The idea of apportionment of damages was created in order to mitigate against the harshness of the rule of common law which held that contributory negligence was an absolute bar to recovery. Comparative negligence standards are adopted under statutes passed by a state legislature. Under the rule of comparative negligence, damages are divided or apportioned according to the proportion of fault attributed to each party. This is accomplished through a procedure known as a special verdict, under which a jury answers specific questions as to the amount of damages and the percentage of fault attributed to each party. Most courts will not employ a comparative negligence standard in a case where the negligence of the plaintiff was equal to or greater than the negligence of the defendant (equal to or more than 50%). Ironically, courts today have expanded this concept beyond negligence and apply comparative negligence standards to both misuse and assumption of risk, apportioning damages. The comparative negligence standard has also been applied to strict liability.

Daly v. General Motors Corporation

Supreme Court of California, 20 Cal. 3d 725; 575 P.2d 1162 (1978)

OPINION BY: RICHARDSON

The most important of several problems which we consider is whether the principles of comparative negligence expressed by us in Li v. Yellow Cab Co. (1975) 13 Cal.3d 804 [119

Cal.Rptr. 858, 532 P.2d 1226, 78 A.L.R.3d 393], apply to actions founded on strict products liability. We will conclude that they do.

* * * In the early hours of October 31, 1970, decedent Kirk Daly, a 36-year-old attorney, was driving his Opel southbound on the Harbor Freeway in Los Angeles. The vehicle, while travelling at a speed of 50-70 miles per hour, collided with and damaged 50 feet of metal divider fence. After the initial impact between the left side of the vehicle and the fence the Opel spun counterclockwise, the driver's door was thrown open, and Daly was forcibly ejected from the car and sustained fatal head injuries. It was equally undisputed that had the deceased remained in the Opel his injuries, in all probability, would have been relatively minor.

* * * The sole theory of plaintiffs' complaint was strict liability for damages allegedly caused by a defective product, namely, an improperly designed door latch claimed to have been activated by the impact. It was further asserted that, but for the faulty latch, decedent would have been restrained in the vehicle and, although perhaps injured, would not have been killed. Thus, the case involves a so-called "second collision" in which the "defect" did not contribute to the original impact, but only to the "enhancement" of injury.

* * * Over plaintiffs' objections, defendants were permitted to introduce evidence indicating that: (1) the Opel was equipped with a seat belt-shoulder harness system, and a door lock, either of which if used, it was contended, would have prevented Daly's ejection from the vehicle; (2) Daly used neither the harness system nor the lock; (3) the 1970 Opel owner's manual contained warnings that seat belts should be worn and doors locked when the car was in motion for "accident security"; and (4) Daly was intoxicated at the time of collision, which evidence the jury was advised was admitted for the limited purpose of determining whether decedent had used the vehicle's safety equipment. After relatively brief deliberations the jury returned a verdict favoring all defendants, and plaintiffs appeal from the ensuing adverse judgment.

Strict Products Liability And Comparative Fault

In response to plaintiffs' assertion that the "intoxication-nonuse" evidence was improperly admitted, defendants contend that the deceased's own conduct contributed to his death. Because plaintiffs' case rests upon strict products liability based on improper design of the door latch and because defendants assert a failure in decedent's conduct, namely, his alleged intoxication and nonuse of safety equipment, without which the accident and ensuing death would not have occurred, there is thereby posed the overriding issue in the case, should comparative principles apply in strict products liability actions?

It may be useful to refer briefly to certain highlights in the historical development of the two principles -- strict and comparative liability. Tort law has evolved from a legal obligation initially imposed without "fault," to recovery which, generally, was based on blameworthiness in a moral sense. For reasons of social policy and because of the unusual nature of defendants' acts, liability without fault continued to be prescribed in a certain restricted area, for example, upon keepers of wild animals, or those who handled explosives or other dangerous substances, or who engaged in ultrahazardous activities. Simultaneously, and more particularly, those who were injured in the use of personal property were permitted recovery on a contract theory if they were the purchasers of the chattel or were in privity. Subsequently, liability was imposed in negligence upon the manufacturer of personalty in favor of the general consumer. Evolving social policies designed to protect the ultimate consumer soon prompted the extension of legal responsibility beyond negligence to express or implied warranty. Thus, in the area of food and drink a form of strict liability predicated upon warranty found wide acceptance. Warranty actions, however, contained their own inherent limitations requiring a precedent notice to the vendor of a breach of the warranty, and absolving him from loss if he had issued an adequate disclaimer.

General dissatisfaction continued with the conceptual limitations which traditional tort and contract doctrines placed upon the consumers and users of manufactured products, this at a time when mass production of an almost infinite variety of goods and products was responding to a myriad of ever-changing societal demands stimulated by wide-spread commercial advertising. From an historic combination of economic and sociological forces was born the doctrine of strict liability in tort.

We, ourselves, were perhaps the first court to give the new principle judicial sanction. In Greenman v. Yuba Power Products, Inc. (1963) 59 Cal.2d 57 [27 Cal.Rptr. 697, 377 P.2d 897, 13 A.L.R.3d 1049], confronted with injury to an ultimate consumer caused by a defective power tool, we fastened strict liability on a manufacturer who placed on the market a defective product even though both privity and notice of breach of warranty were lacking. We rejected both contract and warranty theories, express or implied, as the basis for liability. Strict liability, we said, did not rest on a consensual foundation but, rather, on one created by law. The liability was created judicially because of the economic and social need for the protection of consumers in an increasingly complex and mechanized society, and because of the limitations in the negligence and warranty remedies. Our avowed purpose was "to insure that the costs of injuries resulting from defective products are borne by the manufacturer that put such products on the market rather than by the injured persons who are powerless to protect themselves." (Id., at p. 63.) Subsequently, the Greenman principle was incorporated in section 402A of the Restatement Second of Torts, and adopted by a majority of American jurisdictions. (Prosser, supra, at pp. 657-658.)

From its inception, however, strict liability has never been, and is not now, absolute liability. As has been repeatedly expressed, under strict liability the manufacturer does not thereby become the insurer of the safety of the product's user. On the contrary, the plaintiff's injury must have been caused by a "defect" in the product. Thus the manufacturer is not deemed responsible when injury results from an unforeseeable use of its product. (Cronin, supra, at p. 126; Rest.2d Torts, supra, coms. g, h.) Furthermore, we have recognized that though most forms of contributory negligence do not constitute a defense to a strict products liability action, plaintiff's negligence is a complete defense when it comprises assumption of risk. As will thus be seen, the concept of strict products liability was created and shaped judicially. In its evolution, the doctrinal encumbrances of contract and warranty, and the traditional elements of negligence, were stripped from the remedy, and a new tort emerged which extended liability for defective product design and manufacture beyond negligence but short of absolute liability.

In Li v. Yellow Cab Co., supra, 13 Cal.3d 804, we introduced the other doctrine with which we are concerned, comparative negligence. We examined the history of contributory negligence, the massive criticism directed at it because its presence in the slightest degree completely barred plaintiff's recovery, and the increasing defection from the doctrine. We then weighed the two principal arguments against its removal from California law, namely, that such a sharp change in direction required legislative action, and that there existed a cluster of asserted practical obstacles relating to multiple parties, the apportionment burdens on a jury and the uncertain effect on the defenses of last clear chance, assumption of risk, and willful misconduct. Concluding that none of the obstacles was insurmountable, we announced in Li the adoption of a "pure" form of comparative negligence which, when present, reduced but did not prevent plaintiff's recovery. (Pp. 828-829.) We held that the defense of assumption of risk, insofar as it is no more than a variant of contributory negligence, was merged into the assessment of liability in proportion to fault. (Pp. 824-825.) Within the broad guidelines therein announced, we left to trial courts discretion in the particular implementation of the new doctrine. (Pp. 826-827.)

* * * Those counseling against the recognition of comparative fault principles in strict products liability cases vigorously stress, perhaps equally, not only the conceptual, but also the semantic difficulties incident to such a course. The task of merging the two concepts is said to be impossible, that "apples and oranges" cannot be compared, that "oil and water" do not mix, and that strict liability, which is not founded on negligence or fault, is inhospitable to comparative principles…. While fully recognizing the theoretical and semantic distinctions between the twin principles of strict products liability and traditional negligence, we think they can be blended or accommodated.

The inherent difficulty in the "apples and oranges" argument is its insistence on fixed and precise definitional treatment of legal concepts. In the evolving areas of both products liability and tort defenses, however, there has developed much conceptual overlapping and interweaving in order to attain substantial justice. The concept of strict liability itself, as we have noted, arose from dissatisfaction with the wooden formalisms of traditional tort and contract principles in order to protect the consumer of manufactured goods. Similarly, increasing social awareness of its harsh "all or nothing" consequences led us in Li to moderate the impact of traditional contributory negligence in order to accomplish a fairer and more balanced result. We acknowledged an intermixing of defenses of contributory negligence and assumption of risk and formally effected a type of merger."

As for assumption of risk, we have recognized in this state that this defense overlaps that of contributory negligence to some extent . . . ."

* * * Furthermore, the "apples and oranges" argument may be conceptually suspect. It has been suggested that the term "contributory negligence," one of the vital building blocks upon which much of the argument is based, may indeed itself be a misnomer since it lacks the first element of the classical negligence formula, namely, a duty of care owing to another. A highly respected torts authority, Dean William Prosser, has noted this fact by observing, "It is perhaps unfortunate that contributory negligence is called negligence at all. 'Contributory fault' would be a more descriptive term. Negligence as it is commonly understood is conduct which creates an undue risk of harm to others. Contributory negligence is conduct which involves an undue risk of harm to the actor himself. Negligence requires a duty, an obligation of conduct to another person. Contributory negligence involves no duty, unless we are to be so ingenious as to say that the plaintiff is under an obligation to protect the defendant against liability for the consequences of his own negligence." (Prosser, Law of Torts, supra, § 65, p. 418.)

We think, accordingly, the conclusion may fairly be drawn that the terms "comparative negligence," "contributory negligence" and "assumption of risk" do not, standing alone, lend themselves to the exact measurements of a micrometer-caliper, or to such precise definition as to divert us from otherwise strong and consistent countervailing policy considerations. Fixed semantic consistency at this point is less important than the attainment of a just and equitable result. The interweaving of concept and terminology in this area suggests a judicial posture that is flexible rather than doctrinaire.

We pause at this point to observe that where, as here, a consumer or user sues the manufacturer or designer alone, technically, neither fault nor conduct is really compared functionally. The conduct of one party in combination with the product of another, or perhaps the placing of a defective article in the stream of projected and anticipated use, may produce the ultimate injury. In such a case, as in the situation before us, we think the term "equitable apportionment or allocation of loss" may be more descriptive than "comparative fault."

Given all of the foregoing, we are, in the wake of Li, disinclined to resolve the important issue before us by the simple expedient of matching linguistic labels which have evolved either for convenience or by custom. Rather, we consider it more useful to examine the foundational reasons underlying the creation of strict products liability in California to ascertain whether the purposes of the doctrine would be defeated or diluted by adoption of comparative principles. We imposed strict liability against the manufacturer and in favor of the user or consumer in order to relieve injured consumers "from problems of proof inherent in pursuing negligence . . . and warranty . . . remedies, . . ." (Cronin v. J. B. E. Olson Corp., supra, 8 Cal.3d at p. 133, italics added; Greenman v. Yuba Power Products, Inc., supra, 59 Cal.2d at p. 63; Escola v. Coca Cola Bottling Co. (1944) 24 Cal.2d 453, 461-462

[150 P.2d 436] (conc. opn. by Traynor, J.).) As we have noted, we sought to place the burden of loss on manufacturers rather than ". . . injured persons who are powerless to protect themselves . . . ." (Greenman, supra, at p. 63; italics added; see Escola, supra, at p. 462; Price v. Shell Oil Co. (1970) 2 Cal.3d 245, 251 [85 Cal.Rptr. 178, 466 P.2d 722] ["protection of otherwise defenseless victims of manufacturing defects and the spreading throughout society of the cost of compensating them"] italics added.)

The foregoing goals, we think, will not be frustrated by the adoption of comparative principles. Plaintiffs will continue to be relieved of proving that the manufacturer or distributor was negligent in the production, design, or dissemination of the article in question. Defendant's liability for injuries caused by a defective product remains strict. The principle of protecting the defenseless is likewise preserved, for plaintiff's recovery will be reduced only to the extent that his own lack of reasonable care contributed to his injury. The cost of compensating the victim of a defective product, albeit proportionately reduced, remains on defendant manufacturer, and will, through him, be "spread among society." However, we do not permit plaintiff's own conduct relative to the product to escape unexamined, and as to that share of plaintiff's damages which flows from his own fault we discern no reason of policy why it should, following Li, be borne by others. Such a result would directly contravene the principle announced in Li, that loss should be assessed equitably in proportion to fault.

* * * A second objection to the application of comparative principles in strict products liability cases is that a manufacturer's incentive to produce safe products will thereby be reduced or removed. While we fully recognize this concern we think, for several reasons, that the problem is more shadow than substance. First, of course, the manufacturer cannot avoid its continuing liability for a defective product even when the plaintiff's own conduct has contributed to his injury. The manufacturer's liability, and therefore its incentive to avoid and correct product defects, remains; its exposure will be lessened only to the extent that the trier finds that the victim's conduct contributed to his injury. Second, as a practical matter a manufacturer, in a particular case, cannot assume that the user of a defective product upon whom an injury is visited will be blameworthy. Doubtless, many users are free of fault, and a defect is at least as likely as not to be exposed by an entirely innocent plaintiff who will obtain full recovery. In such cases the manufacturer's incentive toward safety both in design and production is wholly unaffected. Finally, we must observe that under the present law, which recognizes assumption of risk as a complete defense to products liability, the curious and cynical message is that it profits the manufacturer to make his product so defective that in the event of injury he can argue that the user had to be aware of its patent defects. To that extent the incentives are inverted. We conclude, accordingly, that no substantial or significant impairment of the safety incentives of defendants will occur by the adoption of comparative principles.

In passing, we note one important and felicitous result if we apply comparative principles to strict products liability. This arises from the fact that under present law when plaintiff sues in negligence his own contributory negligence, however denominated, may diminish but cannot wholly defeat his recovery. When he sues in strict products liability, however, his "assumption of risk" completely bars his recovery. Under Li, as we have noted, "assumption of risk" is merged into comparative principles. (13 Cal.3d at p. 825.) The consequence is that after Li in a negligence action, plaintiff's conduct which amounts to "negligent" assumption of risk no longer defeats plaintiff's recovery. Identical conduct, however, in a strict liability case acts as a complete bar under rules heretofore applicable. Thus, strict products liability, which was developed to free injured consumers from the constraints imposed by traditional negligence and warranty theories, places a consumer plaintiff in a worse position than would be the case were his claim founded on simple negligence. This, in turn, rewards adroit pleading and selection of theories. The application of comparative principles to strict liability obviates this bizarre anomaly by treating alike the defenses to both negligence and strict products liability actions. In each instance the defense, if established, will reduce but not bar plaintiff's claim.

A third objection to the merger of strict liability and comparative fault focuses on the claim that, as a practical matter, triers of fact, particularly jurors, cannot assess, measure, or compare plaintiff's negligence with defendant's strict liability. We are unpersuaded by the argument and are convinced that jurors are able to undertake a fair apportionment of liability.

* * * We note that the majority of our sister states which have addressed the problem, either by statute or judicial decree, have extended comparative principles to strict products liability.

* * * Moreover, we are further encouraged in our decision herein by noting that the apparent majority of scholarly commentators has urged adoption of the rule which we announce herein. These include, from the academic community: Wade, A Uniform Comparative Fault Act -- What Should It Provide? (1977) 10 Mich. J. L. Ref. 220; Fleming, The Supreme Court of California 1974-1975 -- Foreword: Comparative Negligence at Last -- By Judicial Choice (1976) 64 Cal.L.Rev. 239, 269-271; Schwartz, Comparative Negligence (1974) § 12.1 et seq., p. 195 et seq. (see also Special Cal. Supplement re Nga Li v. Yellow Cab Co. of California (1975) § 4(B), p. 8); Wade, On the Nature of Strict Tort Liability for Products (1973) 44 Miss.L.J. 825, 850; Noel, Defective Products; Abnormal Use, Contributory Negligence, and Assumption of Risk (1972) 25 Vand.L.Rev. 93, 117-118; contra, Levine, Strict Products Liability and Comparative Negligence: The Collision of Fault and No-Fault (1977) 14 San Diego L.Rev. 337, 346 et seq. Among other commentaries urging such a rule are: Posner et al., Comparative Negligence in California: Some Legislative Solutions -- Part II (1977) Los Angeles Daily Journal Report (Aug. 26, 1977) at pages 4, 9-18 (proposed legislation); Brewster, Comparative Negligence In Strict Liability Cases (1976) 42 J. Air L. & Com. 107, 109-117; Comment, Comparative Negligence in Vermont: A Solution or a Problem (1976) 40 Albany L.Rev. 777, 810; Feinberg, The Applicability of a Comparative Negligence Defense in a Strict Products Liability Suit Based on Section 402A of the Restatement of Torts 2d

(1975) 42 Ins.Couns.J. 39, 52; Comment, Tort Defenses to Strict Products Liability (1969) 20 Syracuse L.Rev. 924, 925; Epstein, Products Liability: Defenses Based on Plaintiff's Conduct (1968) 1968 Utah L.Rev. 267, 284; Levine, Buyer's Conduct as Affecting the Extent of Manufacturer's Liability in Warranty (1968) 52 Minn.L.Rev. 627, 652-663; contra, Robinson, Square Pegs (Products Liability) In Round Holes (Comparative Negligence) (1977) 52 State Bar J. 16; Schwartz, Pure Comparative Negligence in Action (1972) 34 Am. Trial Law. J. 117, 129.

* * Having examined the principal objections and finding them not insurmountable, and persuaded by logic, justice, and fundamental fairness, we conclude that a system of comparative fault should be and it is hereby extended to actions founded on strict products liability. In such cases the separate defense of "assumption of risk," to the extent that it is a form of contributory negligence, is abolished. While, as we have suggested, on the particular facts before us, the term "equitable apportionment of loss" is more accurately descriptive of the process, nonetheless, the term "comparative fault" has gained such wide acceptance by courts and in the literature that we adopt its use herein.

In *Daly*, the court noted that the defendant's liability could still be strict (and not based upon its negligence), but that "the share of plaintiff's damage which flows from his own fault should [not] be borne by others." This is an important and unresolved debate (see the Jefferson dissent in *Daly* which states that the application of comparative negligence standards to strict liability is like "asking it to compare apples and oranges"). However, most states today reject this notion, and in fact have applied some type of comparative negligence scheme, even to strict tort liability.

Questions

1. McCown, the appellee, was driving a tractor manufactured by International Harvester Co., the appellant. After making an equipment inspection on the shoulder of the PA turnpike, the appellee reentered the turnpike. Shortly after, the front wheel of the tractor hit a guard rail and the collision caused the steering wheel to spin rapidly and fracture the appellee's wrist. In addition, the design of the steering wheel made the vehicle unusually difficult to maneuver and played a role in the rapid counter rotation of the wheel. The appellant conceded to the defect but argues that the appellee's collision with the guard rail also resulted in his own injury.
   a. Does the appellee face the defense contributory negligence?
2. James Grant and Vernon Grant were working beneath the raised bed of a dump drunk, using hydraulic hoists manufactured by Heil Co., when it somehow descended and crushed James. An engineer for Heil Co. found that there was no malfunction but the pull out cable had been tripped. Moreover, Vernon informed James if the pull out cable was hit, the bed would come down.
   a. How does assumption of risk factor into this case?
   b. Is Heil Co. liable?
3. Kosmos Kountouris worked at Alrimo Pizza Inc. Perfect Paint & Color furnished Alrimo with a lacquer reducer for the purpose of removing a pain film on Alrimo's storage room floor. The reducer was highly flammable and ignited because of an operative gas hot water heater. The fire resulted in the death of Kosmos. Subsequently, his son brought suit.
   a. Does misuse apply to this case?
   b. Is Alrimo liable? Is Perfect Paint & Color liable?
4. How did *Li v. Yellow Cab Co.* help in the development of the principles of contributory negligence?
5. Kirk Daly was driving his Opel at 50-70 mph. He collided with a metal divider, which caused the car to spin counterclockwise. The driver's door was thrown open and Kirk was forcibly ejected from the car. As a result, he sustained fatal head injuries that ultimately led to his death. If he had remained in the Opel, he would have sustained only minor injuries. However, it should be noted that Kirk was not only intoxicated, but he was not using the shoulder harness and his door was unlocked. Regardless, his family brought suit against General Motors Corporation, the manufacturer.
   a. Does comparative negligence apply? If so, how?
   b. Is General Motor Corporation liable?

Chapter Fifteen

Special Topics and Recent Developments

Some interesting theories have recently received attention in the area of products liability. In this Chapter, we will discuss three of the most prominent.

Enterprise Liability Doctrine

The enterprise liability doctrine (*Burnside v. Abbott Laboratories*) is used to assess liability against a defendant where no specific evidence exists against that defendant. This doctrine has been most often applied where fungible (interchangeable) goods are involved and where the harm cannot be traced to any specific producer. For example, a person smoked for over forty years and smoked over forty different brands!

The underlying assumptions inherent in the possible application of this doctrine are:

- The injury-causing product was manufactured by one of a number of manufacturers in an industry who can be identified with reasonable certainty;
- The defendant had joint knowledge of the risks inherent in the product and possessed a joint capacity to reduce those risks;
- Each of the manufacturers failed to take steps to reduce the risk individually, perhaps delegating this responsibility to a trade association or some other third party, who failed to remedy the defect in the product.

Case Study: Burnside v. Abbott Laboratories

Procedural Posture

Appellant women challenged the orders of the Court of Common Pleas of Allegheny County (Pennsylvania). The trial court granted summary judgments as to appellee pharmaceutical companies who were not engaged in the manufacture, promotion, or marketing of a drug during the relevant time period and granted summary judgment against the remaining appellees. Appellants alleged there should have been industry-wide liability.

Overview

Appellant women sought damages for injuries from appellee drug companies who allegedly manufactured a drug. The trial court granted summary judgments in favor of 26 of the named appellees whose products could not have caused the injuries. Appellants conceded that they or their mothers could not have ingested the 26 appellees' products, but they contended that there should have been industry-wide liability for injuries caused by ingestion of the drug. The court rejected the argument and affirmed those judgments. Appellants argued that appellees were individually or jointly liable to them for their failure to exercise due and reasonable care when they marketed and promoted the drug. As the 26 appellees showed that they were not engaged in the manufacture, promotion, or marketing during the relevant time period, those companies had not fallen within the "industry" that allegedly caused the injuries. The court determined that the summary judgment granted against the remaining appellees should have been reversed, as the record failed to disclose facts sufficient to have sustained causes of action based upon an industry-wide conspiracy, concerted industry action, or enterprise liability.

Outcome

The orders that granted summary judgments were affirmed as to appellee drug companies that were not engaged in the manufacture, promotion, or marketing of the drug during the relevant period. The order that granted summary judgment against the remaining appellees was reversed, as the record failed to disclose facts sufficient to have sustained the causes of action. The latter claim was remanded for further proceedings.

In some states, a defendant can exculpate itself from liability if it can prove by clear and convincing proof that it did not market the defective product that could have caused plaintiff's injury. So, in this sense, liability is not strict or absolute without fault.

Alternative Liability

Alternative liability arises where the conduct of two or more parties may have been the cause of damage, the burden of proof is shifted to each actor to prove that he/she has not caused the harm.

Market Share Liability

Market share liability arises once a party has been included as a defendant under the enterprise liability doctrine. The question then becomes: How do we assess the amount (perhaps based on a percentage) of damages to be awarded against an individual enterprise? Each defendant is presumed to have equal liability unless it can establish actual market share in the relevant geographic area or market.

In *Sindell v. Abbott Labs*, the court noted that an application of market share liability permits the court to award damages against an individual enterprise based upon the respective share of the relevant market.

These approaches have been subject to severe criticism as social engineering, more appropriate for the legislature. Courts have raised several interesting questions in their critiques:

- Should liability be transferred to an entire industry irrespective of an individual manufacturer's connection with a particular injury?
- Once the burden of proof is shifted, what amount of proof is required for both the plaintiff and the defendant?
- How do we ascertain the extent of damages that can be apportioned against an individual manufacturer?

No doubt, future cases and future courts (as well as state legislatures or the United States Congress) will attempt to answer these questions as a matter of public policy.

Case Study: Sindell v. Abbott Laboratories

Procedural Posture

In a consolidated appeal, plaintiffs, women diagnosed with cancer, appealed the decisions of the Superior Court of Los Angeles County (California) and the Superior Court of Ventura County (California), which sustained defendant drug manufacturers' demurrers in actions brought by plaintiffs to recover for personal injuries allegedly resulting from prenatal exposure to a drug manufactured by defendants.

Overview

Defendant drug manufacturers produced and sold a drug given to women during pregnancy. Plaintiffs, women diagnosed with cancer, filed suits against defendants alleging that their cancer resulted from prenatal exposure to defendants' drug. In a consolidated appeal, plaintiffs sought review of the trial courts' decisions which sustained defendants' demurrers finding that the complaints failed to state a cause of action because they did not identify the particular defendant which manufactured the drug that allegedly caused plaintiffs injuries. The court reversed the trial courts' decisions and held that the doctrines of concerted action and alternative liability enabled the complaints to withstand a demurrer. The court held that it was not necessary for plaintiffs to identify a particular defendant because the complaints contained factual allegations which, if proven, would establish that defendants were both individually and jointly responsible for plaintiffs' injuries in that they acted in both their individual capacities and in concert in the doing of the wrongful acts which caused those injuries; and that the applicable statute of limitations was Cal. Civ. Proc. Code 340(3).

Outcome

The court reversed the trial courts' decisions, sustaining defendant drug manufacturers' demurrers, and held that plaintiffs, women diagnosed with cancer, included sufficient factual allegations in their complaints to establish actions based on the theories of concerted action and alternative liability even though plaintiffs were unable to identify the particular defendant that manufactured the drug that allegedly caused plaintiffs' injuries.

In *George v. Parke-Davis*, the court cited *Martin v. Abbott Labs*. The court determined that the plaintiff (or mother) used DES, the breast implant; that DES caused the subsequent injury; the defendant or defendants produced or marketed the type of DES taken by her mother; and the production or marketing of DES constituted the breach of a legal duty to the plaintiff and was a cause of the injury.

However, the court refused to find the pharmaceutical company (Parke-Davis) liable on the basis of its status as a successor corporation.

Case Study: George v. Parke-Davis

Procedural Posture

Plaintiff injured party filed a products liability action against defendant pharmaceutical company for personal injuries allegedly sustained by her as a result of her mother's ingestion of diethylstilbestrol (DES) while pregnant with her. The pharmaceutical company filed a motion for summary judgment.

Overview

Although the injured party's mother was unable to identify the manufacturer of the DES she took, it was undisputed that she purchased the prescriptions from a particular pharmacy. The injured party filed suit against the pharmaceutical company because its predecessor may have manufactured the DES in question. The court granted summary judgment for the pharmaceutical company because none of the exceptions to the general rule of non-liability of a successor corporation existed. Since the pharmaceutical company did not continue to produce DES after its acquisition of the manufacturer, it was not liable for injuries caused by DES under the product-line exception. The purchase agreement did not clearly express either the inclusion or exclusion of any liability for tort or product liability actions. The purchase of the manufacturer's assets did not amount to a statutory merger or de facto merger. The pharmaceutical company was not a mere continuation of the manufacturer because the two common shareholders owned only minority interests, and the treasurer's involvement in both corporations was insufficient to show the control necessary to meet the continuity requirement.

Outcome

The court granted summary judgment for the pharmaceutical company and dismissed the injured party's product liability complaint with prejudice.

Questions

1. Find modern day examples where the following are applicable:
    a. Enterprise Liability Doctrine
    b. Alternative Liability Doctrine
    c. Market Share Liability Doctrine
2. How does the Enterprise Liability Doctrine apply to the *Burnside v. Abbott Laboratories* case?
3. Abbott laboratories manufactured, produced, and sold a drug given to women during pregnancy. Users alleged that they developed cancer as a result of drug use.
    a. Does the alternative liability apply?
    b. Does market share liability apply?
    c. Is Abbott liable?
4. George, the plaintiff, used DES, which was sold by the pharmaceutical company Parke-Davis, the defendant. George suffered injuries as a result of ingesting DES and brought suit.
    a. How does the product line exception apply?
    b. Is Parke-Davis liable?

Table of Cases

Index

~ C ~

~ G ~

~ H ~

~ I ~

~ J ~

~ K ~

~ L ~

~ M ~

~ N ~

~ O ~

~ P ~

~ R ~

~ S ~

~ T ~

~ U ~

~ V ~

~ W ~